A Reader's Guide to
Contemporary Literary Theory

A Reader's Guide to Contemporary Literary Theory
Third Edition

Raman Selden and Peter Widdowson

The University Press of Kentucky

Copyright © Peter Widdowson 1993

Published by The University Press of Kentucky

Scholarly publisher for the Commonwealth,
serving Bellarmine College, Berea College, Centre
College of Kentucky, Eastern Kentucky University,
The Filson Club, Georgetown College, Kentucky
Historical Society, Kentucky State University,
Morehead State University, Murray State University,
Northern Kentucky University, Transylvania University,
University of Kentucky, University of Louisville,
and Western Kentucky University.

Editorial and Sales Offices: Lexington, Kentucky 40508–4008

Library of Congress Cataloging-in-Publication Data

Selden, Raman.
    A reader's guide to contemporary literary theory. — 3rd ed./
Raman Selden and Peter Widdowson.
        p.   cm.
    Earlier eds. by Raman Selden; this ed. rev. by Peter Widdowson.
    Includes bibliographical references and index.
    ISBN 0–8131–0816–0
    1. Criticism—History—20th century.   I. Widdowson, Peter.
II. Title.
PN94.S46   1993
801'.95'0904—dc20   92–47056

Printed and bound in Great Britain

To the memory of Raman Selden, the original maker, and for his widow, Jane.

Contents

Preface to the Third Edition

Writing this preface is a sad task. Some little while after revising the second edition of *A Reader's Guide*, Raman Selden prematurely and tragically died of a brain tumour. Raman was much loved and highly respected – not least for the remarkable achievement of producing a short, clear, informative and unpolemical volume on contemporary literary theory. As the person asked (and honoured) to revise his book for a third edition, I salute Ray and sincerely hope that my labours do not obscure the work he so intelligently and lucidly initiated.

Four years have elapsed since the book was last revised, and the terrain of literary theory has, of course, again undergone radical change. The whole of *A Reader's Guide*, therefore, has been extensively revised and the reading lists substantially updated. In addition, there are two new complete chapters – on New Criticism and F. R. Leavis, and on postmodernism and postcolonialism – and one other, on feminist theories, which is so fundamentally revised as to be effectively a new one. The second and third of these major revisions clearly signal the directions in which critical theory has been most dynamically moving, and the reordering of the chapters for this edition – with 1–5 already being of a more historical cast – underscores this.

In all of this work I have been generously assisted by the three advisors I recruited to the project, without whom it simply would not have been done: Peter Brooker, Maggie Humm and

Francis Mulhern. My sincerest thanks to them. Peter Brooker supplied, among other things, most of the materials for the chapter on postmodernist and postcolonialist theories. The material on Baudrillard and Lyotard in particular draws on and extends the discussion in his *Modernism/Postmodernism* (Longman, 1992) and elsewhere. Drawing directly on Maggie Humm's *Feminisms: A Reader* (Harvester Wheatsheaf, 1992) enabled me to write the chapter on feminist theories. For a fuller introduction to the range and diversity of feminist criticism, I refer the reader to Maggie Humm's forthcoming book, *A Reader's Guide to Feminist Criticism*, also from Harvester Wheatsheaf. And Francis Mulhern exercised his customary critical intelligence at all points of the book – but most extensively in relation to Marxist theory (on which he, too, published a Longman Critical Reader in 1992). Raman Selden thanked others whose books had contributed to his revision of the second edition, and the debt still stands. I must add a couple more: Coyle, Garside, Kelsall and Peck's *Encyclopaedia of Literature and Criticism* (1990), and various essays in it, have been immensely helpful; Elizabeth Wright's work there, and in her *Psychoanalytic Criticism: Theory and Practice* (1984), was essential for parts of the book: and Mary Eagleton's 'Critical Reader', *Feminist Literary Criticism* (1991), was also fundamental to my writing of the last chapter.

I should thank too my new colleagues at the University of Brighton who allowed me to do this work without complaint even though I had only just arrived there, and, in particular, Amanda Moore who typed my pre-IT script with speed, intelligence and good humour. With all these people to thank, it only remains for me to say that any failings in this new *Reader's Guide* are entirely my responsibility, not theirs – and, sadly, certainly not Ray's.

Introduction

Until relatively recently, in the English-speaking world at least, ordinary readers of literature and even professional literary critics had no reason to trouble themselves about developments in literary theory. Theory seemed a rather rarefied specialism which concerned a few individuals in literature departments who were, in effect, philosophers pretending to be literary critics. Discussions about literature, whether book reviews in the press, or in arts magazines on radio and television, were addressed to the ordinary reader. Most critics assumed, like Dr Johnson, that great literature was universal and expressed general truths about human life, and that therefore readers required no special knowledge or language. Critics talked comfortable good sense about the writer's personal experience, the social and historical background of the work, the human interest, imaginative 'genius', and poetic beauty of great literature. In other words, criticism spoke about literature without disturbing our picture of the world or of ourselves as readers. Then, at the end of the 1960s, things began to change.

During the past twenty years or so students of literature have been troubled by a seemingly endless series of challenges to the consensus of common sense, many of them deriving from European (and especially French and Russian) intellectual sources. To the Anglo-Saxon tradition, this was a particularly nasty shock. 'Structuralism', for example, hit the headlines

1

when Colin MacCabe failed to obtain a tenured appointment at Cambridge University in 1980. The protests of the structuralists and their allies at Cambridge alerted the quality papers to the existence of an intruder in the bed of Dr Leavis's *alma mater*. The *Times Literary Supplement* duly published a special number on the scandal and its intellectual background. Most general readers of the newspaper accounts must have emerged more confused about 'structuralism' than they were before the 'MacCabe affair' gave the theorists a chance to explain themselves to the public. To be told that there was a touch of *Marxism* about MacCabe's structuralism, that his approach to structuralism was really a *poststructuralist* critique of structuralism, and that the main influence on his work was the *psychoanalytic* structuralism of the French writer Jacques Lacan only confirmed ingrained prejudices.

Raman Selden decided to undertake the daunting task of writing a reader's guide to this subject mainly because he believed that the questions raised by modern literary theory were important enough to justify the effort of clarification. Many readers now feel that the conventional contemptuous dismissal of theory will not do. They would like to know exactly what they are being asked to reject. Inevitably any attempt to put together a brief summation of complex and contentious concepts will drain much of the blood from the body of a theory, and leave it even more vulnerable to the teeth of sceptics. However, we have assumed that the reader is *interested* and *curious* about the subject, and therefore ready to accept lightly seasoned fare as a preparation for the more authentic and pungent flavours of the original theories. We acknowledge that we have perpetrated some gross over-simplifications in an attempt to say much in little, and hope that the reader will not be seriously misled by such unavoidable compressions and sweeping generalisations. We provide at the end of each section graded 'further reading' to enable the reader to follow up particular approaches at various levels of difficulty.

Why should we trouble ourselves about literary theory? Can we not simply wait for the fuss to die down? The signs are that the graft of theory has taken rather well, and may remain intact for the foreseeable future. New journals have been launched, new courses established, conferences are devoted to theoretical questions, and it is already clearly apparent that this new critical self-awareness is manifesting itself in the newer generations of secondary and tertiary teachers of literature. How does all this affect our experience and understanding of reading and writing? First, an emphasis on theory tends to undermine reading as an *innocent* activity. If we ask ourselves questions about the construction of meaning in fiction or the presence of ideology in poetry, we can no longer naïvely accept the 'realism' of a novel or the 'sincerity' of a poem. Some readers may cherish their illusions and mourn the loss of innocence, but, if they are serious readers, they cannot ignore the deeper issues raised by the major literary theorists in recent years. Secondly, far from having a sterile effect on our reading, new ways of seeing literature can revitalise our engagement with texts. Of course, if one has no desire to reflect upon one's reading, literary criticism of any sort will have little to offer. Alternatively, readers may believe that theories and concepts will only deaden the spontaneity of their response to literary works. They may not realise that *no* discourse about literature is theory-free, that even apparently 'spontaneous' discussion of literary texts is dependent on the *de facto* (if less self-conscious) theorising of older generations. Their talk of 'feeling', 'imagination', 'genius', 'sincerity' and 'reality' is full of dead theory which is sanctified by time and has become part of the language of common sense. If we are to be adventurous and exploratory in our reading of literature, we must also be adventurous in our thinking about literature.

One can think of the various literary theories as raising different questions about literature. Theories may ask questions from the particular point of view of the writer, of the work, of the reader, or of what we usually call 'reality', although most will, in effect, also involve aspects of the other approaches. The following diagram of linguistic communication, devised by Roman Jakobson, helps to distinguish the various viewpoints:

$$\begin{array}{ccc} & \text{CONTEXT} & \\ \text{ADDRESSER} \rightarrow & \text{MESSAGE} & \rightarrow \text{ADDRESSEE} \\ & \text{CONTACT} & \\ & \text{CODE} & \end{array}$$

An addresser sends a message to an addressee; the message

uses a code (usually a language familiar to both addresser and addressee); the message has a context (or 'referent') and is transmitted through a contact (a medium, such as live speech, a telephone, or writing). For the purposes of discussing literature, the 'contact' is usually now the printed word (except in drama or 'performance poetry'); and so we may restate the diagram thus:

	CONTEXT	
WRITER	WRITING	READER
	CODE	

If we adopt the addresser's viewpoint, we draw attention to the *writer* and his or her 'emotive' or 'expressive' use of language; if we focus on the 'context', we isolate the 'referential' use of language and invoke its historical dimension at the point of its production; if we are principally interested in the addressee, we study the *reader's* 'reception' of the 'message', hence introducing a different historical context (no longer the moment of a text's production but of its *reproduction*), and so on. The different literary theories also tend to place an emphasis upon one function rather than another. Taking some of the dominant theories of our time, we might place them diagrammatically as follows:

	MARXIST	
ROMANTIC-	FORMALISTIC	READER-
HUMANIST	STRUCTURALIST	ORIENTED

Romantic-humanist theories emphasise the *writer's* life and mind as expressed in his or her work; 'reader-criticism' (phenomenological criticism) centres itself on the *reader's*, or 'affective', experience; formalist theories concentrate on the nature of the *writing* itself in isolation; Marxist criticism regards the social and historical *context* as fundamental, though it must be added that Western Marxists do not hold a strictly referential view of language; and structuralist poetics draws attention to the *codes* we use to construct meaning. At their best none of the approaches totally ignores the other dimensions of literary communication. For example, in Marxist criticism, the writer, the audience, and the text are all included within a generally sociological perspective. Feminist criticism, it may significantly be noted, is not given a place in our diagram because its project by definition is to attempt a global reinterpretation and redeployment of all approaches as an aspect of a revolutionary sexual politics. And that word 'politics', which feminism has here foregrounded, is a key term in understanding theory in general and its specific present manifestations. We will return to it briefly in a moment.

This *Reader's Guide* does not try to give a comprehensive picture of modern critical theory, but rather a map of the most challenging and prominent trends. For example, myth criticism, which has a long and various history, and includes the work of Gilbert Murray, James Frazer, Maud Bodkin, Carl Jung and Northrop Frye, has been omitted because it seemed to us that it has not entered the main stream of academic or popular culture, and has not challenged received ideas as vigorously as the theories which we will examine. This admission/omission too will, in its selectivity and partiality, direct us back to the *politics* of literary theory, and to one of the major lessons delivered to us by the alarums and excursions of the theoretical debates of the last twenty years or so. But first, a further brief explanation of apparent oddities in the composition of this Guide.

A new chapter in this revised edition is the first one on New Criticism and F. R. Leavis. The question is: why have we put it *first* when even a cursory glance at the original opening chapter on Russian Formalism would indicate that chronologically the high point of the latter arguably *precedes* the former? Two points of interest can be made here. First, because of the determinations of political and cultural history Russian Formalism, albeit mainly *produced* in the second two decades of the twentieth century, did not have widespread impact until the late 1960s and 1970s, when it was effectively rediscovered and translated (made accessible and given currency) by Western intellectuals who were themselves part of the newer Marxist and structuralist movements of that time. In this sense the Russian Formalists 'belong' to this later moment of their *reproduction* and are mobilised by the new left critics in their assault, precisely, on established literary criticism – represented most centrally in the Anglo-Saxon cultures by New Criticism and Leavisism. The second point, therefore, is that despite the apparently later and longer mid-twentieth-century chronology of these Anglo-American movements they are *anterior*, in terms of critical-theoretical ideology, to the older but more latterly reproduced work of the Russian Formalists. Periodicity in any context is problematical; here we have partially solved it by putting New Criticism and the 'moral formalism' of Leavis first because, in a very real sense, they are the traditions of criticism with which contemporary critical theory, from the onset and principally, had to engage.

Developments in critical theory and practice have diversified in geometric progression since Raman Selden was first brave enough to write this book. Revised editions, including the present one, have attempted to keep up with this profusion – witness here the separation out of a new chapter on 'Postmodernism' from the one on 'Poststructuralism'; the inclusion of a preliminary section on postcolonial theory; and the extensive but still no doubt inadequate revision of the chapter on feminist criticism. But all such attempts are doomed to failure – because to some they will be partial (in both senses), tendentious, exclusive, wrong-headed or whatever. For example, it has already been pointed out to me that the book will inevitably be seen to be – indeed is – ethnocentric and homophobic, and the absences and naturalised prejudicial emphases are, I am afraid, readily apparent: little if anything on African-American, Asian, Caribbean or black British theory – especially in relation to feminism; nothing on queer theory or lesbian theory, and so on. Perhaps a still later edition will be able to overcome this one's inadequacy and accommodate these dynamic manifestations of postmodern theoretical fission.

But this is indeed the point which begins to emerge from the gap between the moment when Ray Selden began in 1985 and the moment of revision now: 'theory', even 'literary theory', can no longer be usefully regarded as a progressively emerging body of work, evolving through a series of definable phases or 'movements' – of delivery, critique, advancement, reformulation and so on. This appeared to be the case – no doubt it was never true – in the later 1970s and very early 1980s, when the 'moment of theory' seemed to have arrived and there was a danger even to those enthusiastically participating in it that a new academic subject, even a new scholasticism – radical and subversive, yes, but also potentially exclusive in its abstraction – was emerging. Books poured from the presses, conferences

abounded, 'theory' courses on undergraduate degree pro-
grammes became *de rigeur*, MAs proliferated, and residual
notions of 'practice' and of 'the empirical' had to be defined and
defended very carefully and exactly. To me, such a 'moment of
theory' seems no longer to obtain – whether because it
paradoxically coincided with the rise to power of the new right,
whether because in a postmodern world it could not by
definition survive in a more or less unitary state, or whether it
contained, as itself a postmodern creature, the catalysing agents
for its own dispersal, I could not confidently say. But a change
has occurred – a change very different to that increasingly
abstract and self-obsessed intellectual field the first edition of
this book felt itself just about able to describe and contain. The
moment of theory has instead spawned a hugely diverse tribe of
praxes, or theorised practices, at once self-conscious about their
project and representing forms of political action in the cultural
domain at least. This is in particular the case with the various
critical theories and practices which focus on gender and
sexuality, and with those which seek to deconstruct ethno- and
Eurocentricity. Herein, too, lies the explanation for our reordering of the chapters in this revised *Reader's Guide* – where 1–5
already have an *historical* feel to them, and 6–8 represent 'the
state of the art' or where the action is.

The lesson that has been learnt from the theoretical debates of
the past twenty years, and learnt not only by radicals but also by
some of those who wish to defend more conventional or
traditionally humanistic positions and approaches, is that *no*
literary-critical activity is not underpinned by theory; that the
theory, whatever it may be, represents an ideological – if not
expressly political – attitude; that it is more effective, if not more
honest, to have a praxis which is explicitly theorised than to
operate with naturalised and unexamined assumptions; that
theoretical praxis may be tactical and strategic rather than
seemingly philosophically absolute; that 'theory' is no longer
awesome (although still 'difficult'); and that it is to be *put to use*
rather than studied for its own sake.

The demystification of theory, then – which has resulted in
the great plurality of theorised praxes for specific interests and
purposes – allows us to be rather more self-questioning about it.
How far is it appropriate to force the autonomous study of

critical theory onto every undergraduate literature course? Is theory something which can, in fact, be studied as though it were a separate philosophical genre? Is there ever a universally applicable theory? Do we need to comprehend the informing philosophical history of a critical position or practice? How far is a 'theory' often no more than a *technique*? Are particular theories tied, in effect, to particular kinds of text or to particular periods – will the same theory be usefully applicable to Renaissance and to Romantic literature, to a poem and to a novel? How far and with what justification does a theoretical position 'rewrite' or transform its object of study? All such questions demand answers in particular contexts and are part of a properly pragmatic politics in the field of cultural study. In this new edition of *A Reader's Guide* and as an aid to this process, we have attempted to suggest, where appropriate, instances of practical applications of particular theories – for the most part, for reasons of space, ones included in Raman Selden's companion volume to the present work, *Practising Theory and Reading Literature: An Introduction* (referred to in the text as *PTRL* after the first citing in each chapter). In no sense is this an attempt to diminish the force and importance of theoretical work or to promote a new empiricism: it is merely to recognise that all literary criticism is a theoretical practice and that to understand the theory – and be able to theorise one's *own* practice – is to enfranchise oneself in the constituency of cultural politics.

GENERAL READING

Introductions and reference works

Atkins, G. Douglas and Morrow, Laura (eds), *Contemporary Literary Theory* (Macmillan, Basingstoke and London, 1989).

Coyle, Martin, Garside, Peter, Kelsall, Malcolm and Peck, John (eds), *Encyclopaedia of Literature and Criticism* (Routledge, London, 1990). Among its 100 essays on 'English Literature' are many which introduce categories of criticism to be found in the present volume.

Eagleton, Terry, *Literary Theory: An Introduction* (Blackwell, Oxford, 1983).

Hawthorn, Jeremy, *Unlocking The Text: Fundamental Issues in Literary Theory* (Arnold, London, 1987).

Hawthorn, Jeremy (ed.), *A Glossary of Contemporary Literary Theory*

(Arnold, London, 1992). Also *A Concise Glossary of Contemporary Literary Theory* in paperback. Useful, dictionary-like reference books.
Jefferson, Ann and Robey, David (eds), *Modern Literary Theory: A Comparative Introduction* (Batsford, London, 2nd edn, 1986).
Newton, Ken (ed.), *Theory into Practice: A Reader in Modern Criticism* (Macmillan, Basingstoke and London, 1992). A collection of practical 'applications' of critical theories. See also Newton's 'Reader' of theory below.
Selden, Raman, *Practising Theory and Reading Literature: An Introduction*, (Harvester Wheatsheaf, Hemel Hempstead, 1989).
Tallack, Douglas (ed.), *Literary Theory at Work: Three Texts* (Batsford, London, 1987). Theory applied to specific literary works.
Webster, Roger, *Studying Literary Theory: An Introduction* (Arnold, London, 1990). Has all the advantages and disadvantages of being a really short 'Introduction'.

Anthologies of literary theory

Davis, Robert Con and Schleifer, Ronald (eds), *Contemporary Literary Criticism: Literary and Cultural Studies: 1900 to the Present* (Longman, London and New York, 2nd edn, 1989).
Lambropoulos, V. and Miller, D. N. (eds), *Twentieth-Century Literary Theory: An Introductory Anthology* (State University of New York Press, Albany, New York, 1987). Concentrates on New Criticism and Russian and Czech Formalism.
Lodge, David (ed.), *Twentieth-Century Literary Criticism* (Longman, London and New York, 1972). Mainly pre-1960 material.
Lodge, David (ed.), *Modern Criticism and Theory: A Reader* (Longman, London and New York, 1988). Authoritative on most post-1960 theories.
Newton, K. M. (ed.), *Twentieth-Century Literary Theory* (Macmillan, Basingstoke and London, 1988).
Rice, Philip and Waugh, Patricia (eds), *Modern Literary Theory: A Reader* (Arnold, London, 2nd edn, 1992). Helpful introductions to the sections and extracts.
Rylance, Rick (ed.), *Debating Texts: A Reader in Twentieth-Century Literary Theory and Method* (Open University, Milton Keynes, 1987).
Selden, Raman (ed.), *The Theory of Criticism from Plato to the Present: A Reader* (Longman, London and New York, 1988). Extracts from contemporary theories placed in historical context.
Walder, Dennis (ed.), *Literature in the Modern World* (Oxford University Press with the Open University, Oxford, 1990). Interestingly structured collection of 'documents' and critical essays ranging right across the field.

1 New Criticism, moral formalism and F. R. Leavis

ORIGINS: ELIOT, RICHARDS AND EMPSON

The origins of the dominant Anglo-American traditions of criticism in the mid-twentieth century (roughly from the 1920s to the 1970s) are of course complex and often apparently contradictory – as are their theoretical and critical positions and practices. But we may crudely say that the influence of the British nineteenth-century poet and literary and cultural critic Matthew Arnold is strongly perceptible in them – especially the Arnold who proposed that philosophy and religion would be 'replaced by poetry' in modern society and who held that 'Culture' – representing 'the best that has been known and thought in the world' – could mount a humanistic defence against the destructive 'Anarchy' (Arnold's word) of what F. R. Leavis was later to call the 'technologico-Benthamite' civilisation of urban, industrialised societies. The principal twentieth-century mediator of Arnold into the new critical movements, and himself the single most influential common figure behind them – British or American – was the American (and then naturalised English) poet, dramatist and critic, T. S. Eliot (see below).

To over-simplify, what is central to all the diverse inflections of the Anglo-American tradition – and itself derived from the two sources mentioned above – is a profound, almost reverential regard for literary works themselves. This may manifest

10

itself as an obsessive concern with 'the text itself', 'the words on the page', nothing more nor less; with literary works as icons of human value deployed against twentieth-century cultural barbarism; or as an 'objective', 'scientific', 'disinterested' (Arnold's word) criticism of the text – but at heart it represents the same aesthetico-humanist idealisation of works of Literature. We capitalise 'Literature' because one of the most influential – and later most crucially deconstructed – effects of this critical tradition was the elevation of some literary works over others by way of close and 'disinterested' textual analysis ('scrutiny' leading to 'discrimination', both key Leavisite terms). Only some literary writing, in other words, was 'Literature' (the best that has been thought and *written*), and could become part of the 'tradition' (Eliot's key term and then Leavis's, as in *The Great Tradition*) or, more recognisably these days, of *the canon*. By its nature, the canon is exclusive and hierarchical, and would clearly be seen to be artificially constructed by choices and selections made by human agency (critics) were it not for its endemic tendency to naturalise itself as, precisely, *natural*: self-evidently, unarguably *given*, *there*, and not created by critical 'discrimination', by taste, preference, partiality, etc. This is its great danger; and of course it disenfranchises huge tracts of literary writing from serious study and status. It is why, in the post-1960s critical revolution, it had to be demystified and dismantled, so that all the writing which had been 'hidden from criticism' – 'gothic' and 'popular' fiction, working-class and women's writing, for example – could be put back on the agenda in an environment relatively free of pre-emptive evaluation.

T. S. Eliot was central to many of the tendencies sketched in so far, and his early essay 'Tradition and the Individual Talent' (1919) has been perhaps the singly most influential work in Anglo-American criticism. In it, Eliot does two things in particular: he emphasises that writers must have 'the historical sense' – that is, a sense of the tradition of writing in which they must situate themselves; and that this process reinforces the necessary 'depersonalisation' of the artist if his or her art is to attain the 'impersonality' it must have if it is 'to approach the condition of science'. Famously, he wrote: 'Poetry is not a turning loose of emotion, but an escape from emotion; it is not the expression of personality, but an escape from personality.'

The poet (and we may note Eliot's privileging of poetry as the dominant genre, for this was to become the main focus of much New Criticism – and an instance therefore of the way particular theories relate most closely to particular kinds of writing: see Introduction, p. 8) becomes a kind of impersonal 'catalyst' of experience, a 'medium' not of his or her 'consciousness' or 'personality' but of that which in the end makes up the 'medium' itself – the poem – and our sole object of interest. In another famous phrase from a different essay ('Hamlet', 1919), Eliot describes the work of art as an 'objective correlative' for the experience which may have engendered it: an impersonal recreation which is the autonomous object of attention. (It is closely related to the notion of the 'image' which is central to the poetics of Ezra Pound, Imagism and Eliot's own poetic practice.) What emerges from all this in the context of the diverse developments of New Criticism is the (seemingly) anti-romantic thrust of Eliot's thinking (a new 'classicism'); the emphasis on 'science', 'objectivity', 'impersonality', and the 'medium' as the focal object of analysis; and the notion of a 'tradition' of works which most successfully hold an 'essence' of human experience in their constituent 'medium'.

In the immediate post-First-World-War period when Eliot was developing these ideas, 'English' was emerging (most particularly at Cambridge University) as a (some would say *the*) central subject in the Arts higher-education syllabus, and with it a new, younger generation of academics determined to transcend the older 'bellettrist' critical tradition which had dominated 'English' hitherto. In a sense, they can be regarded as the first proponents of a 'professional' criticism working from within the academy, and it was to them that Eliot's critical precepts appealed most strongly. It is worth registering – both in the present context and in the later one of contemporary critical theory's assault on the earlier tradition, and of *its* consonance with *post*modernism – that this new criticism had a thoroughly symbiotic relationship with literary modernism, finding its premises borne out in such works and using these as its model texts for analysis. To put it over simply, perhaps: this new critical movement *was* 'modernist' criticism.

I. A. Richards, William Empson and, slightly later, F. R. Leavis (see below) were the main proponents of the new English at Cambridge. Richards, whose background was in philosophy (aesthetics, psychology and semantics), produced his widely influential *Principles of Literary Criticism* in 1924. In it he innovatively attempted to lay down an explicit theoretical base for literary study. Arguing that criticism should emulate the precision of science, he attempted to articulate the special character of literary language, differentiating the 'emotive' language of poetry from the 'referential' language of non-literary discourse (his *Science and Poetry* was to follow in 1926). Even more influential – certainly in terms of its title and the praxis it enunciates – was *Practical Criticism* (1929), in which Richards included examples of his students' attempts to analyse short, unidentified poems, showed how slack their reading equipment was, and attempted to establish basic tenets for the close reading of poetry. Practical Criticism became, in both the United States and England, the central compulsory critical and pedagogic tool of the higher-education (and then secondary) English syllabus – rapidly and damagingly becoming untheorised, and thus naturalised, as *the* fundamental critical practice. Its virtues were, however – and we may yet come to regret its obloquy in the demystifying theoretical initiatives of the past twenty years – that it encouraged attentive close reading of texts and, in its intellectual and historical abstraction, a kind of democratisation of literary study in the classroom, in which nearly everyone was placed on an equal footing in the face of a 'blind' text – a point we will re-emphasise in the context of American New Criticism. Indeed Richards left Cambridge in 1929, later settling at Harvard University, and his influence, particularly through *Practical Criticism*, substantially underpinned native developments in the States which were moving in similar directions.

William Empson, who transferred from mathematics to English as an undergraduate and became Richards's pupil, is most important in our context here for his first, famously precocious and astoundingly quickly produced work (written when he was Richards's student), *Seven Types of Ambiguity* (1930). It would be inaccurate to characterise Empson as purely a New Critic (his later work and career constantly refused easy labelling or placing) but that first book, with its emphasis on 'ambiguity' as the defining characteristic of poetic language, its virtuoso feats of close, creative 'practical criticism' in action, and its detaching of literary texts from their contexts in the process of 'reading' their ambiguities was particularly influential on New Criticism.

THE AMERICAN NEW CRITICS

American New Criticism, emerging in the 1920s and especially dominant in the 1940s and 1950s, is equivalent to the establishing of the new professional criticism in the emerging discipline of 'English' in British higher education during the inter-war period. As always, origins and explanations for its rise – in its heyday to almost hegemonic proportions – are complex and finally indefinite, but some suggestions may be sketched in. First, a number of the key figures were also part of a group called the Southern Agrarians, or 'Fugitives', a traditional, conservative, Southern-oriented movement which was hostile to the hard-nosed industrialism and materialism of a United States dominated by 'the North'. Without stretching the point too far, a consanguinity with Arnold, Eliot and, later, Leavis in his opposition to modern 'inorganic' civilisation may be discerned here. Second, New Criticism's high point of influence was during the Second World War and the Cold War succeeding it, and we may see that its privileging of literary texts (their 'order', 'harmony' and 'transcendence' of the historically and ideologically determinate) and of the 'impersonal' analysis of what makes them great works of art (their innate value lying in their superiority to material history: see below Cleanth Brooks's essay about Keats's 'Ode on a Grecian Urn') might represent a haven for alienated intellectuals and, indeed, for whole generations of quietistic students. Third, with the huge expansion of the student population in the States in this period, catering for second-generation products of the American 'melting pot', New Criticism with its 'practical criticism' basis was at once pedagogically economical (copies of short texts could be distributed equally to everyone) and also a way of coping with masses of individuals who had no 'history' in common. In other words, its ahistorical, 'neutral' nature – the study only of 'the words on the page' – was an apparently equalising, democratic activity appropriate to the new American experience. (Frank

Lentricchia's important book, *After the New Criticism*, 1980, is an attempt to chart the flux (1955–77) of American critical theory after the 'death' of New Criticism sometime in the mid-to-late 1950s.)

But whatever the socio-cultural explanations for its provenance, New Criticism is clearly characterised in premise and practice: it is not concerned with *context* – historical, biographical, intellectual and so on; it is not interested in the 'fallacies' of 'intention' or 'affect'; it is concerned solely with the 'text in itself', with its language and organisation; it does not seek a text's 'meaning', but how it 'speaks itself' (see Archibald MacLeish's poem 'Ars Poetica', itself a synoptic New Critical document, which opens: 'A poem must not mean/But be'); it is concerned to trace how the parts of the text relate, how it achieves its 'order' and 'harmony', how it contains and resolves 'irony', 'paradox', 'tension', 'ambivalence' and 'ambiguity'; and it is concerned essentially with articulating the very 'poem-ness' – the formal quintessence – of the poem itself (and it usually *is* a poem – but see Mark Schorer below).

RANSOM AND BROOKS

An early, founding essay in the self-identification of New Criticism is John Crowe Ransom's 'Criticism, Inc.' (1937). (His book on Eliot, Richards and others, entitled *The New Criticism*, 1941, gave the movement its name.) Ransom, one of the 'Fugitives' and editor of the *Kenyon Review* 1939–59, here lays down the ground rules: 'Criticism, Inc.' is the 'business' of professionals – professors of literature in the universities in particular; criticism should become 'more scientific, or precise and systematic'; students should 'study literature, and not merely about literature'; Eliot was right to denounce romantic literature as 'imperfect in objectivity, or "aesthetic distance"'; criticism is *not* ethical, linguistic or historical studies, which are merely 'aids'; the critic should be able to exhibit not the 'prose core' to which a poem may be reduced but 'the differentia, residue, or tissue, which keeps the object poetical or entire. The character of the poem resides for the good critic in its way of exhibiting the residuary quality.'

Many of these precepts are given practical application in the work of Cleanth Brooks, himself also a 'Fugitive', professional academic, editor of the *Southern Review* (with Robert Penn Warren) 1935–42, and one of the most skilled and exemplary practitioners of the New Criticism. His and Warren's textbook anthologies, *Understanding Poetry* (1938) and *Understanding Fiction* (1943), are often regarded as having spread the New Critical doctrine throughout generations of American university literature students, but his most characteristic book of close readings is the significantly titled *The Well-Wrought Urn: Studies in the Structure of Poetry* (1947), in which the essay on the eponymous urn of Keats's Ode, 'Keats's Sylvan Historian: History Without Footnotes' (1942), is in our view the best exemplificaton, explicitly and implicitly, of New Critical practice one could hope to find. Brooks at once quotes the opening of MacLeish's 'Ars Poetica' (see above); refers to Eliot and his notion of the 'objective correlative'; rejects the relevance of biography; reiterates throughout the terms 'dramatic propriety', 'irony', 'paradox' (repeatedly) and 'organic context'; performs a bravura reading of the poem which leaves its 'sententious' final dictum as a dramatically organic element of the whole; constantly admires the poem's 'history' above the 'actual' histories of 'war and peace', of 'our time-ridden minds', of 'meaningless' 'accumulations of facts', of 'the scientific and philosophical generalisations which dominate our world'; explicitly praises the poem's 'insight into essential truth'; and confirms the poem's value to us (in 1942, in the midst of the nightmare of wartime history) precisely because, like Keats's urn, it is 'All breathing human passion for above' – thus stressing 'the ironic fact that all human passion *does* leave one cloyed; hence *the superiority of art*' (our italics). (For Raman Selden's own example of a 'New Critical' approach to Keats, based on Brooks, see *Practising Theory and Reading Literature*, chapter 1, section 2.)

THE 'INTENTIONAL' AND 'AFFECTIVE' FALLACIES: WIMSATT AND BEARDSLEY

As New Criticism is, by definition, a praxis, much of its 'theory' occurs along the way in more specifically practical essays (as with Brooks above) and not as theoretical writing (see below, also, ιͻr Leavis's refusal to theorise his position or engage in 'philosophical' extrapolation). But there are two New Critical essays in particular which are overtly theoretical and which have become influential texts more generally in modern critical discourse: 'The Intentional Fallacy' (1946) and 'The Affective Fallacy' (1949) written by W. K. Wimsatt – a professor of English at Yale University and author of the symptomatically titled book, *The Verbal Icon: Studies in the Meaning of Poetry* (1954) – in collaboration with Monroe C. Beardsley, a philosopher of aesthetics. Both essays, influenced by Eliot and Richards, engage with the 'addresser' (writer)–'message' (text)–'addressee' (reader) nexus outlined in the Introduction, in the pursuit of an 'objective' criticism which abjures both the personal input of the writer ('intention') and the emotional effect on the reader ('affect') in order purely to study the 'words on the page' and how the artifact 'works'. The first essay argues that 'the design or intention of the author is neither available nor desirable as a standard for judging the success of a work of literary art'; that a poem 'goes about the world beyond [the author's] power to intend about it or control it' – it 'belongs to the public'; that it should be understood in terms of the 'dramatic *speaker*' of the text, not the author; and be judged only by whether it 'works' or not. Much critical debate has since raged about the place of intention in criticism, and continues to do so: Wimsatt and Beardsley's position strikes a chord, for example, with poststructualist notions of the 'death of the author' (see below, p.2) and with deconstruction's freeing of the text from 'presence' and 'meaning'. But there the resemblance ends, for the New Critics still basically insist that there is a determinate, ontologically stable 'poem itself', which is the ultimate arbiter of its own 'statement', and that an 'objective' criticism is possible. This runs quite counter to deconstruction's notion of the 'iterability' of a text in its multiplex 'positioned' rereadings.

This difference becomes very much clearer in the second essay, which argues that the 'affective fallacy' represents 'a confusion between the poem and its *results*': 'trying to derive the standard of criticism from the psychological effects of the poem

. . . ends in impressionism and relativism'. Opposing the 'classical objectivity' of New Criticism to 'romantic reader psychology', it asserts that the outcome of both fallacies is that 'the poem itself, as an object of specifically critical judgment, tends to disappear'. And the importance of a poem in classic New Critical terms is that by 'fixing emotions and making them more permanently perceptible', by the 'survival' of 'its clear and nicely interrelated meanings, its completeness, balance, and tension', it represents 'the most precise emotive report on customs': 'In short, though cultures have changed, poems remain and explain.' Poems, in other words, are our cultural heritage, permanent and valuable artifacts; and therein lies the crucial difference from more contemporary theoretical positions.

TECHNIQUE AS DISCOVERY: MARK SCHORER

Finally in the context of American New Criticism we may briefly mention the work of Mark Schorer, professor of English at Berkeley, California, whose two essays 'Technique as Discovery' (1948) and 'Fiction and the Analogical Matrix' (1949) mark the attempt to deploy New Critical practice, so extensively and sophisticatedly applied to poetry, in relation to prose fiction. In the first essay Schorer notes: 'Modern criticism has shown us that to speak of content as such is not to speak of art at all, but of experience; and that it is only when we speak of the *achieved* content, the form, the work of art as a work of art, that we speak as critics. The difference between content, or experience, and achieved content, or art, is technique.' This, he adds, has not been followed through in regard to the novel, whose own 'technique' is language, and whose own 'achieved content' – or 'discovery' of what it is saying – can only, as with a poem, be analysed in terms of that 'technique'. In the second essay Schorer extends his analysis of the language of fiction by revealing the unconscious patterns of imagery and symbolism (way beyond the author's 'intention') present in all forms of fiction and not just those which foreground a 'poetic' discourse. He shows how the author's 'meaning', often contradicting the surface sense, is embedded in the matrix of linguistic analogues which constitute the text. In this we may see connections with later poststructuralist theories' concern with the sub-texts, 'silences', 'ruptures', 'raptures' and 'play' inherent in all texts, however seemingly stable – although Schorer himself, as a good New Critic, does not deconstruct modern novels, but reiterates the coherence of their 'technique' in seeking to capture 'the whole of the modern consciousness . . . the complexity of the modern spirit'. Perhaps it is, rather, that we should sense an affinity between the American New Critic, Schorer, and the English moral formalist, F. R. Leavis (see below), some of whose most famous criticism of fiction in the 1930s and beyond presents 'the Novel as Dramatic Poem'.

THE CHICAGO SCHOOL: RHETORIC OF FICTION

As a footnote to the New Criticism, however, and before we turn to Leavis, it is worth mentioning another American 'movement' of the mid-century which was especially influential in the study of fiction: the so-called 'Chicago School' of 'Neo-Aristotelians'. Theoretically offering a challenge to the New Critics but in fact often seen as only a New Critical 'heresy' in their analysis of formal structure and in their belief, with T. S. Eliot, that criticism should study 'poetry as poetry and not another thing', the Neo-Aristotelians were centred, from the later 1930s through the 1940s and 1950s, on R. S. Crane at the University of Chicago. Establishing a theoretical basis derived principally from Aristotle's *Rhetoric* and *Poetics*, Crane and his group sought to emulate the logic, lucidity and scrupulous concern with evidence found there; were worried by the limitations of New Critical practice (its rejection of historical analysis, its tendency to present subjective judgements as though they were objective, its concern primarily with poetry); and attempted therefore to develop a more inclusive and catholic criticism which would cover all genres and draw for its techniques, on a 'pluralistic and instrumentalist' basis, from whatever method seemed appropriate to a particular case. The anthology *Critics and Criticism: Ancient and Modern* (1952; abridged edition with preface by Crane, 1957) contains many examples of their approach, including Crane's own exemplary reading of Fielding's *Tom Jones*, 'The Concept of Plot and the Plot of *Tom Jones*'.

In effect, the Neo-Aristotelians were most influential in the study of narrative structure in the novel, and most particularly by way of the work of a slightly later critic, Wayne C. Booth, who nevertheless acknowledged that he was a Chicago Aristotelian. His book *The Rhetoric of Fiction* (1961) has been widely read and highly regarded, although latterly contemporary critical theory has demonstrated its limitations and inadequacies (see below, by Jameson, p.95, and implicitly by much 'reader-oriented' theory, chapter 3). Booth's project was to examine 'the art of communicating with readers – the rhetorical resources available to the writer of epic, novel or short story as he tries, consciously or unconsciously, to impose his fictional world upon the reader'. Although accepting in New Critical terms that a novel is an 'autonomous' text, Booth develops a key concept with the notion that it nevertheless contains an authorial 'voice' – the 'implied author' (his or her 'official scribe' or 'second self') – whom the reader invents by deduction from the attitudes articulated in the fiction. Once this distinction between author and the 'authorial voice' is made, the way is open to analyse, in and for themselves, the many and various forms of narration which construct the text. A major legacy of Booth's is his separating out of 'reliable' and 'unreliable' narrators – the former, usually in the third person, coming close to the values of the 'implied author'; the latter, often a character within the story, a deviant from them. What Booth did was at once to enhance the formal equipment available for analysis of the 'rhetoric of fiction' and, paradoxically perhaps, to promote the belief that authors *do* mean to 'impose' their values on the reader and that 'reliability' is therefore a good thing. We may see here a consonance with the 'moral formalism' of Leavis, and the reason why poststructuralist narratology has gone beyond Booth. (A reading of Henry James's *The Aspern Papers*, based on Booth's concepts, is included in chapter 1, section 3 of *PTRL*.)

MORAL FORMALISM: F. R. LEAVIS

Despite, or rather because of, the fact that F. R. Leavis (and 'Leavisite criticism' more generally, flowing from the journal *Scrutiny* [1932–53]) became the major single target for the New Critical theory of the 1970s and beyond in the British context at least, both Raymond Williams in *Politics and Letters* (1979) and Terry Eagleton in *Literary Theory: An Introduction* (1983) bear witness to his enormous, ubiquitous influence in English Studies from the 1930s onwards. Apropos of Leavis's *The Great Tradition* (1948), Williams remarks that by the early 1970s, in relation to the English novel, Leavis 'had completely won. I mean if you talked to anyone about [it], including people who were hostile to Leavis, they were in fact reproducing his sense of the shape of its history.' And more generally, Eagleton writes: 'Whatever the "failure" or "success" of *Scrutiny* . . . the fact remains that English students in England today [1983] are "Leavisites" whether they know it or not, irremediably altered by that historic intervention.'

   Leavis, profoundly influenced by Matthew Arnold and by T. S. Eliot (Leavis's *New Bearings in English Poetry* [1932] in effect first taught the English how to 'read' *The Waste Land*), was, like Richards and Empson above, one of the new academics in Cambridge in the late 1920s and early 1930s who turned the English syllabus away from the bellettrism of Sir Arthur Quiller-Couch and others, and put it at the centre of arts education in the university. His *Education and the University* (1943) – in part made up of essays published earlier, including the widely influential 'A Sketch for an "English School"' and 'Mass Civilisation and Minority Culture' – bears witness (as do later works like *English Literature in Our Time and the University*, 1969, *The Living Principle: English as a Discipline of Thought*, 1975, and *Thought, Words and Creativity*, 1976), to the fact that Leavis was an *educator* as much as he was a critic, and to the practical, empirical, strategically anti-theoretical nature of his work. In a famous exchange with the American critic René Wellek, for example (see Leavis's essay 'Literary Criticism and Philosophy', 1937, in *The Common Pursuit*, 1952), he defends his refusal to theorise his work by saying that criticism and philosophy are quite separate activities and that the business of the critic is to 'attain a peculiar completeness of response [in order] to enter into possession of the given poem . . . in its concrete fulness'.

In addition to editing *Scrutiny*, to teaching generations of students – many of whom themselves became teachers and writers – and to being the informing presence, behind, for example, the widely selling, ostensibly neutral but evidently Leavisite *Pelican Guide to English Literature* (1954–61) edited by Boris Ford in seven volumes, Leavis produced many volumes of criticism and cultural commentary: all of which are indelibly imbued with his 'theory', although resolutely untheorised in abstract terms – a theory which has, therefore, to be extrapolated from his work *passim*.

Following Richards, Leavis is a kind of 'practical critic', but also, in his concern with the concrete specificity of the 'text itself', the 'words on the page', a kind of 'New Critic' too: '[the critic] is concerned with the work in front of him [sic] as something that should contain within itself the reason why it is so and not otherwise' ('The Function of Criticism' in *The Common Pursuit*, 1952 – note the sideways reference to both Arnold and Eliot in the essay's title). But to regard Leavis simply in this way, with its inherent formalism and ahistoricism, is a mistake; for his close address to the text is only ever to establish the vitality of its 'felt life', its closeness to 'experience', to prove its moral force, and to demonstrate (by close *scrutiny*) its excellence. The passage from Eliot which gave Leavis his title for *The Common Pursuit* speaks of the critic's task as engaging in: 'the common pursuit of true judgment', and *Revaluation* (1936) is an Eliot-like sorting-out of the 'true' tradition of English poetry, just as *The Great Tradition* itself opens with the classic Leavisian 'discrimination' that 'The great English novelists are' Jane Austen, George Eliot, Henry James and Joseph Conrad – a list which may immediately suggest just how tendentious Leavis's 'true judgment' always, in fact, is: James and Conrad 'English'? A major plank in Leavis's platform, in other words, is to identify the 'great works' of literature, to sift out the dross ('mass' or 'popular' fiction, for example), and to establish the Arnoldian and Eliotian 'tradition' or 'canon'. This is necessary because these are the works which should be taught in a university 'English' course as part of the process of cultural filtering, refining and revitalising which such courses undertake on behalf of the nation's cultural health. In particular, such works will promote the values of 'Life' (the crucial Leavisian word, never defined: 'the major novelists . . . are significant in terms of that human awareness they promote; awareness of the poss-ibilities of life') against the forces of materialism, barbarism, industrialism and so on in a 'technologico-Benthamite' society: they represent a 'minority culture', in other words, embattled with a 'mass civilisation'.

Just as Leavis's *moral* fervour distinguishes him from the more abstract or aesthetic formalism of the New Critics (for an illustration of Leavis's 'moral criticism' at work see Raman Selden's discussion of it in relation to Bunyan's *A Pilgrim's Progress*, in chapter 1, section 1 of *PTRL*), so too does his emphatically sociological and historical sense. Literature is a weapon in the battle of cultural politics, and much of the 'great' literature of the past (as for Eliot – especially but not exclusively – from the pre-'dissociation of sensibility' seventeenth century) bears witness to the 'organic' strength of pre-industrial cultures. The past and past literature, as for Arnold and Eliot once more, act as a measure of the 'wasteland' of the present age – although the work of the 'great' moderns (Eliot and D. H. Lawrence, for example). in its 'necessary' difficulty, complexity and commit-ment to cultural values, is also mobilised on 'Life's' behalf in the inimical world of the twentieth century. As for the New Critics, too, great works of literature are vessels in which humane values survive; but for Leavis they are also to be actively deployed in an ethico-sociological cultural politics. Paradoxically then, and precisely because of this, Leavis's project is both elitist and culturally pessimistic. It is perhaps not surprising therefore that in the twentieth century it became so profoundly popular and influential; had indeed until quite recently become natural-ised *as* 'Literary Studies'. (In this context, see Perry Anderson's critique of Leavisism in 'Components of the National Culture', 1968, in which he asserts that Leavisian literary criticism, in mid-century Britain, filled the vacuum left by the failure to develop a British Marxism or sociology.) Hence the absence of theory: not *being* a theory, but merely 'true judgment' and common sense based on lived experience ('"This – doesn't it? – bears such a relation to that; this kind of thing – don't you find it so? – wears better than *that*"' ['Literary Criticism and Philosophy']: see above, p.21), Leavisian criticism had no need of theory – could not in fact be theorised. Paradoxically, and for many years, that was its greatest strength.

SELECTED READING

Basic texts

Arnold, Matthew, *Culture and Anarchy* (1869), ed. J. Dover Wilson (Cambridge University Press, Cambridge [1932], 1971).

Arnold, Matthew, *Essays in Criticism*, Second Series, 1888.

Booth, Wayne C., *The Rhetoric of Fiction* (University of Chicago Press, Chicago, 1961).

Brooks, Cleanth, *Modern Poetry and the Tradition* (1939) (Galaxy/Oxford University Press, New York, 1965).

Brooks, Cleanth, *The Well-Wrought Urn: Studies in the Structure of Poetry* (1947) (Methuen, London, 1968).

Brooks, Cleanth and Warren, Robert Penn (eds), *Understanding Poetry: An Anthology for College Students* (Henry Holt, New York, 1938).

Brooks, Cleanth and Warren, Robert Penn (eds), *Understanding Fiction* (Appleton-Century-Crofts, New York, 1943).

Crane, R. S. (ed.), *Critics and Criticism: Ancient and Modern* (Chicago, 1952). Abridged edition with Crane's preface, 1957.

Eliot, T. S., *Selected Essays* (1932) (Faber, London, 1965).

Eliot, T. S., *Notes Towards the Definition of Culture* (Faber, London, 1948).

Empson, William, *Seven Types of Ambiguity* (1930) (Penguin, Harmondsworth, 1961).

Empson, William, *Some Versions of Pastoral* (1935) (Penguin, Harmondsworth, 1966).

Leavis, F. R., *New Bearings in English Poetry* (1932) (Penguin, Harmondsworth, 1963).

Leavis, F. R., *Revaluation* (1936) (Penguin, Harmondsworth, 1978).

Leavis, F. R., *Education and the University* (1943) (Cambridge University Press, Cambridge, 1979).

Leavis, F. R., *The Great Tradition* (1948) (Penguin, Harmondsworth, 1962).

Leavis, F. R., *The Common Pursuit* (1952) (Penguin, Harmondsworth, 1978).

Leavis, F. R., *D. H. Lawrence: Novelist* (1955) (Penguin, Harmondsworth, 1964).

Leavis, F. R., *English Literature in Our Time and the University* (1969) (Cambridge University Press, Cambridge, 1979).

Leavis, F. R., *Nor Shall My Sword* (Chatto & Windus, London, 1972).
Leavis, F. R., *The Living Principle: English as a Discipline of Thought* (Chatto & Windus, London, 1975).
Leavis, F. R., *Thought, Words and Creativity* (Chatto & Windus, London, 1976).
Ransom, John Crowe, 'Criticism, Inc.' (1937) in *The World's Body* (1938) (Kennikat Press, New York, 1964).
Ransom, John Crowe, *The New Criticism* (New Directions, Norfolk, Conn., 1941).
Richards, I. A., *Principles of Literary Criticism* (1924) (Routledge, London, 1970).
Richards, I. A., *Practical Criticism* (1929) (Routledge, London, 1964).
Schorer, Mark, 'Technique as Discovery', *The Hudson Review* (1948).
Schorer, Mark, 'Fiction and the Analogical Matrix', *Kenyon Review* (1949).
Wellek, René and Warren, Austin, *Theory of Literature* (1949) (Penguin, Harmondsworth, 1966).
Wimsatt, W. K., Jr and Beardsley, Monroe C., 'The Intentional Fallacy' (1946), reprinted in Wimsatt, *The Verbal Icon: Studies in the Meaning of Poetry* (1954) (Methuen, London, 1970).
Wimsatt, W. K., Jr and Beardsley, Monroe C., 'The Affective Fallacy' (1949), reprinted in Wimsatt, *The Verbal Icon: Studies in the Meaning of Poetry* (1954) (Methuen, London, 1970).

Introductions

Eagleton, Terry, *Literary Theory: An Introduction* (Basil Blackwell, Oxford, 1983), chap. 1, 'The Rise of English'.
Newton, K. M., *Interpreting the Text: A Critical Introduction to the Theory and Practice of Literary Interpretation* (Harvester Wheatsheaf, Hemel Hempstead, 1990).
Parrinder, Patrick, *Authors and Authority: English and American Criticism, 1750–1990* (Macmillan, Basingstoke, 2nd end, 1991), chaps 6 and 7.
Robey, David, 'Anglo-American New Criticism' in *Modern Literary Theory: A Comparative Introduction*, Ann Jefferson and David Robey (eds) (Batsford, London, 1982).
Rylance, Rick, 'The New Criticism' in *Encyclopaedia of Literature and Criticism*, Martin Coyle, Peter Garside, Malcolm Kelsall and John Peck (eds) (Routledge, London, 1990).
Watson, George, *The Literary Critics* (Penguin, Harmondsworth, 1962), chaps 9 and 10.
Webster, Roger, *Studying Literary Theory: An Introduction* (Edward Arnold, London, 1990), chap 2.

Further reading

Baldick, Chris, *The Social Mission of English Criticism* (Oxford University Press, Oxford, 1983).

Bell, Michael, *F. R. Leavis* (Routledge, London, 1988).

Doyle, Brian, *English and Englishness* (Routledge, London, 1989).

Fekete, John, *The Critical Twilight: Explorations in the Ideology of Anglo-American Literary Theory from Eliot to McLuhan* (Routledge, London, 1977).

Fry, Paul H., *William Empson: Prophet Against Sacrifice* (Routledge, London, 1991).

Graff, Gerald, *Professing Literature: An Institutional History* (Chicago University Press, Chicago, 1987).

Krieger, Murray, *The New Apologists for Poetry* (1956) (Greenwood Press, Newport, 1977).

Lentricchia, Frank, *After the New Criticism* (1980) (Methuen, London, 1983).

MacCullum, Patricia, *Literature and Method: Towards a Critique of I. A. Richards, T. S. Eliot and F. R. Leavis* (Gill & Macmillan, Dublin, 1983).

Mathieson, Margaret, *Preachers of Culture* (Allen & Unwin, London, 1975).

Mulhern, Francis, *The Moment of 'Scrutiny'* (Verso, London, 1979).

Norris, Christopher, *William Empson and the Philosophy of Literary Criticism* (London, 1978).

Palmer, D. J., *The Rise of English Studies* (Oxford University Press, Oxford, 1965).

Samson, Anne, *F. R. Leavis* (Harvester Wheatsheaf, Hemel Hempstead, 1992).

Stewart, John L., *The Burden of Time: The Fugitives and Agrarians* (Princeton University Press, Princeton, 1965).

Thompson, E. M., *Russian Formalism and Anglo-American New Criticism: A Comparative Study* (Mouton, The Hague, 1971).

2 Russian formalism

Students of literature brought up in the tradition of Anglo-American New Criticism with its emphasis on 'practical criticism' and the organic unity of the text might expect to feel at home with Russian Formalism. Both kinds of criticism aim to explore what is specifically *literary* in texts, and both reject the limp spirituality of late Romantic poetics in favour of a detailed and empirical approach to reading. That being said, it must be admitted that the Russian Formalists were much more interested in 'method', much more concerned to establish a 'scientific' basis for the theory of literature. As we have seen, the New Critics combined attention to the specific verbal ordering of texts with an emphasis on the *non-conceptual* nature of literary meaning: a poem's complexity embodied a subtle response to life, which could not be reduced to logical statements or paraphrases. Their approach, despite the emphasis on close reading of texts, remained fundamentally humanistic. For example, Cleanth Brooks (see also above, p. 16) insisted that Marvell's 'Horatian Ode' is not a political statement of Marvell's position on the Civil War but a dramatisation of opposed views, unified into a poetic whole. Brooks concluded his account by arguing that like all 'great poetry' the poem embodies 'honesty and insight and whole-mindedness'. The first Russian Formalists on the other hand considered that human 'content' (emotions, ideas and 'reality' in general) possessed no literary significance in itself, but merely provided a context for the functioning of literary 'devices'. As we shall see, this sharp division of form and content was modified by the later Formalists, but it remains true that the Formalists avoided the New Critics' tendency to endow aesthetic form with moral and cultural significance. They aimed rather to outline models and hypotheses (in a scientific spirit) to explain how aesthetic effects are produced by literary devices, and how the 'literary' is distinguished from and related to the 'extra-literary'. While the New Critics regarded literature as a form of human understanding, the Formalists thought of it as a special use of language.

Peter Steiner has argued convincingly against a monolithic view of Russian Formalism. His own account threatens at times to become utterly pluralistic, but he comes up with a helpful way of discriminating between formalisms when he highlights three metaphors which act as generative models for three phases in the history of Russian Formalism. The model of the 'machine' governs the first phase which sees literary criticism as a sort of mechanics and the text as a heap of devices. The second is an 'organic' phase which sees literary texts as fully functioning 'organisms' of interrelated parts. The third phase adopts the metaphor of 'system' and tries to understand literary texts as the products of the entire literary system and even of the meta-system of interacting literary and non-literary systems.

THE HISTORICAL DEVELOPMENT OF FORMALISM

Formalist studies were well established before the 1917 Revolution – in the Moscow Linguistic Circle, founded 1915, and in Opojaz (the letters stand for 'The Society for the Study of Poetic Language'), started in 1916. The leading figures of the former group were Roman Jakobson and Petr Bogatyrev, who both later helped to found the Prague Linguistic Circle in 1926. Viktor Shklovsky, Yury Tynyanov and Boris Eikhenbaum were prominent in Opojaz. The initial impetus was provided by the Futurists whose artistic efforts before the First World War were directed against 'decadent' bourgeois culture and especially against the anguished soul-searching of the Symbolist movement in poetry and the visual arts. They derided the mystical posturing of poets such as Briusov who insisted that the poet was 'the guardian of the mystery'. In place of the 'absolute', Mayakovsky, the extrovert Futurist poet, offered the noisy materialism of the machine age as the home of poetry. However, it should be noted that the Futurists were as opposed to Realism as the Symbolists had been: their slogan of the 'self-sufficient word' placed a stress on the self-contained sound patterning of words as distinct from their ability to refer to things. The Futurists threw themselves behind the Revolution and emphasised the artist's role as (proletarian) producer of crafted objects. Dmitriev declared that 'the artist is now simply a constructor and technician, a leader and foreman'. The Constructivists took these arguments to their logical extreme and entered actual factories to put into practice their theories of 'production art'.

From this background the Formalists set about producing a theory of literature concerned with the writer's *technical* prowess and *craft* skill. They avoided the proletarian rhetoric of the poets and artists, but they retained a somewhat mechanistic view of the literary process. Shklovsky was as vigorously materialistic in his attitudes as Mayakovsky. The former's famous definition of literature as 'the sum total of all stylistic devices employed in it' sums up well this early phase of formalism.

At first, the Formalists' work developed freely, especially between 1921 and 1925 when the weary USSR was emerging from 'War Communism'. Non-proletarian economics and literature were allowed to flourish during this breathing space, and by 1925 formalism was the dominant method in literary scholarship. Trotsky's sophisticated criticisms of formalism in *Literature and Revolution* (1924) ushered in a defensive phase, culminating in the Jakobson/Tynyanov theses (1928). Some regard the later developments as signalling the defeat of pure formalism and a capitulation to the Communist 'social command'. We would argue that, before official disapproval brought an end to the movement in about 1930, the need to take account of the sociological dimension produced some of the best work of the period, especially in the writings of the 'Bakhtin School' which combined formalist and Marxist traditions in fruitful ways that anticipated later developments. The more structuralist type of formalism, initiated by Jakobson and Tynyanov, was continued in Czech formalism (notably by the Prague Linguistic Circle), until Nazism brought it to an end. Some of this group, including René Wellek and Roman Jakobson, emigrated to the United States where they helped shape the development of New Criticism during the 1940s and 1950s.

ART AS DEVICE: SHKLOVSKY AND TOMASHEVSKY

The Formalists' technical focus led them to treat literature as a special use of language which achieves its distinctness by deviating from and distorting 'practical' language. Practical language is used for acts of communication, while literary language has no practical function at all and simply makes us *see* differently. One might apply this fairly easily to a writer such as Gerard Manley Hopkins, whose language is 'difficult' in a way which draws attention to itself as 'literary', but it is also easy to show that there is no intrinsically literary language. Opening Hardy's *Under the Greenwood Tree* at random, we read the exchange ' "How long will you be?" "Not long. Do wait and talk to me." ' There is absolutely no linguistic reason to regard the words as 'literary'. We read them as literary rather than as an act of communication only because we read them in what we take to be a literary work. As we shall see, Tynyanov and others developed a more dynamic view of 'literariness' which avoids this problem.

What distinguishes literature from 'practical' language is its *constructed* quality. Poetry was treated by the Formalists as the quintessentially literary use of language: it is 'speech organised in its entire phonic texture'. Its most important constructive factor is rhythm. Consider a line from Donne's 'A Nocturnall upon St Lucies Day', stanza 2:

For I am every dead thing

A Formalist analysis would draw attention to an underlying iambic impulse (laid down in the equivalent line in the first stanza: 'The Sunne is spent, and now his flasks'). In the line from stanza 2, our anticipation is frustrated by a dropped syllable between 'dead' and 'thing'; we perceive a deviation from the norm, and this is what produces aesthetic significance. A Formalist would also note finer differences of rhythm produced by syntactical differences between the two lines (for example, the first has a strong caesura, the second none). Poetry exercises a controlled violence upon practical language, which is thereby deformed in order to compel our attention to its constructed nature.

The earlier phase of Formalism was dominated by Viktor Shklovsky, whose theorising, influenced by the Futurists, was lively and iconoclastic. While the Symbolists had viewed poetry as the expression of the Infinite or some unseen reality, Shklovsky adopted a down-to-earth approach, seeking to define the techniques which writers use to produce specific effects.

Shklovsky called one of his most attractive concepts 'defamiliarisation' (*ostranenie*: 'making strange'). He argued that we can never retain the freshness of our perceptions of objects; the demands of 'normal' existence require that they must become to a great extent 'automatised' (a later term). That Wordsworthian innocent vision through which Nature retains 'the glory and the freshness of a dream' is not the normal state of human consciousness. It is the special task of art to give us back the awareness of things which have become habitual objects of our everyday awareness. It must be stressed that the Formalists, unlike the Romantic poets, were not so much interested in the perceptions themselves as in the nature of the devices which produce the effect of 'defamiliarisation'. The purpose of a work of art is to change our mode of perception from the automatic and practical to the artistic. In 'Art as Technique' (1917), Shklovsky makes this clear:

> The purpose of art is to impart the sensation of things as they are perceived, and not as they are known. The technique of art is to make objects 'unfamiliar', to make forms difficult, to increase the difficulty and length of perception, because the process of perception is an aesthetic end in itself and must be prolonged. *Art is a way of experiencing the artfulness of an object; the object is not important.* (Shklovsky's emphasis)

The Formalists were fond of citing two English eighteenth-century writers, Laurence Sterne and Jonathan Swift. Tomashevsky shows how devices of defamiliarisation are used in *Gulliver's Travels*:

> In order to present a satirical picture of the European social-political order, Gulliver . . . tells his master (a horse) about the customs of the ruling class in human society. Compelled to tell everything with the utmost accuracy, he removes the shell of euphemistic phrases and fictitious traditions which justify such things as war, class strife, parliamentary intrigue and so on. Stripped of their verbal justification and thus defamiliarised, these topics emerge in all their horror. Thus criticism of the political system – nonliterary material – is artistically motivated and fully involved in the narrative.

At first this account seems to stress the content of the new perception itself ('horror' at 'war' and 'class strife'). But in fact, what interests Tomashevsky is the artistic transformation of 'non-literary material'. Defamiliarisation changes our response to the world but only by submitting our habitual perceptions to a processing by literary form. (For a discussion of this term in relation to Craig Raine's poem 'A Martian Sends a Postcard Home', and then to William Golding's novel *The Inheritors*, see chapter 2, section 5 of *Practising Theory and Reading Literature*.)

In his monograph on Sterne's *Tristram Shandy*, Shklovsky draws attention to the ways in which familiar actions are defamiliarised by being slowed down, drawn out or interrupted. This technique of delaying and protracting actions makes us attend to them, so that familiar sights and movements cease to be perceived automatically and are thus 'defamiliarised'. Mr Shandy, lying despondently on his bed after hearing of his son Tristram's broken nose, might have been described conventionally ('he lay mournfully upon his bed'), but Sterne chose to defamiliarise Mr Shandy's posture:

> The palm of his right hand, as he fell upon the bed, receiving his forehead, and covering the greatest part of both his eyes, gently sunk down with his head (his elbow giving way backwards) till his nose touch'd the quilt; – his left arm hung insensible over the side of the bed, his knuckles reclining upon the handle of the chamber pot . . .

The example is interesting in showing how often defamiliarisation affects not a perception as such but merely the presentation of a perception. By slowing down the description of Mr Shandy's posture, Sterne gives us no new insight into grief, no new perception of a familiar posture, but only a heightened verbal presentation. It is Sterne's very lack of concern with perception in the non-literary sense which seems to attract Shklovsky's admiration. This emphasis on the actual process of presentation is called 'laying bare' one's technique. Many readers find Sterne's novel irritating for its continual references to its own novelistic structure, but 'laying bare' its own devices is, in Shklovsky's view, the most essentially *literary* thing a novel can do. (There is a fuller discussion of Sterne and 'baring the device' in chapter 2, section 4 of *PTRL*.)

'Defamiliarisation' and 'laying bare' are notions which directly influenced Bertolt Brecht's famous 'alienation effect' (see below, pp. 79–80, for further treatment of this). The classical ideal that art should *conceal* its own processes (*ars celare artem*) was directly challenged by the Formalists and by Brecht. For literature to present itself as a seamless unity of discourse and as a natural representation of reality would be deceitful and, for Brecht, politically regressive – which is why he rejected realism and embraced modernism (for the Lukács/Brecht debate about this, see below pp. 75–81). For example, in a Brechtian production a male character may be played by an actress in order to destroy the naturalness and familiarity of the role and by defamiliarising the role to make the audience attend to its specific maleness. The possible political uses of the device were not foreseen by the Formalists, since their concerns were purely technical.

NARRATIVE

Greek tragedians drew upon traditional stories which consisted of a series of incidents. In section 6 of the *Poetics*, Aristotle defines 'plot' ('mythos') as the 'arrangement of the incidents'. A 'plot' is clearly distinguished from a story upon which a plot may be based. A plot is the artful disposition of the incidents which make up a story. A Greek tragedy usually starts with a 'flashback', a recapitulation of the incidents of the story which occurred prior to those which were selected for the plot. In Virgil's *Aeneid* and in Milton's *Paradise Lost*, the reader is plunged *in medias res* ('into the middle of things'), and earlier incidents in the story are introduced artfully at various stages in the plot, often in the form of retrospective narration: Aeneas narrates the Fall of Troy to Dido in Carthage, and Raphael relates the War in Heaven to Adam and Eve in Paradise.

The distinction between 'story' and 'plot' is given a prominent place in the Russian Formalists' theory of narrative. They stress that only 'plot' (*sjuzet*) is strictly literary, while 'story' (*fabula*) is merely raw material awaiting the organising hand of the writer. However, as Shklovsky's essay on Sterne reveals, the Formalists had a more revolutionary concept of plot than Aristotle. The plot of *Tristram Shandy* is not merely the arrangement of story-incidents but also all the 'devices' used to interrupt and delay the narration. Digressions, typographical games, displacement of parts of the book (preface, dedication, etc.) and extended descriptions are all devices to make us attend to the novel's form. In a sense, 'plot', in this instance, is actually the violation of the expected formal arrangements of incidents. By frustrating familiar plot arrangement, Sterne draws attention to plotting itself as a literary object. In this way, Shklovsky is not at all Aristotelian. In the end, a carefully ordered Aristotelian 'plot' should give us the essential and familiar truths of human life; it should be plausible and have a certain inevitability. The Formalists, on the other hand, often linked theory of plot with the notion of defamiliarisation: the plot *prevents* us from regarding the incidents as typical and familiar. Instead, we are made constantly aware how artifice constructs or forges (makes/counterfeits) the 'reality' presented to us. In its display of *poiesis* ('poet' = 'maker') rather than *mimesis* ('copying' = realism), this looks forward, as does Sterne, to postmodernist self-reflexivity.

MOTIVATION

Boris Tomashevsky called the smallest unit of plot a 'motif', which we may understand as a single statement or action. He makes a distinction between 'bound' and 'free' motifs. A bound motif is one which is required by the story, while a 'free' motif is inessential from the point of view of the story. However, from the literary point of view, the 'free' motifs are potentially the focus of art. For example, the device of having Raphael relate the War in Heaven is a 'free' motif, because it is not part of the story in question. However, it is formally *more* important than the narration of the War itself, because it enables Milton to insert the narration artistically into his overall plot.

This approach reverses the traditional subordination of formal devices to 'content'. The Formalists rather perversely seem to regard a poem's ideas, themes, and references to 'reality' as merely the external excuse the writer required to justify the use of formal devices. They called this dependence on external, non-literary assumptions 'motivation'. According to Shklovsky, *Tristram Shandy* is remarkable for being totally without 'motivation'; the novel is entirely made up of formal devices which are 'bared'.

The most familiar type of 'motivation' is what we usually call 'realism'. No matter how formally constructed a work may be, we still often expect it to give us the illusion of the 'real'. We expect literature to be 'life-like', and may be irritated by characters or descriptions which fail to match our common-sense expectations of what the real world is like. 'A man in love wouldn't behave like that' and 'people of that class wouldn't talk like that' are the kind of remarks we might make when we notice a failure of realistic motivation. On the other hand, as Tomashevsky pointed out, we become accustomed to all kinds of absurdities and improbabilities once we learn to accept a new set of conventions. We fail to notice the improbable way in which heroes are always rescued just before they are about to be killed by the villains in adventure stories. Indeed, realism's central strategy is to disguise its artificiality, to pretend there is no art between it and the reality it shows us; in this respect, it does the exact opposite of 'baring its device'.

The theme of 'motivation' turned out to be important in a great deal of subsequent literary theory. Jonathan Culler summed up the general theme neatly when he wrote: 'To assimilate or interpret something is to bring it within the modes of order which culture makes available, and this is usually done by talking about it in a mode of discourse which a culture takes as natural.' Human beings are endlessly inventive in finding ways of making sense of the most random or chaotic utterances or inscriptions. We refuse to allow a text to remain alien and outside our frames of reference; we insist on 'naturalising' it, and effacing its textuality. When faced with a page of apparently random images, we prefer to naturalise it by attributing the images to a disordered mind or by regarding it as a reflection of a disordered world, rather than to accept its disorder as strange and inexplicable. The Formalists anticipated structuralist and poststructuralist thought by attending to those features of texts which resist the relentless process of naturalisation. Shklovsky refused to reduce the bizarre disorder of *Tristram Shandy* to an expression of Tristram's quirky mind, and instead drew attention to the novel's insistent literariness which checks naturalisation.

THE DOMINANT: JAKOBSON

It gradually became apparent that literary devices were not fixed pieces that could be moved at will in the literary game. Their value and meaning changed with time and also with context. With this realisation, 'device' gave way to 'function' as the leading concept. The effect of this shift was far-reaching. Formalists were no longer plagued by an unresolved rejection of 'content', but were able to internalise the central principle of 'defamiliarisation'; that is to say, instead of having to talk about literature defamiliarising reality, they could begin to refer to the defamiliarising of literature itself. Elements *within* a work may become 'automatised' or may have a positive aesthetic function. The same device may have different aesthetic functions in different works or may become totally automatised. For example, archaisms and Latinate word order may have an 'elevating' function in an epic poem, or an ironic function in a satire, or even become totally automatised as general 'poetic diction'. In the last case, the device is not 'perceived' by the reader as a functional element, and is effaced in the same way as ordinary perceptions become automatised and taken for granted. Literary works are seen as *dynamic systems* in which elements are structured in relations of foreground and background. If a particular element is 'effaced' (perhaps archaic diction), other elements will come into play as dominant (perhaps plot or rhythm) in the work's system. Writing in 1935, Jakobson regarded 'the dominant' as an important late Formalist concept, and defined it as 'the focusing component of a work of art: it rules, determines and transforms the remaining components'. He rightly stresses the non-mechanistic aspect of this view of artistic structure. The dominant provides the work with its focus of crystallisation and facilitates its unity or *gestalt* (total order). The very notion of defamiliarisation implied *change* and historical development. Rather than look for eternal verities which bind all great literature into a single canon, the Formalists were disposed to see the history of literature as one of permanent revolution. Each new development is an attempt to repulse the dead hand of familiarity and habitual response. This dynamic notion of the dominant also provided the Formalists with a useful way of explaining literary history. Poetic forms change and develop not at random but as a result of a 'shifting dominant': there is a continuing shift in the mutual relationships among the various elements in a poetic system. Jakobson added the interesting idea that the poetics of particular periods may be governed by a 'dominant' which derives from a non-literary system. The dominant of Renaissance poetry was derived from the visual arts; Romantic poetry oriented itself towards music; and Realism's dominant is verbal art. But whatever the dominant may be, it organises the other elements in the individual work, relegating to the background of aesthetic attention elements which in works of earlier periods might have been 'foregrounded' as dominant. What changes is not so much the elements of the system (syntax, rhythm, plot, diction, etc.) but the *function* of particular elements or groups of elements. When Pope wrote the following lines satirising the antiquarian, he could rely on the dominance of the values of prose clarity to help him achieve his purpose:

> But who is he, in closet close y-pent,
> Of sober face, with learned dust besprent?
> Right well mine eyes arede the myster wight,
> On parchment scraps y-fed, and Wormius hight.

The Chaucerian diction and archaic word order are immediately treated by the reader as comically pedantic. In an earlier period

Spenser was able to hark back to Chaucer's style without calling up the satiric note. The shifting dominant operates not only within particular texts but within particular literary periods.

THE BAKHTIN SCHOOL

The so-called Bakhtin School arose in the later period of formalism. The authorship of several key works of the group is disputed and we are compelled simply to refer to the names which appear on the original title pages – Mikhail Bakhtin, Pavel Medvedev and Valentin Voloshinov. These works have been differently interpreted and employed in liberal and left criticism. Medvedev's *The Formal Method in Literary Scholarship: A Critical Introduction to Sociological Poetics* (1928) was a serious attempt at a rapprochement between Marxism and formalism. Indeed Medvedev had begun his career as an orthodox Marxist whose earliest essays were anti-formalist. The School remained formalist in its concern for the linguistic structure of literary works, but works authored by Voloshinov, particularly, were deeply influenced by Marxism in the belief that language could not be separated from ideology. This intimate connection between language and ideology, discussed in Voloshinov's *Marxism and the Philosophy of Language* (1973), immediately drew literature into the social and economic sphere, the homeland of ideology. This approach departs from classical Marxist assumptions about ideology by refusing to treat it as a purely mental phenomenon which arises as a reflex of a material (real) socio-economic substructure. Ideology is not separable from its medium – language. As Voloshinov put it, 'consciousness itself can arise and become a viable fact only in the material embodiment of signs'. Language, a socially constructed sign-system, is itself a material reality.

The Bakhtin School was not interested in abstract linguistics of the kind which later formed the basis of structuralism. They were concerned with language or discourse as a social phenomenon. Voloshinov's central insight was that 'words' are active, dynamic social signs, capable of taking on different meanings and connotations for different social classes in different social and historical situations. He attacked those linguists (including

Saussure) who treated language as a synchronic (unhistorical) and abstract system. He rejected the whole notion of 'The isolated, finished, monologic utterance, divorced from its verbal and actual context and standing open not to any possible sort of active response but to passive understanding.' The Russian *slovo* may be translated 'word' but is used by the Bakhtin School with a strongly social flavour (nearer to 'utterance' or 'discourse'). Verbal signs are the arena of continuous class struggle: the ruling class will always try to narrow the meaning of words and make social signs 'uni-accentual', but in times of social unrest the vitality and basic 'multi-accentuality' of linguistic signs becomes apparent as various class interests clash and intersect upon the ground of language. 'Heteroglossia' is a fundamental concept, most clearly defined in Bakhtin's 'Discourse in the Novel' (written 1934–5). The term refers to the basic condition governing the production of meaning in all discourse. It asserts the way in which *context* defines the meaning of utterances, which are heteroglot in so far as they put in play a multiplicity of social voices and their individual expressions. A single voice may give the impression of unity and closure, but the utterance is constantly (and to some extent unconsciously) producing a plenitude of meanings, which stem from social interaction (dialogue). Monologue is not really possible.

It was Mikhail Bakhtin who developed the implications of this dynamic view of language for literary texts. However, he did not, as one might have expected, treat literature as a direct reflection of social forces, but retained a formalist concern with literary structure, showing how the dynamic and active nature of language was given expression in certain literary traditions. He stressed not the way texts reflect society or class interests, but rather the way language is made to disrupt authority and liberate alternative voices. A libertarian language is entirely appropriate in describing Bakhtin's approach, which is very much a celebration of those writers whose work permits the freest play of different value systems and whose authority is not imposed upon the alternatives. Bakhtin is profoundly un-Stalinist. His classic work is *Problems of Dostoevsky's Poetics* (1929), in which he developed a bold contrast between the novels of Tolstoy and those of Dostoevsky. In the former, the various voices we hear are strictly subordinated to the author's controlling purpose: there is only one truth – the author's. In contrast to this 'monologic' type of novel, Dostoevsky developed a new 'polyphonic' (or dialogic) form, in which no attempt is made to orchestrate or unify the various points of view expressed in the various characters. The consciousness of the various characters does not merge with the author's nor do they become subordinated to the author's viewpoint; they retain an integrity and independence, and are 'not only objects of the author's word, but subjects of their own directly significant word as well'. In this book and in his later one on Rabelais, Bakhtin explores the liberating and often subversive use of various dialogic forms in classical satire and in medieval and Renaissance cultural forms.

Bakhtin's discussion of 'Carnival' has important applications both to particular texts and to the history of literary genres. The festivities associated with Carnival are collective and popular; hierarchies are turned on their heads (fools become wise, kings become beggars); opposites are mingled (fact and fantasy, heaven and hell); the sacred is profaned. The 'jolly relativity' of all things is proclaimed. Everything authoritative, rigid or serious is subverted, loosened and mocked. This essentially popular and libertarian social phenomenon has a formative influence on literature of various periods, but becomes especially dominant in the Renaissance. (For a practical example of Bakhtinian Carnival in action, see Raman Selden's analysis of Shakespeare's *King Lear* and *Twelfth Night* in chapter 6, section 24 of *PTRL*.) 'Carnivalisation' is the term Bakhtin uses to describe the shaping effect of Carnival on literary genres. The earliest carnivalised literary forms are the Socratic dialogue and the Menippean satire. The former is in its origins close to the immediacy of oral dialogue, in which the discovery of truth is conceived as an unfolding exchange of views rather than as an authoritative monologue. The Socratic dialogues come down to us in the sophisticated literary forms devised by Plato. Some of the 'jolly relativity' of Carnival survives in the written works, but there is also, in Bakhtin's view, some dilution of that collective quality of enquiry in which points of view collide without a strict hierarchy of voices being established by the 'author'. In the last Platonic dialogues, argues Bakhtin, the later image of Socrates as the 'teacher' begins to emerge and to replace the carnivalistic image of Socrates as the grotesque hen-pecked provoker of argument, who was midwife rather than author of truth.

In Menippean satire, the three planes of Heaven (Olympus), the Underworld, and Earth are all treated to the logic of Carnival. For example, in the underworld earthly inequalities are dissolved; emperors lose their crowns and meet on equal terms with beggars. Dostoevsky brings together the various traditions of carnivalised literature. The 'fantastic tale' *Bobok* (1873) is almost pure Menippean satire. A scene in a cemetery culminates in a weird account of the brief 'life outside life' of the dead in the grave. Before losing their earthly consciousness completely, the dead enjoy a period of a few months when they are released from all the obligations and laws of normal existence and are able to reveal themselves with a stark and unlimited freedom. Baron Klinevich, 'king' of the corpses, declares 'I just want everyone to tell the truth . . . On earth it is impossible to live without lying, because life and lie are synonyms; but here we will tell the truth just for fun.' This contains the seed of the 'polyphonic' novel, in which voices are set free to speak subversively or shockingly, but without the author stepping between character and reader.

Bakhtin raises a number of themes developed by later theorists. Both Romantics and Formalists (including the New Critics) regarded texts as organic unities, as integrated structures in which all loose ends are finally gathered up into aesthetic unity by the reader. Bakhtin's emphasis on Carnival breaks up this unquestioned organicism and promotes the idea that major literary works may be multi-levelled and resistant to unification. This leaves the author in a much less dominant position in relation to his or her writings. The notion of individual identity is left problematic: 'character' is elusive, insubstantial and quirky. This anticipates a major concern of recent poststructuralist and psychoanalytic criticism, although one should not exaggerate this, or forget that Bakhtin still retains a firm sense of the writer's controlling artistry. His work does not imply the radical questioning of the role of author which arises in the work of Roland Barthes and other poststructuralists. However, Bakhtin does resemble Barthes in his 'privileging' of the polyphonic novel. Both critics prefer liberty and pleasure to authority and decorum. There is a tendency among recent critics to treat polyphonic and other kinds of 'plural' text as normative rather than as eccentric; that is, they treat them as more truly literary than more univocal (monologic) kinds of writing. This may appeal to modern readers brought up on Joyce and Beckett, but we must also recognise that both Bakhtin and Barthes are indicating *preferences* which arise from their own social and ideological predispositions. Nevertheless, it remains true that, in asserting the openness and instability of literary texts, Bakhtin, or rather the readings of Bakhtin, have confirmed that such preferences have a central place in the inescapable 'politics' of criticism.

THE AESTHETIC FUNCTION: MUKAŘOVSKÝ

We have already discussed the shift from Shklovsky's notion of the text as a heap of devices to Tynyanov's of the text as a functioning system. The high point of this 'structural' phase was the series of statements known as the Jakobson-Tynyanov theses (1928). The theses reject a mechanical formalism and attempt to reach beyond a narrowly literary perspective by trying to define the relationship between the literary 'series' (system) and other 'historical series'. The way in which the literary system develops historically cannot be understood, they argue, without understanding the way in which other systems impinge on it and partly determine its evolutionary path. On the other hand, they insist, we must attend to the 'immanent laws' of the literary system itself if we are to understand correctly the correlation of the systems.

The Prague Linguistic Circle, founded in 1926, continued and developed the 'structural' approach. Mukařovský, for example, developed the formalist concept of 'defamiliarisation' into the more systematic 'foregrounding' which he defined as 'the aesthetically intentional distortion of the linguistic components'. He also underlined the folly of excluding extra-literary factors from critical analysis. Taking over Tynyanov's dynamic view of aesthetic structures, he placed great emphasis on the dynamic tension between literature and society in the artistic product. Mukařovský's most powerful argument concerned the 'aesthetic function', which proves to be an ever-shifting boundary and not a watertight category. The same object can possess several functions: a church may be both a place of worship and a work of art; a stone may be a door-stop, a missile, building material and an object of artistic appreciation. Fashions are especially complex signs and may possess social, political, erotic and aesthetic functions. The same variability of function can be seen in literary products. A political speech, a biography, a letter and a piece of propaganda may or may not possess aesthetic value in different societies and periods. The circumference of the sphere of 'art' is always changing, and always dynamically related to the structure of society.

Mukařovský's insight has been taken up recently by Marxist critics to establish the social bearings of art and literature. We can never talk about 'literature' as if it were a fixed canon of works, a specific set of devices, or an unchanging body of forms and genres. To endow an object or artifact with the dignity of aesthetic value is a *social* act, ultimately inseparable from prevailing ideologies. Modern social changes have resulted in certain artifacts, which once had mainly non-aesthetic function, being regarded as primarily art-objects. The religious function of icons, the domestic functions of Greek vases, and the military function of breast plates have been subordinated in modern times to a primarily aesthetic function. What people choose to regard as 'serious' art or 'high' culture is also subject to changing values. Jazz, for example, once 'popular' music in brothels and bars, has become serious art, although its 'low' social origins still give rise to conflicting evaluations. From this perspective, art and literature are not eternal verities but are always open to new definitions – hence the increasing presence, as the literary canon is deconstructed, of 'popular' writing on 'Cultural Studies' (rather than 'Literature') courses. The dominant class in any historical era will have an important influence on definitions of art, and where new trends arise will normally wish to incorporate them into its ideological world.

The theories of Bakhtin, the Jakobson-Tynyanov theses and the work of Mukařovský pass beyond the 'pure' Russian Formalism of Shklovsky, Tomashevsky and Eikhenbaum, and will form an apt prelude to our later chapter on Marxist criticism, which in any case influenced their more sociological interests. The Formalists' isolation of the literary system is evidently at odds with the Marxist subordination of literature to society, but we shall discover that not all Marxist critics follow the harsh anti-formalist line of the official, socialist-realist Soviet tradition. However, first, we will survey another school of critical theory which primarily situates the differential nature of the 'aesthetic function' with the 'addressee' or 'reader' of literary texts (see Jakobson's diagram in the Introduction above, p. 3).

SELECTED READING

Basic texts

Bakhtin, Mikhail, *Problems of Dostoevsky's Poetics*, trans. R. W. Rotsel (Ardis, Ann Arbor, 1973).

Bakhtin, Mikhail, *The Dialogic Imagination: Four Essays*, ed. Michael Holquist, trans. C. Emerson and M. Holquist (University of Texas Press, Austin, 1981). Has good introduction.

Bann, Stephen and Bowlt, John E. (eds), *Russian Formalism* (Scottish Academic Press, Edinburgh, 1973).

Garvin, Paul L. (trans.), *A Prague School Reader* (Georgetown University Press, Washington DC, 1964).

Lemon, Lee T. and Reis, Marion J. (eds), *Russian Formalist Criticism: Four Essays* (Nebraska University Press, Lincoln, 1965). Contains classic essays, including Shklovsky's on Sterne.

Matejka, Ladislav and Pomorska, Krystyna (eds), *Readings in Russian Poetics: Formalist and Structuralist Views* (MIT Press, Cambridge, Mass. and London, 1971).

Medvedev, P. N. and Bakhtin, Mikhail, *The Formal Method in Literary Scholarship: A Critical Introduction to Sociological Poetics*, trans. A. J. Wehrle (Johns Hopkins University Press, Baltimore and London, 1978).

Mukařovský, Jan, *Aesthetic Function, Norm and Value as Social Facts*, trans. M. E. Suino (Michigan University Press, Ann Arbor, 1979).

Voloshinov, Valentin, *Marxism and the Philosophy of Language*, trans. L. Matejka and I. R. Titunik (Seminar Press, New York, 1973; reprint Harvard University Press, Cambridge, Mass., 1986).

Introductions

Bennett, Tony, *Formalism and Marxism* (Routledge, London, 1979).

Erlich, Victor, *Russian Formalism: History Doctrine* (Yale University Press, New Haven and London, 3rd edn, 1981). The classic introduction.

Jefferson, Ann, 'Russian Formalism' in *Modern Literary Theory: A Comparative Introduction*, Ann Jefferson and David Robey (eds) (Batsford, London, 2nd edn, 1986).

Further reading

Clark, Katerina and Holquist, Michael, *Mikhail Bakhtin* (Harvard University Press, Cambridge, Mass. and London, 1984).

Eagleton, Terry, 'Wittgenstein's Friends' in *Against The Grain* (Verso, London, 1986).

Galan, F. W., *Historic Structures: The Prague School Project 1928–1946* (University of Texas Press, Austin, 1985).

Gardiner, Michael, *The Dialogics of Critique: M. M. Bakhtin and the Theory of Ideology* (Routledge, London, 1992).

Hirschkop, Ken and Shepherd, David (eds), *Bakhtin and Cultural Theory* (Manchester University Press, Manchester, 1991). A collection of essays.

Holquist, Michael, *Dialogism: Bakhtin and His World* (Routledge, London, 1990).

Jameson, Fredric, *The Prison-House of Language: A Critical Account of Structuralism and Russian Formalism* (Princeton University Press, Princeton, NJ and London, 1972).

Lodge, David, *After Bakhtin: Essays on Fiction and Criticism* (Routledge, London, 1990).

Pike, Christopher (ed.), *The Futurists, the Formalists, and the Marxist Critique* (Ink Links, London, 1979). An anthology.

Selden, Raman, *Criticism and Objectivity* (Allen & Unwin, London, Boston, Sydney, 1984), chap. 4, 'Russian Formalism, Marxism and "Relative Autonomy"'.

Steiner, Peter, *Russian Formalism: A Metapoetics* (Cornell University Press, Ithaca, 1984).

Thompson, E. M., *Russian Formalism and Anglo-American New Criticism: A Comparative Study* (Mouton, The Hague, 1971).

Trotsky, L., *Literature and Revolution* (Michigan University Press, Ann Arbor, 1960).

Williams, Raymond, *Marxism and Literature* (Oxford University Press, Oxford, 1977).

Young, Robert, 'Back to Bakhtin,' *Cultural Critique*, vol. 2 (1985/6), 71–92.

3 Reader-oriented theories

THE SUBJECTIVE PERSPECTIVE

The twentieth century has seen a steady assault upon the objective certainties of nineteenth-century science. Einstein's theory of relativity alone cast doubt on the belief that objective knowledge was simply a relentless and progressive accumulation of facts. The philosopher, T. S. Kuhn, has shown that what emerges as a 'fact' in science depends upon the frame of reference which the scientific observer brings to the object of understanding. *Gestalt* psychology argues that the human mind does not perceive things in the world as unrelated bits and pieces but as *configurations* of elements, themes, or meaningful, organised wholes. Individual items look different in different contexts, and even within a single field of vision they will be interpreted according to whether they are seen as 'figure' or 'ground'. These approaches and others have insisted that the perceiver is active and not passive in the act of perception. In the case of the famous duck–rabbit puzzle, only the perceiver can decide how to orient the configuration of lines. Is it a duck looking left, or a rabbit looking right?

How does this modern emphasis on the observer's active role affect literary theory?

Consider once more (see Introduction, 3) Jakobson's model of linguistic communication:

CONTEXT
ADDRESSER →   MESSAGE   → ADDRESSEE
CONTACT
CODE

Jakobson believed that literary discourse is different from other kinds of discourse by having a 'set to the message'; a poem is about itself (its form, its imagery, its literary meaning) before it is about the poet, the reader, or the world. However, if we reject formalism and adopt the perspective of the reader or audience, the whole orientation of Jakobson's diagram changes. From this angle, we can say that the poem has no real existence until it is read; its meaning can only be discussed by its readers. We differ about interpretations only because our ways of reading differ. It is the reader who applies the code in which the message is written and in this way *actualises* what would otherwise remain only potentially meaningful. If we consider the simplest examples of interpretation, we see that the addressee is often actively involved in constructing a meaning. For example, consider the system used to represent numerals in electronic displays. The basic configuration consists of seven segments: ⷀ. One might regard this figure as an imperfect square (⸫) surmounted by three sides of a similar square (⸪), or as the reverse. The viewer's eye is invited to interpret this shape as an item in the familiar numerical system, and has no difficulty in 'recognising' an 'eight'. The viewer is able to construct the numerals without difficulty from variations of this basic configuration of segments, even though the forms offered are sometimes poor approximations: ⷀ is 2, ⷀ is 5 (not 'S'), and ⷀ is 4 (not a defective 'H'). The success of this piece of communication depends on (1) the viewer's knowledge of the number system and (2) the viewer's ability to complete what is incomplete, or select what is significant and ignore what is not. Seen in this way the addressee is not a passive recipient of an entirely formulated meaning, but an active agent in the making of meaning. However, in this case, the addressee's task is very simply performed, because the message is stated within a completely closed system.

But take the following poem by Wordsworth (a second poem by Wordsworth, 'To H. C., Six Years Old', is given a 'phenomenological' [see below, pp. 51–2] reading by Raman Selden in chapter 5, section 14, *Practising Theory and Reading Literature*):

> A slumber did my spirit seal;
> I had no human fears;
> She seemed a thing that could not feel
> The touch of earthly years.
>
> No motion has she now, no force;
> She neither hears nor sees;
> Rolled round in earth's diurnal course,
> With rocks, and stones, and trees.

Leaving aside many preliminary and often unconscious steps which readers must make to recognise that they are reading a lyric poem, and that they accept the speaker as the authentic voice of the poet and not as a dramatic persona, we can say that there are two 'statements' made, one in each stanza: (1) I thought she could not die; (2) She is dead. As readers we ask ourselves what sense we make of the *relationship* between the statements. Our interpretation of every phrase will turn on the answer to this question. How are we to regard the speaker's attitude towards his earlier thoughts about the female (baby, girl, or woman)? Is it good and sensible to have 'no human fears', or is it naïve and foolish? Is the 'slumber' which sealed his spirit a sleep of illusion or an inspired reverie? Does 'she seemed' suggest that she had all the visible marks of an immortal being, or that the speaker was perhaps mistaken? Does the second stanza suggest that she has no spiritual existence in death and is reduced to mere inanimate matter? The first two lines of the stanza invite this view. However, the last two lines open another possible interpretation – that she has become part of a natural world and partakes of an existence which is in some sense greater than the naïve spirituality of stanza one; her individual 'motion' and 'force' are now subsumed in the grand motion and force of Nature.

From the perspective of reader-oriented criticism the answers to these questions cannot simply be derived from the text. The meaning of the text is never self-formulated; the reader must act upon the textual material in order to produce meaning. Wolfgang Iser (see below, pp. 55–7) argues that literary texts always contain 'blanks' which only the reader can fill. The 'blank' between the two stanzas of Wordsworth's poem arises because the relationship between the stanzas is unstated. The act of interpretation requires us to fill this blank. A problem for theory centres on the question of whether or not the text itself triggers the reader's act of interpretation, or whether the reader's own interpretative strategies impose solutions upon the problems thrown up by the text. Even before the growth of reader-response theory, semioticians had developed the field with some sophistication. Umberto Eco's *The Role of the Reader* (1979, comprising essays dating from 1959) argues that some texts are 'open' (Joyce's *Finnegans Wake*, atonal music) and invite the reader's collaboration in the production of meaning, while others are 'closed' (comics, detective fiction) and predetermine the reader's response. He also speculates on how the codes available to the reader determine what the text means as it is read.

But before we survey the various ways in which the reader's role in constructing meaning has been theorised, we must ask the question: *who is* 'the reader'?

GERALD PRINCE: THE 'NARRATEE'

The narratologist Gerald Prince poses the question: why, when we study novels, do we take such pains to discriminate between the various kinds of narrator (omniscient, unreliable, implied author, etc.), but never ask questions about the different kinds of person to whom the narrator addresses the discourse. Prince calls this person the 'narratee'. We must not confuse the narratee with the reader. The narrator may specify a narratee in terms of sex ('Dear Madam . . .'), class ('gentlemen'), situation (the 'reader' in his armchair), race (white), or age (mature). Evidently actual readers may or may not coincide with the person addressed by the narrator. An actual reader may be a black, male, young factory-worker reading in bed. The narratee is also distinguished from the 'virtual reader' (the sort of reader whom the author has in mind when developing the narrative) and the 'ideal reader' (the perfectly insightful reader who understands the writer's every move).

How do we learn to identify narratees? When the novelist Anthony Trollope writes 'Our archdeacon was worldly – who among us is not so?', we understand that the narratees here are people who, like the narrator, recognise the fallibility of all human beings, even the most pious. There are many 'signals', direct and indirect, which contribute to our knowledge of the narratee. The assumptions of the narratee may be attacked, supported, queried, or solicited by the narrator who will thereby strongly imply the narratee's character. When the narrator apologises for certain inadequacies in the discourse ('I cannot convey this experience in words'), this indirectly tells us something of the narratee's susceptibilities and values. Even in a novel which appears to make no direct reference to a narratee we pick up tiny signals even in the simplest of literary figures. The second term of a comparison, for example, often indicates the kind of world familiar to the narratee ('the song was as sincere as a TV jingle'). Sometimes the narratee is an important character. For example, in *A Thousand and One Nights* the very survival of the narrator, Scheherazade, depends on the continued attention of the narratee, the caliph; if he loses interest in her stories, she must die. The effect of Prince's elaborated theory is to highlight a dimension of narration which had been understood intuitively by readers but which had remained shadowy and undefined. He contributes to reader-oriented theory by drawing attention to ways in which narratives produce their own 'readers' or 'listeners', who may or may not coincide with actual readers. Many of the writers discussed in the following pages ignore this distinction between reader and narratee.

PHENOMENOLOGY: HUSSERL, HEIDEGGER AND GADAMER

A modern philosophical tendency which stresses the perceiver's central role in determining meaning is known as 'phenomeno- logy'. According to Edmund Husserl the proper object of philosophical investigation is the contents of our consciousness and not objects in the world. Consciousness is always of something, and it is the 'something' which appears to our consciousness which is truly real to us. In addition, argued Husserl, we discover in the things which appear in conscious- ness ('phenomena' in Greek, meaning 'things appearing') their universal or essential qualities. Phenomenology claims to show us the underlying nature both of human consciousness and of 'phenomena'. This was an attempt to revive the idea (eclipsed since the Romantics) that the individual human mind is the centre and origin of all meaning. In literary theory this approach did not encourage a purely subjective concern for the critic's mental structure but a type of criticism which tries to enter into the world of a writer's works and to arrive at an understanding of the underlying nature or essence of the writings as they appear to the critic's consciousness. The early work of J. Hillis Miller, the American (later deconstructionist – see below, p.156– 7) critic, was influenced by the phenomenological theories of the so-called 'Geneva School' of critics, who included Georges Poulet and Jean Starobinski. For example, Miller's first study of Thomas Hardy, *Thomas Hardy: Distance and Desire* (1970; he wrote further 'deconstructive' studies later), uncovers the novels' pervasive mental structures, namely 'distance' and 'desire'. The act of interpretation is possible, because the texts allow the reader access to the author's consciousness, which, says Poulet, 'is open to me, welcomes me, lets me look deep inside itself, and . . . allows me . . . to think what it thinks and feel what it feels'. Derrida (see chapter 6) would consider this kind of thinking 'logocentric' for supposing that a meaning is centred on a 'transcendental subject' (the author) and can be recentred on another such subject (the reader).

The shift towards a reader-oriented theory is prefigured in the rejection of Husserl's 'objective' view by his pupil Martin

Heidegger. The latter argued that what is distinctive about human existence is its *Dasein* ('givenness'): our consciousness both *projects* the things of the world and at the same time *is subjected to* the world by the very nature of existence in the world. We find ourselves 'flung down' into the world, into a time and place we did not choose, but simultaneously it is our world in so far as our consciousness projects it. We can never adopt an attitude of detached contemplation, looking down upon the world as if from a mountain top. We are inevitably merged with the very object of our consciousness. Our thinking is always in a situation and is therefore always *historical*, although this history is not external and social but personal and inward. It was Hans-Georg Gadamer who, in *Truth and Method* (1975), applied Heidegger's situational approach to literary theory. Gadamer argued that a literary work does not pop into the world as a finished and neatly parcelled bundle of meaning; rather meaning depends on the historical situation of the interpreter. Gadamer influenced 'reception theory' (see Jauss below).

HANS ROBERT JAUSS: HORIZONS OF EXPECTATIONS

Jauss, an important German exponent of 'reception' theory (*Rezeptionästhetik*), gave a historical dimension to reader-oriented criticism. He tries to achieve a compromise between Russian Formalism which ignores history, and social theories which ignore the text. Writing during a period of social unrest at the end of the 1960s, Jauss and others wanted to question the old canon of German literature *and* to show that it was perfectly reasonable to do so. The older critical outlook had ceased to make sense in the same way that Newton's physics no longer seemed adequate in the early twentieth century. He borrows from the philosophy of science (T. S. Kuhn) the term 'paradigm' which refers to the scientific framework of concepts and assumptions operating in a particular period. 'Ordinary science' does its experimental work within the mental world of a particular paradigm, until a new paradigm displaces the old one and throws up new problems and establishes new assumptions.

Jauss uses the term 'horizon of expectations' to describe the criteria readers use to judge literary texts in any given period. These criteria will help the reader decide how to judge a poem as, for example, an epic or a tragedy or a pastoral; it will also, in a more general way, cover what is to be regarded as poetic or literary as opposed to unpoetic or non-literary uses of languages. Ordinary writing and reading will work within such a horizon. For example, if we consider the English Augustan period, we might say that Pope's poetry was judged according to criteria which were based upon values of clarity, naturalness and stylistic decorum (the words should be adjusted according to the dignity of the subject). However, this does not establish once and for all the value of Pope's poetry. During the second half of the eighteenth century, commentators began to question whether Pope was a poet at all and to suggest that he was a clever versifier who put prose into rhyming couplets and lacked the imaginative power required of true poetry. Leapfrogging the nineteenth century, we can say that modern readings of Pope work within a changed horizon of expectations: we now often value his poems for their wit, complexity, moral insight and their renewal of literary tradition.

The original horizon of expectations only tells us how the work was valued and interpreted when it appeared, but does not establish its meaning finally. In Jauss's view it would be equally wrong to say that a work is universal, that its meaning is fixed forever and open to all readers in any period: 'A literary work is not an object which stands by itself and which offers the same face to each reader in each period. It is not a monument which reveals its timeless essence in a monologue.' This means, of course, that we will never be able to survey the successive horizons which flow from the time of a work down to the present day and then, with an Olympian detachment, to sum up the work's final value or meaning. To do so would be to ignore our own historical situation. Whose authority are we to accept? That of the first readers? The combined opinion of readers over time? Or the aesthetic judgement of the present? The first readers may have been incapable of seeing the revolutionary significance of a writer (for example, William Blake; but also see *PTRL*, chapter 5, section 18, for an application of Jaussian 'reception theory' to Arnold Wesker's play, *Roots*, and

Samuel Beckett's *Endgame*), and the same objection must also apply to succeeding readers' judgements, including our own.

Jauss's answers to these questions derive from the philosophical 'hermeneutics' of Hans–Georg Gadamer, a follower of Heidegger (see above, p. 52). Gadamer argues that all interpretations of past literature arise from a dialogue between past and present. Our attempts to understand a work will depend on the questions which our own cultural environment allows us to raise. At the same time, we seek to discover the questions which the work itself was trying to answer in its own dialogue with history. Our present perspective always involves a relationship to the past, but at the same time the past can only be grasped through the limited perspective of the present. Put in this way, the task of establishing a *knowledge* of the past seems hopeless. But a hermeneutical notion of 'understanding' does not separate knower and object in the familiar fashion of empirical science; rather it views understanding as a 'fusion' of past and present: we cannot make our journey into the past without taking the present with us. 'Hermeneutics' was a term originally applied to the interpretation of sacred texts; its modern equivalent preserves the same serious and reverent attitude towards the secular texts to which it tries to gain access.

Jauss recognises that a writer may directly affront the prevailing expectations of his or her day. Indeed, reception theory itself developed in Germany during the 1960s in a climate of literary change: writers such as Rolf Hochhuth, Hans Magnus Enzenberger and Peter Handke were challenging accepted literary formalism by increasing the direct involvement of reader or audience. Jauss himself examines the case of the French poet Baudelaire whose *Les Fleurs du mal* had in the late nineteenth century created uproar and attracted legal prosecution, by offending the norms of bourgeois morality *and* the canons of romantic poetry. However, the poems also immediately produced a new aesthetic horizon of expectations; the literary avant-garde saw the book as a trail-blazing work of decadence, and the poems were 'concretised' (Iser's term – see below pp. 55–7) as expressions of the aesthetic cult of nihilism. Jauss assesses later psychological, linguistic and sociological interpretations of Baudelaire's poems, but often disregards them, thus casting doubt upon a method which recognises its own historical limitations while still feeling able to regard certain other interpretations as raising 'falsely posed or illegitimate questions'. The 'fusion of horizons' is not, it seems, a total merging of all the points of view which have arisen but only those which to the hermeneutical sense of the critic appear to be part of the gradually emerging totality of meanings which make up the true unity of the text.

WOLFGANG ISER: THE 'IMPLIED READER'

A leading member of the so-called 'Constance School' of German reception theory, Wolfgang Iser draws heavily on the phenomenological aesethetician Roman Ingarden and on the work of Gadamer (above). Unlike Jauss, Iser decontextualises and dehistoricises text and reader. A key work is his *The Act of Reading: A Theory of Aesthetic Response* (1978) in which, as elsewhere, he presents the text as a potential structure which is 'concretised' by the reader in relation to his or her extra-literary norms, values and experience. A sort of oscillation is set up between the power of the text to control the way it is read and a reader's 'concretisation' of it in terms of his or her own experience – an experience which will itself be modified in the act of reading. 'Meaning', in this theory, lies in the adjustments and revisions to expectations which are brought about in the reader's mind in the process of making sense of his or her dialectical relationship to the text. Iser himself does not entirely resolve the relative weight of the text's determinacy and the reader's experience in this relationship, although it would seem that his emphasis falls more heavily on the latter.

In Iser's view the critic's task is to explain not the text as an object but rather its effects on the reader. It is in the nature of texts to allow a spectrum of possible readings. The term 'reader' can be subdivided into 'implied reader' and 'actual reader'. The first is the reader whom the text creates for itself and amounts to 'a network of response-inviting structures' which predispose us to read in certain ways. The 'actual reader' receives certain mental images in the process of reading; however, the images will inevitably be coloured by the reader's 'existing stock of experience'. If we are atheists we will be affected differently by the Wordsworth poem above (p. 48) than if we are Christians. The experience of reading will differ according to our past experiences.

The words we read do not represent actual objects but human speech in fictional guise. This fictional language helps us to construct in our minds *imaginary* objects. To take one of Iser's own examples (Raman Selden also does an Iser-based reading of Harold Pinter's *The Homecoming* in *PTRL*, chapter 5, section 17): in *Tom Jones* Fielding presents two characters, Allworthy (the perfect man) and Captain Blifil (the hypocrite). The reader's imaginary object, 'the perfect man', is subject to modification: when Allworthy is taken in by Blifil's feigned piety, we adjust the imaginary object in view of the perfect man's lack of judgement. The reader's journey through the book is a continuous process of such adjustments. We hold in our minds certain expectations, based on our memory of characters and events, but the expectations are continually modified, and the memories transformed as we pass through the text. What we grasp as we read is only a series of changing viewpoints, not something fixed and fully meaningful at every point.

While a literary work does not represent objects, it does refer to the extra-literary world by selecting certain norms, value systems or 'world-views'. These norms are concepts of reality which help human beings to make sense of the chaos of their experience. The text adopts a 'repertoire' of such norms and suspends their validity within its fictional world. In *Tom Jones*, various characters embody different norms: Allworthy (benevolence), Squire Western (ruling passion), Square (the eternal fitness of things), Thwackum (the human mind as a sink of iniquity), Sophia (the ideality of natural inclinations). Each norm asserts certain values at the expense of others, and each tends to contract the image of human nature to a single principle or perspective. The reader is therefore impelled by the unfinished nature of the text to relate the values of the hero (good nature) to the various norms which are violated by the hero in specific incidents. *Only the reader* can actualise the degree to which particular norms are to be rejected or questioned. *Only the reader* can make the complex moral judgement on Tom, and see that, while his 'good nature' disrupts the restrictive norms of other characters, it does so partly because Tom lacks 'prudence' and 'circumspection'. Fielding does not tell us this, but as readers we insert this into the interpretation in order to fill a 'gap' or 'blank' (key terms in Iser's theory) in the text. In real life we sometimes meet people who appear to represent certain world-views ('cynicism', 'humanism'), but we assign such descriptions ourselves on the basis of received ideas. The value systems we encounter are met at random: no author selects and predetermines them and no hero appears in order to test their validity. So, even though there are 'gaps' in the text to be filled, the text is much more definitely structured than life.

If we apply Iser's method to our Wordsworth poem, we see that the reader's activity consists in first adjusting his or her viewpoint ((a), (b), (c), then (d)), and secondly in filling a 'blank' between the two stanzas (between transcendent spirituality and pantheistic immanence). This application may seem rather unwieldy because a short poem does not require the reader to make the long sequence of adjustments necessary when reading a novel. However, the concept of 'gaps' remains valid.

As we have suggested, it remains unclear whether Iser wishes to grant the reader the power to fill up at will the blanks in the text or whether he regards the text as the final arbiter of the reader's actualisations. Is the gap between 'the perfect man' and 'the perfect man's lack of judgement' filled by a freely judging reader or by a reader who is *guided* by the text's instructions? Iser's emphasis is ultimately phenomenological: the reader's experience of reading is at the centre of the literary process. By resolving the contradictions between the various viewpoints which emerge from the text or by filling the 'gaps' between viewpoints in various ways, the readers take the text into their consciousnesses and make it their own *experience*. It seems that, while texts do set the terms on which the reader actualises meanings, the reader's own 'store of experience' will take some part in the process. The reader's existing consciousness will have to make certain internal adjustments in order to receive and process the alien viewpoints which the text presents as reading takes place. This situation produces the possibility that the reader's own 'world-view' may be modified as a result of internalising, negotiating and realising the partially indeterminate elements of the text: to use Iser's words, reading 'gives us the chance to formulate the unformulated'.

STANLEY FISH: THE READER'S EXPERIENCE

Stanley Fish, the American critic of seventeenth-century English literature, developed a reader-oriented perspective called an 'affective stylistics'. Like Iser, he concentrates on the adjustments of expectation to be made by readers as they pass along the text, but considers this at the immediately local level of the sentence. He separates his approach very self-consciously from all kinds of formalism (including American New Criticism) by denying literary language any special status; we use the same reading strategies to interpret literary and non-literary sentences. His attention is directed to the developing responses of the reader in relation to the words of sentences as they succeed one another in time. Describing the fallen angels' state of awareness, having plummeted from heaven to hell, Milton wrote in *Paradise Lost*: 'Nor did they not perceive the evil plight'. This cannot be treated as a statement equivalent to 'they perceived the evil plight'. We must attend, argues Fish, to the sequence of words which creates a state of suspension in the reader, who hangs between two views of the fallen angels' awareness. His point is weakened though not refuted by the fact that Milton was evidently imitating the double negative in the style of classical epic. But the following sentence by Walter Pater receives an especially sensitive analysis by Fish: 'This at least of flame-like, our life has, that it is but the concurrence, renewed from moment to moment, of forces parting sooner or later on their ways.' He points out that by interrupting 'concurrence of forces' with 'renewed from moment to moment' Pater prevents the reader from establishing a definite or stable image in the mind, and at each stage in the sentence forces the reader to make an adjustment in expectation and interpretation. The idea of 'the concurrence' is disrupted by 'parting', but then 'sooner or later' leaves the 'parting' temporally uncertain. The reader's expectation of meaning is thus continuously adjusted: the meaning is the total movement of reading.

Jonathan Culler (see also chapter 5 and pp. 62–4 below) has lent general support to Fish's aims, but has criticised him for failing to give us a proper theoretical formulation of his reader criticism. Fish believes that his readings of sentences simply follow the natural practice of informed readers. In his view a reader is someone who possesses a 'linguistic competence', has internalised the syntactic and semantic knowledge required for reading. The 'informed reader' of literary texts has also acquired a specifically 'literary competence' (knowledge of literary conventions). Culler makes two trenchant criticisms of Fish's position:

1. He fails to theorise the conventions of reading: that is, he fails to ask the question 'What conventions do readers follow when they read?'
2. His claim to read sentences word by word in a temporal sequence is misleading: there is no reason to believe that readers actually do take in sentences in such a piecemeal and gradual way. Why does he assume, for example, that the reader, faced with Milton's 'Nor did they not perceive', will experience a sense of being suspended between two views?

There is something factitious about Fish's continual willingness to be surprised by the next word in a sequence. Also, Fish himself admits that his approach tends to privilege those texts which proceed in a self-undermining way (*Self-Consuming Artifacts* [1972] is the title of one of his earlier books). Elizabeth Freund points out that in order to sustain his reader orientation Fish has to suppress the fact that the actual experience of reading is not the same thing as a verbal rendering of that experience. By treating his own reading experience as itself an act of interpretation he is ignoring the gap between experience and the understanding of an experience. What Fish gives us, therefore, is not a definitive account of the nature of reading but Fish's understanding of his own reading experience.

In *Is There a Text in This Class?* (1980) Fish acknowledges that his earlier work treated his own experience of reading as the norm, and goes on to justify this position by introducing the idea of 'interpretative communities'. This meant that he was trying to persuade readers to adopt 'a set of community assumptions so that when they read they would do what I did'. Of course, there may be many different groups of readers who adopt particular kinds of reading strategies, but in this later phase of his work the strategies of a particular interpretative community determine the entire process of reading – the stylistic facts of the texts and the experience of reading them. If we accept the category of interpretative communities, we no longer need to choose between asking questions about the text or about the reader; the whole problem of subject and object disappears. However, the price that must be paid for this solution is high: by reducing the whole process of meaning-production to the already existing conventions of the interpretative community, Fish seems to abandon all possibility of deviant interpretations or resistances to the norms which govern acts of interpretation. As Elizabeth Freund points out: 'The appeal to the imperialism of agreement can chill the spines of readers whose experience of the community is less happily benign than Fish assumes.'

MICHAEL RIFFATERRE: LITERARY COMPETENCE

The French semiotician Michael Riffaterre agrees with the Russian Formalists in regarding poetry as a special use of language. Ordinary language is practical and is used to refer to some sort of 'reality', while poetic language focuses on the message as an end in itself. He takes this formalist view from Jakobson, but in a well-known essay he attacks Jakobson's and Lévi-Strauss's interpretation of Baudelaire's 'Les Chats'. Riffaterre shows that the linguistic features they discover in the poem could not possibly be perceived even by an informed reader. All manner of grammatical and phonemic patterns are thrown up by their structuralist approach, but not all the features they note can be part of the poetic structure for the reader. In a telling example he objects to their claim that by concluding a line with the word *volupté* (rather than, say, *plaisir*) Baudelaire is making play with the fact that a feminine noun (*la volupté*) is used as a 'masculine' rhyme, thus creating sexual ambiguity in the poem. Riffaterre rightly points out that a reasonably practised reader may well never have heard of the technical terms 'masculine' and 'feminine' rhyme. However, Riffaterre has some difficulty in explaining why something perceived by Jakobson does not count as evidence of what readers perceive in a text.

Riffaterre developed his theory in *Semiotics of Poetry* (1978), in which he argues that competent readers go beyond surface meaning. If we regard a poem as a string of statements, we are limiting our attention to its 'meaning', which is merely what it can be said to represent in units of information. If we attend only to a poem's 'meaning' we reduce it to a (possibly nonsensical) string of unrelated bits. A true response starts by noticing that the elements (signs) in a poem often appear to depart from normal grammar or normal representation: the poem seems to be establishing significance only *indirectly* and in doing so 'threatens the literary representation of reality'. It requires only ordinary linguistic competence to understand the poem's 'meaning', but the reader requires 'literary competence' to deal with the frequent 'ungrammaticalities' encountered in reading a poem. Faced with the stumbling-block of ungrammaticalness the reader is forced, during the process of reading, to uncover a second (higher) level of significance which will explain the ungrammatical features of the text. What will ultimately be uncovered is a structural 'matrix', which can be reduced to a single sentence or even a single word. The matrix can be deduced only indirectly and is not actually present as a word or statement in the poem. The poem is connected to its matrix by actual versions of the matrix in the form of familiar statements, clichés, quotations, or conventional associations. These versions are called 'hypograms'. It is the matrix which ultimately gives a poem unity. This reading process can be summarised as follows:

1. Try to read for ordinary 'meaning';
2. Highlight those elements which appear ungrammatical and which obstruct an ordinary mimetic interpretation;
3. Discover the 'hypograms' (or commonplaces) which receive expanded or unfamiliar expression in the text;
4. Derive the 'matrix' from the 'hypograms'; that is, find a single statement or word capable of generating the 'hypograms' and the text.

If we tried, hesitantly, to apply this theory to the Wordsworth poem 'A slumber did my spirit seal' (see above, p. 48), we might finally arrive at the matrix 'spirit and matter'. The 'hypograms' which are reworked in the text appear to be (1) death is the end of life; (2) the human spirit cannot die; (3) in death we return to the earth from which we came. The poem achieves unity by reworking these commonplaces in an unexpected way from a basic matrix. No doubt Riffaterre's theory would look stronger if we had given one of his own examples from Baudelaire or Gautier, for his approach seems much more appropriate as a way of reading difficult poetry which goes against the grain of 'normal' grammar or semantics. As a general theory of reading it has many difficulties, not least that it disallows several kinds of reading that you or I might think perfectly straightforward (for example, reading a poem for its political message).

JONATHAN CULLER: CONVENTIONS OF READING

Jonathan Culler (see also chapter 5) has argued that a theory of reading has to uncover the interpretative operations used by readers. We all know that different readers produce different interpretations. While this has led some theorists to despair of developing a theory of reading at all, Culler argues in *The Pursuit of Signs* (1981) that it is this variety of interpretation which theory has to explain. While readers may differ about meaning, they may well follow the same set of interpretative conventions. His first example is New Criticism's basic assumption – that of unity; different readers may discover unity in different ways in a particular text, but the basic forms of meaning they look for (forms of unity) may be the same. While we may feel no compulsion to perceive the unity of our experiences in the real world, in the case of poems we often expect to find it. Returning to the Wordsworth poem discussed above, a reader will find it very difficult not to ask the question 'How can I unify the two halves of the poem?' However, the variety of interpretations arises because there are several models of unity which one may bring to bear, and within a particular model there are several ways of applying it to the poem. One model is thematic unity: the Wordsworth poem may be unified as 'pantheistic' or 'nihilistic'. Alternatively we may discover unity by using a model of what Culler calls 'alethic reversal: first a false or inadequate vision, then its true or adequate counterpart'. If we apply this to the Wordsworth poem, we might see a transition from an inadequate vision of the superiority of otherworldly spirituality to a more adequate vision of union with nature. It can certainly be claimed for Culler's approach that it allows a genuine prospect of a theoretical advance – unlike Fish's, which gives us a useful method but shuts its eyes to the fundamental issues of theory, or Riffaterre's which produces a theoretical strait-jacket. On the other hand, one can object to Culler's refusal to examine the *content* of particular interpretative moves. For example, he examines two political readings of Blake's 'London' and concludes: 'The accounts different readers offer of what is wrong with the social system will, of course, differ, but the formal interpretative operations that give them a structure to fill in seem very similar.' There is something limiting about a theory which treats interpretative moves as substantial and the content of the moves as immaterial. After all, there may be historical grounds for regarding one way of applying an interpretative model as more valid or plausible than another. Readings of different degrees of plausibility may well share the same interpretative conventions. It is, for example, more plausible to regard the Wordsworth poem as 'pantheistic' than 'nihilistic' (although neither view is fully satisfactory). (An example of Culler's notion of 'literary competence' applied to Edgar Allan Poe's novella, *The Fall of the House of Usher*, is given in chapter 5, section 16 of *PTRL*.)

As we will see in chapter 5, Culler, in *Structuralist Poetics* (1975), argued that a theory of the structure of texts or genres is not possible because there is no underlying form of 'competence' which produces them. We can talk only about the competence of readers to make sense of what they read. Poets and novelists write on the basis of this competence: they write what can be read. In order to read texts as literature we must possess a 'literary competence', just as we need a more general 'linguistic competence' to make sense of the ordinary linguistic utterances we encounter. We acquire this 'grammar' of literature in educational institutions. Culler recognised that the conventions which apply to one genre will not apply to another, and that the conventions of interpretation will differ from one period to another, but as a structuralist he believed that theory is concerned with static, synchronic systems of meaning and not diachronic historical ones. However, in his later work – *On Deconstruction: Theory and Criticism after Structuralism* (1983), and more particularly *Framing the Sign* (1988) – Culler has moved away from such purist structuralism and towards a more radical questioning of the institutional and ideological foundations of literary competence. In the latter book, for instance, he explores and challenges the powerful tendency in postwar Anglo-American criticism, sustained by its institutionalisation in the academy, to promote crypto-religious doctrines and values by way of the authority of 'special texts' in the literary tradition.

NORMAN HOLLAND AND DAVID BLEICH: READER PSYCHOLOGY

Two American critics have derived approaches to reader theory from psychology. Norman Holland adopts a specific theory – 'ego-psychology' – according to which every child receives the imprint of a 'primary identity' from its mother. The adult has an 'identity theme' which, like a musical theme, is capable of variation but remains a central structure of stable identity. When we read a text, we process it in accordance with our identity theme: we 'use the literary work to symbolize and finally replicate ourselves'. We recast the work, in other words, to discover our own characteristic strategies for coping with the deep fears and wishes that shape our psychic lives. The reader's inbuilt defence mechanisms must be placated to allow access to the text. A dramatic example is a case cited by Holland of a boy compulsively driven to read detective stories to satisfy his aggressive feelings towards his mother by allying himself with the murderer. The stories not only took the imprint of his desires but also allowed him to assuage his guilt by associating himself with the victim and also the detective. In this way the boy was able to gratify his instincts *and* set up defences against anxiety and guilt. The example is untypical but raises a number of questions about Holland's theory. In more typical instances, readers assert control over texts by discovering unifying themes and structures in them which enable the readers to internalise the text: 'Putting within yourself and so controlling something that is outside where it cannot be controlled but seeks to control you.' Holland emphasises the interplay between the reader's identity theme and the text's unity: the latter is discovered by the reader as an expression of his or her identity theme. However, the example of the boy seems to invalidate the notions of textual 'unity' and 'identity theme'. *Any* detective story allowed him to construct the meanings he needed psychically; if there was a textual unity it seemed to lie in the narrative structure of detective stories rather than in specific texts. In any case the boy's reading seems to have *disrupted* the text's unity by producing contradictory subject positions for him to enter. Indeed this example (admittedly not pursued by Holland) throws into doubt the whole notion of an identity theme as a principle of psychic *unity*. Our discussion of Lacan will suggest one alternative model (chapter 6.) See too *PTRL*, chapter 5, section 15, for an application of Holland's theory – to Wallace Stevens's poem 'A High-toned Old Christian Woman' – which also distinguishes it from Lacan's.

David Bleich's *Subjective Criticism* (1978) is a sophisticated argument in favour of a shift from an objective to a subjective paradigm in critical theory. He argues that modern philosophers of science (especially T. S. Kuhn) have correctly denied the existence of an objective world of facts. Even in science, the perceiver's mental structures will decide what counts as an objective fact: 'Knowledge is made by people and not found [because] the object of observation appears changed by the act of observation.' He goes on to insist that the advances of 'knowledge' are determined by the *needs of the community*. When we say that 'science' has replaced 'superstition', we are describing not a passage from darkness to light, but a change in paradigm which occurs when certain urgent needs of the community come into conflict with old beliefs and demand new beliefs.

The child's acquisition of language, argues Bleich, enables it to establish a subjective control of experience. We can understand another's words only as a 'motivated act' – as a way of establishing some grasp of things which has importance for the speaker. Every utterance indicates an *intention* and every act of interpreting an utterance is a *conferring* of meaning. Since this is true of all human attempts to explain experience, we can best understand the arts if we ask: what are the motives of those who create 'symbolic' renderings of experience?; what are the individual and communal occasions for their response and creativity?

'Subjective criticism' is based on the assumption that 'each person's most urgent motivations are to understand himself'. In his classroom experiments, Bleich was led to distinguish between (1) the reader's spontaneous 'response' to a text and (2) the 'meaning' the reader attributed to it. The latter is usually presented as an 'objective' interpretation (something offered for negotiation in a pedagogic situation), but is necessarily developed from the *subjective response* of the reader. Whatever system of thought is being employed (moralist, Marxist, structuralist, psychoanalytic, etc.), interpretations of particular texts will normally reflect the subjective individuality of a personal 'response'. Without a grounding in 'response', the application of systems of thought will be dismissed as empty formulae derived from received dogma. Particular interpretations make more sense when critics take the trouble to explain the growth and origin of their views. In the teaching situation this is provided by a 'response statement', which gives the 'motivational substrate' of the subsequent interpretative judgement. For example, Ms A's 'response' to Kafka's story 'Metamorphosis' was one of initial repulsion, 'like taking cod-liver oil'. Ms A felt sadness at the plight of Gregor because she identified him with her brother who was similarly humiliated by and alienated from his father. The transformation of Gregor to a dung beetle produced a conflicting repulsion, since Ms A confessed to her sadistic insensitivity to insects. There was a further association between Gregor and memories of an ugly schoolgirl about which Ms A also felt guilty. Her predominant feelings for all the characters, but especially Gregor, were ambivalent ('attraction-repulsion'). The final judgement of 'meaning' which emerges from Ms A's statement has an objective appearance but is evidently built upon the initial 'response': the story is 'structured on the drama of the victim/victimiser dualism', victims and victimisers, she argues, depend on one another, and cannot in the end be distinguished. In other words, Ms A projects her own inconsistency of attitudes towards people into the text, and discovers there a 'dualism'. Anyone taking part in a seminar on the story would be inclined to see Ms A's interpretation as an 'objective' statement, offered in a suitably detached literary critical idiom. However, 'subjective criticism' would wish to reconnect the interpretation to Ms A's personal 'response' and its subjective motivation.

Reader-oriented theory has no single or predominant philosophical starting point. The writers we have considered belong to quite different traditions of thought. The German writers, Iser and Jauss, draw upon phenomenology and hermeneutics in their attempts to describe the process of reading in terms of the reader's consciousness. Riffaterre presupposes a reader who possesses a specifically *literary* competence, while Stanley Fish believes that readers respond to the sequence of words in sentences whether or not the sentences are literary. Jonathan Culler tries to establish a 'structuralist' theory of interpretation which seeks to disclose the regularities in readers' strategies, while recognising that the same strategies can produce different interpretations, and in chapter 6 we will see how Roland Barthes celebrates the end of structuralism's reign by granting the reader the power to create meanings by 'opening' the text to the interminable play of 'codes'. The Americans, Holland and Bleich, regard reading as a process which satisfies or at least depends upon the psychological needs of the reader. Whatever one thinks of these reader-oriented theories, there is no doubt that they seriously challenge the predominance of the text-oriented theories of New Criticism and Formalism. We can no longer talk about the meaning of a text without considering the reader's contribution to it.

SELECTED READING

Basic texts

Bleich, David, *Subjective Criticism* (Johns Hopkins University Press, Baltimore and London, 1978).

Culler, Jonathan, *The Pursuit of Signs: Semiotics, Literature, Deconstruction* (Routledge & Kegan Paul, London and Henley, 1981), especially Part Two.

Culler, Jonathan, *On Deconstruction: Theory and Criticism After Structuralism* (Routledge, London, 1983).

Culler, Jonathan, *Framing the Sign* (Basil Blackwell, Oxford, 1988).

Eco, Umberto, *The Role of the Reader: Explorations in the Semiotics of Texts* (Indiana University Press, Bloomington, 1979).

Fish, Stanley, *Self-Consuming Artifacts: The Experience of Seventeenth-Century Literature* (California University Press, Berkeley, 1972).

Fish, Stanley, *Is There a Text in This Class? The Authority of Interpretive Communities* (Harvard University Press, Cambridge, Mass., 1980).

Fish, Stanley, *Doing What Comes Naturally: Changes, Rhetoric, and the Practice of Theory in Literary and Legal Studies* (Clarendon Press, Oxford, 1990).

Holland, Norman, *5 Readers Reading* (Yale University Press, New Haven and London, 1975).

Ingarden, Roman, *The Literary Work of Art*, trans. George G. Grabowicz (Northwestern University Press, Evanston, Ill., 1973).

Iser, Wolfgang, *The Act of Reading: A Theory of Aesthetic Response* (Johns Hopkins University Press, Baltimore, 1978).

Jauss, Hans R., *Toward An Aesthetic of Reception*, trans. T. Bahti (Harvester Press, Brighton, 1982). The important first chapter is also in Ralph Cohen (ed.), *New Directions in Literary History* (Routledge & Kegan Paul, London, 1974).

Miller, J. Hillis, *Thomas Hardy: Distance and Desire* (Oxford University Press, Oxford, 1970).

Miller, J. Hillis, *Theory Now and Then* (Harvester Wheatsheaf, Hemel Hempstead, 1991).

Prince, Gerald, 'Introduction to the study of the narratee' in Tompkins (below). French original in *Poétique* no. 14 (1973), 177–96.

Riffaterre, Michael, 'Describing Poetic Structures: Two Approaches to Baudelaire's *Les Chats*' in *Structuralism*, J. Ehrmann (ed.) (Doubleday, Garden City, New York, 1970).

Riffaterre, Michael, *Semiotics of Poetry* (Indiana University Press, Bloomington; Methuen, London, 1978).

Suleiman, Susan and Crosman, Inge (eds), *The Reader in the Text: Essays on Audience and Interpretation* (Princeton University Press, Princeton, NJ, 1980). Includes essays by Iser, Culler, Prince and Holland.

Tompkins, Jane P. (ed.), *Reader-Response Criticism: From Formalism to Post-Structuralism* (Johns Hopkins University Press, Baltimore and London, 1980). Basic anthology of texts.

Walder, Dennis (ed.), *Literature in the Modern World* (Oxford University Press/Open University, Oxford, 1990), Part One, II, 'Interpretation'.

Introductions

Introductions to Suleiman and Crosman, *The Reader in the Text* (above) and Tompkins, *Reader-Response Criticism* (above).

Eagleton, Terry, *Literary Theory: An Introduction* (Basil Blackwell, Oxford, 1983). chap. 2.

Fokkema, D. W. and Kunne-Ibsch, E., *The Theories of Literature in the Twentieth Century: Structuralism, Marxism, Aesthetics of Reception, Semiotics* (C. Hurst, London, 1977).

Freund, Elizabeth, *The Return of the Reader: Reader-Response Criticism* (Methuen, London and New York, 1987).

Holland, Norman N., *Holland's Guide to Psychoanalytic Psychology and Literature-and-Psychology* (Oxford University Press, Oxford, 1990).

Holub, Robert C., *Reception Theory: A Critical Introduction* (Methuen, London and New York, 1984).

McGregor, Graham and White, R. S. (eds), *Reception and Response: Hearer Creativity and the Analysis of Spoken and Written Texts* (Routledge, London, 1990).

Ray, William, *Literary Meaning: From Phenomenology to Deconstruction* (Blackwell, Oxford, 1984).

Sutherland, John, 'Production and Reception of the Literary Book' in *Encyclopaedia of Literature and Criticism*, Martin Coyle, Peter Garside, Malcolm Kelsall and John Peck (eds) (Routledge, London, 1990).

4 Marxist theories

Of the kinds of criticism represented in this guide, Marxist criticism has the longest history. Marx himself made important general statements about culture and society in the 1850s. Even so, it is correct to think of Marxist *criticism* as a twentieth-century phenomenon.

The basic tenets of Marxism are no easier to summarise than the essential doctrines of Christianity, but two well-known statements by Marx provide a sufficient point of departure:

> It is not the consciousness of men that determines their being, but, on the contrary, their social being that determines their consciousness.

> The philosophers have only *interpreted* the world in various ways; the point is to *change* it.

Both statements were intentionally provocative. By contradicting widely accepted doctrines, Marx was trying to put people's thought into reverse gear. First, philosophy has been merely airy contemplation; it is time that it engaged with the real world. Secondly, Hegel and his followers in German philosophy have persuaded us that the world is governed by thought, that the process of history is the gradual dialectical unfolding of the laws of Reason, and that material existence is the expression of an immaterial spiritual essence. People have been led to believe

70

that their ideas, their cultural life, their legal systems, and their religions were the creations of human and divine reason, which should be regarded as the unquestioned guides to human life. Marx reverses this formulation and argues that all mental (ideological) systems are the products of real social and economic existence. The material interests of the dominant social class determine how people see human existence, individual and collective. Legal systems, for example, are not the pure manifestations of human or divine reason, but ultimately reflect the interests of the dominant class in particular historical periods.

In one account, Marx described this view in terms of an architectural metaphor: the 'superstructure' (ideology, politics) rests upon the 'base' (socio-economic relations). To say 'rests upon' is not quite the same as saying 'is caused by'. Marx was arguing that what we call 'culture' is not an independent reality but is inseparable from the historical conditions in which human beings create their material lives; the relations of exploitation and domination which govern the social and economic order of a particular phase of human history will in some sense 'determine' the whole cultural life of the society.

In its crudest formulations, the theory is evidently far too mechanical. For example, in *The German Ideology* (1846) Marx and Engels talk about morality, religion and philosophy as 'phantoms formed in the brains of men', which are the 'reflexes and echoes' of 'real life-processes'. On the other hand, in a famous series of letters written in the 1890s Engels insists that, while he and Marx always regarded the economic aspect of society as the *ultimate* determinant of other aspects, they also recognised that art, philosophy and other forms of consciousness are 'relatively autonomous' and possess an independent ability to alter men's existence. After all, how else do Marxists expect to alter people's awareness except by political discourse? Were we to examine the novels of the eighteenth century or the philosophy of the seventeenth century in Europe, we would recognise, if we were Marxists, that these writings arose at particular phases in the development of early capitalist society. The conflict of social classes establishes the ground upon which ideological conflicts arise. Literature and art belong to the ideological sphere, but possess a relationship to ideology which is often less direct even than is found in the case of religious, legal and philosophical systems.

The special status of literature is recognised by Marx in a celebrated passage in his *Grundrisse,* in which the problem of an apparent discrepancy between economic and artistic development is discussed. Greek tragedy is considered a peak of literary development and yet it coincides with a social system and a form of ideology (Greek myth) which are no longer valid for modern society. The problem for Marx was to explain how an art and literature produced in a long-obsolete social organisation can still give us aesthetic pleasure and be regarded as 'a standard and unattainable ideal'. He seems to be accepting reluctantly a certain 'timelessness' and 'universality' in literature and art; reluctantly, because this would be a major concession to one of bourgeois ideology's premisses. However, it is now possible to see that Marx was simply falling back on received (Hegelian) ways of thinking about literature and art. Our discussion of Mukařovský in chapter 2 established what can now be regarded as a Marxist view: that canons of great literature are socially generated. The 'greatness' of Greek tragedy is not a universal and unchanging fact of existence, but a *value* which must be reproduced from generation to generation.

Even if we reject a privileged status for literature, there remains the question of how far literature's historical development is independent of historical development in general. In his attack on the Russian Formalists in *Literature and Revolution,* Trotsky conceded that literature had its own principles and rules. 'Artistic creation,' he admits, is 'a changing and a transformation of reality in accordance with the peculiar laws of art.' He still insists that the 'reality' remains the crucial factor and not the formal games which writers play. Nevertheless, his remarks point forward to a continuing debate in Marxist criticism about the relative importance of literary form and ideological content in literary works.

SOVIET SOCIALIST REALISM

Marxist criticism written in the West has often been adventurous and exhilarating, but Socialist Realism, as the official

Communist 'artistic method', seems drab and blinkered to Western readers. The doctrines expounded by the Union of Soviet Writers (1932–4) appealed to certain of Lenin's pre-Revolutionary statements as these were interpreted during the 1920s. The theory addressed certain major questions about the evolution of literature, its reflection of class relations and its function in society.

As we have seen, when the Revolution of 1917 encouraged the Formalists to continue developing a revolutionary theory of art, there emerged at the same time an orthodox Communist view, which frowned upon formalism and regarded the nineteenth-century tradition of Russian realism as the only suitable foundation for the aesthetics of the new Communist society. The 'modernist' revolutions in European art, music and literature which occurred around 1910 (Picasso, Stravinsky, Schoenberg, Joyce, Woolf, T. S. Eliot) were to be regarded by Soviet critics as the decadent products of late capitalist society. The modernist rejection of traditional realism paradoxically left Socialist Realism as the leading custodian of bourgeois aesthetics. In Tom Stoppard's play *Travesties* (1975), the Dadaist poet Tzara is made to complain that 'the odd thing about revolution is that the further left you go politically, the more bourgeois they like their art'. The combination of nineteenth-century aesthetics and revolutionary politics remained the essential recipe of Soviet theory.

The principle of *partinost'* (commitment to the working-class cause of the Party) is derived almost exclusively from Lenin's essay 'Party Organisation and Party Literature' (1905), and there remains some doubt about Lenin's intentions in arguing that, while all writers were free to write what they liked, they could not expect to be published in Party journals unless they were committed to the Party's political line. While this was a reasonable demand to make in the precarious circumstances of 1905, it took on a much more despotic significance after the Revolution, when the Party controlled publishing.

The quality of *narodnost'* ('popularity') is central to both the aesthetics and the politics. A work of art of any period achieves this quality by expressing a high level of social awareness, revealing a sense of the true social conditions and feelings of a particular epoch. It will also possess a 'progressive' outlook, glimpsing the developments of the future in the lineaments of the present, and giving a sense of the ideal possibilities of social development from the point of view of the mass of working people. In the 1844 'Paris Manuscripts', Marx argues that the capitalist division of labour destroyed an earlier phase of human history in which artistic and spiritual life were inseparable from the processes of material existence, and craftsmen still worked with a sense of beauty. The separation of mental and manual work dissolved the organic unity of spiritual and material activities, with the result that the masses were forced to produce commodities without the joy of creative engagement in their work. Only folk art survived as the people's art. The appreciation of high art was professionalised, dominated by the market economy and limited to a privileged section of the ruling class. The truly 'popular' art of socialist societies, argued Soviet critics, will be accessible to the masses and will restore their lost wholeness of being.

The theory of the class nature of art (*klassovost'*) is a complex one. In the writings of Marx, Engels and the Soviet tradition, there is a double emphasis – on the writer's commitment or class interests on the one hand, and the social realism of the writer's work on the other. Only the crudest forms of Socialist Realism treat the class nature of art as a simple matter of the writer's explicit class allegiance. In his letter (1888) to Margaret Harkness on her novel *City Girl*, Engels praises her for not writing an explicitly socialist novel. He argues that Balzac, a reactionary supporter of the Bourbon dynasty, provides a more penetrating account of French society in all its economic details than 'all the professed historians, economists and statisticians of the period together'. Balzac's insights into the downfall of the nobility and the rise of the bourgeoisie compelled him to 'go against his own class sympathies and political prejudices'. Realism transcends class sympathies. This argument was to have a powerful influence not only on the theory of Socialist Realism but on later Marxist criticism.

Socialist Realism is considered to be a continuation and development of bourgeois realism at a higher level. Bourgeois writers are judged not according to their class origins or explicit political commitment, but by the extent to which their writings reveal insights into the social developments of their time. The

Soviet hostility to modernist novels can best be understood in this context. Karl Radek's contribution to the Soviet Writers' Congress in 1934 posed the choice 'James Joyce or Socialist Realism?' During a discussion Radek directed a vitriolic attack against another Communist delegate, Herzfelde, who had defended Joyce as a great writer. Radek regards Joyce's experimental technique and his 'petty bourgeois' content as all of a piece. Joyce's preoccupation with the sordid inner life of a trivial individual indicates his profound unawareness of the larger historical forces at work in modern times. For Joyce 'the whole world lies between a cupboard of medieval books, a brothel and a pot house'. He concludes 'if I were to write novels, I would learn how to write them from Tolstoy and Balzac, not from Joyce.'

This admiration for nineteenth-century realism was understandable. Balzac, Dickens, George Eliot, Stendhal and others developed a sophisticated literary form which explores the individual's involvement in the complex network of social relations. Modernist writers abandoned this project and began to reflect a more fragmented image of the world, which was often pessimistic and introverted, exploring the alienated individual consciousness in retreat from the 'nightmare of history' which is modern society. Nothing could be further from the 'revolutionary romanticism' of the Soviet school, which wanted to project a heroic image. Andrey Zhdanov, who gave the keynote speech at the 1934 Congress, reminded writers that Stalin had called upon them to be the 'engineers of the human soul'. At this stage, the political demands upon writers became brutally insistent. Engels was clearly doubtful of the value of overly committed writing, but Zhdanov dismissed all such doubts: 'Yes, Soviet literature is tendentious, for in epochs of class struggle there is not and cannot be a literature which is not class literature, not tendentious, allegedly non-political.'

GEORG LUKÁCS

It is appropriate to consider next the first major Marxist critic, Georg Lukács, since his work is inseparable from orthodox

Socialist Realism. It can be argued that he anticipated some of the Soviet doctrines, but, at any rate, he developed the realist approach with great subtlety. He inaugurated a distinctively Hegelian style of Marxist thought, treating literary works as reflections of an unfolding system. A realist work must reveal the underlying pattern of contradictions in a social order. His view is Marxist in its insistence on the material and historical nature of the structure of society.

Lukács' use of the term 'reflection' is characteristic of his work as a whole. Rejecting the 'naturalism' of the then recent European novel, he returns to the old realist view that the novel reflects reality, not by rendering its mere surface appearance, but by giving us 'a truer, more complete, more vivid and more dynamic reflection of reality'. To 'reflect' is 'to frame a mental structure' transposed into words. People ordinarily possess a reflection of reality, a consciousness not merely of objects but of human nature and social relationships. Lukács would say that a reflection may be more or less concrete. A novel may conduct a reader 'towards a more concrete insight into reality', which transcends a merely common-sense apprehension of things. A literary work reflects not individual phenomena in isolation, but 'the full process of life'. However, the reader is always aware that the work is not itself reality but rather 'a special form of reflecting reality'.

A 'correct' reflection of reality, therefore, according to Lukács, involves more than the mere rendering of external appearances. Interestingly, his view of reflection undermines at the same time both naturalism and modernism. A randomly presented sequence of images may be interpreted either as an *objective* and impartial reflection of reality (as Zola and the other exponents of 'naturalism' might be taken as saying) or as a purely *subjective* impression of reality (as Joyce and Virginia Woolf seem to show). The randomness can be seen as a property either of reality or of perception. Either way, Lukács rejects such merely 'photographic' representation. Instead, he describes the truly realistic work which gives us a sense of the 'artistic necessity' of the images presented; they possess an 'intensive totality' which corresponds to the 'extensive totality' of the world itself. Reality is not a mere flux, a mechanical collision of fragments, but possesses an 'order', which the novelist renders in an 'intensive' form. The writer does not impose an abstract order upon the world, but rather presents the reader with an image of the richness and complexity of life from which emerges a sense of the order within the complexity and subtlety of lived experience. This will be achieved if all the contradictions and tensions of social existence are realised in a formal whole.

Lukács is able to insist on the principle of underlying order and structure because the Marxist tradition borrowed from Hegel the 'dialectical' view of history. Development in history is not random or chaotic, nor is it a straightforward linear progression, but rather a dialectical development. In every social organisation, the prevailing mode of production gives rise to inner contradictions which are expressed in class struggle. Capitalism developed by destroying the feudal mode of production and replacing it with one based on absolute private property and the market, which made possible far higher levels of productivity (commodity production). However, while the process of production was increasingly socialised, the ownership of the means of production became concentrated in private hands. Workers who had owned their looms or tools eventually had nothing to sell but their labour. The inherent contradiction is expressed in the conflict of interest between capitalist and worker. The private accumulation of capital was the foundation of factory working, and thus the contradiction (privatisation/ socialisation) is a necessary unity, which is central to the nature of the capitalist mode of production. The 'dialectical' resolution of the contradiction is always already implied in the contradiction itself: if people are to re-establish control over their labour power, the ownership of the means of production must also be socialised. This brief excursus is intended to show how Lukács' whole view of realism is shaped by the nineteenth-century inheritance of Marxism.

In a series of brilliant works, especially *The Historical Novel* (1937) and *Studies in European Realism* (1950), Lukács refines and extends his theory, and in *The Meaning of Contemporary Realism* (1957) he advances the Communist attack on modernism. He refuses to deny Joyce the status of a true artist, but asks us to reject his view of history, and especially the way in which Joyce's 'static' view of events is reflected in an epic structure which is itself essentially static. For Lukács, this failure to perceive human existence as part of a dynamic historical environment infects the whole of contemporary modernism, as reflected in the works of writers such as Kafka, Beckett and Faulkner. These writers, he argues, are preoccupied with formal experiment – with montage, inner monologues, the technique of 'stream of consciousness', the use of reportage, diaries, etc. All this formalistic virtuosity is the result of a narrow concern for subjective impressions, a concern which itself stems from the advanced individualism of late capitalism. Instead of an objective realism we have an *angst*-ridden vision of the world. The fullness of history and its social processes are narrowed down to the bleak inner history of absurd existences. This 'attenuation of actuality' is contrasted to the dynamic and developmental view of society to be found in the great nineteenth-century novelists and in their latterday heirs like Thomas Mann, who, though not 'socialist', achieve a genuinely 'Critical Realism'.

By divorcing the individual from the outer world of objective reality, the modernist writer, in Lukács' view, is compelled to see the inner life of characters as 'a sinister, inexplicable flux', which ultimately also takes on a timeless static quality. Lukács seems unable to perceive that in rendering the impoverished and alienated existence of modern subjects some modern writers achieve a kind of realism, or at any rate develop new literary forms and techniques which articulate modern reality. Insisting on the reactionary nature of modernist *ideology*, he refused to recognise the *literary* possibilities of modernist writings. Because he thought the *content* of modernism was reactionary, he treated modernist *form* as equally unacceptable. During his brief stay in Berlin during the early 1930s, he found himself attacking the use of modernist techniques of montage and reportage in the work of fellow radicals, including the outstanding dramatist Bertolt Brecht.

Erich Auerbach, an exile from Hitler's Germany who later became Professor of Romance Languages at Yale University, also promotes a Lukácsian conception of Realism in his wide-ranging and influential work, *Mimesis: The Representation of Reality in Western Literature* (1946). Like Lukács, Auerbach is interested in what, and how, historical forces shape behaviour, and how the artist establishes telling links between individual activity and its particular social and historical context. The work of art's ability to comprehend and enact such a 'totalising' view is what makes it important, and for Auerbach therefore, as for Lukács, modern realism should represent at once a kind of repository of cultural history and an intervention in the moral and political lives of human beings.

BERTOLT BRECHT

Brecht's early plays were radical, anarchistic and anti-bourgeois, but not anti-capitalist. After reading Marx in about 1926, his youthful iconoclasm was converted to conscious political commitment, although he always remained a maverick and never a Party man. Around 1930 he was writing the so-called *Lehrstücke*, didactic plays intended for working-class audiences, but he was forced to leave Germany when the Nazis took power in 1933. He wrote his major plays in exile, mainly in Scandinavian countries. Later, in America, he was brought before the McCarthy Committee for un-American Activities and finally settled in East Germany in 1949. He had trouble too with the Stalinist authorities of the GDR, who regarded him as both an asset and a liability.

His opposition to Socialist Realism certainly offended the East German authorities. His best-known theatrical device, the alienation effect (*Verfremdungseffekt*), recalls the Russian Formalists' concept of 'defamiliarisation' (see above, pp. 31–3). Socialist Realism favoured realistic illusion, formal unity and 'positive' heroes. He called *his* theory of realism 'anti-Aristotelian', a covert way of attacking the theory of his opponents. Aristotle emphasised the universality and unity of the tragic action, and the identification of audience and hero in empathy which produces a 'catharsis' of emotions. Brecht rejected the entire tradition of 'Aristotelian' theatre. The dramatist should avoid a smoothly interconnected plot and any sense of inevitability or universality. The facts of social injustice needed to be presented as if they were shockingly unnatural and totally surprising. It is all too easy to regard 'the price of bread, the lack of work, the declaration of war as if they were phenomena of nature:

earthquakes or floods', rather than as the results of exploitative human agency.

To avoid lulling the audience into a state of passive acceptance, the illusion of reality must be shattered by the use of the alienation effect. The actors must not lose themselves in their roles or seek to promote a purely empathic audience identification. They must present a role to the audience as both recognisable and unfamiliar, so that a process of critical assessment can be set in motion. The situation, emotions and dilemmas of the characters must be understood from the outside and presented as strange and problematic. This is not to say that actors should avoid the use of emotion, but only the resort to empathy. This is achieved by 'baring the device', to use the Formalist term (see above, p. 31–3). The use of gesture is an important way of externalising a character's emotions. Gesture or action is studied and rehearsed as a device for conveying in a striking way the specific social meaning of a role. One might contrast this with the Stanislavskian 'method acting', which encourages total identification of actor and role. Improvisation rather than calculation is encouraged in order to create a sense of 'spontaneity' and individuality. This foregrounding of a character's inner life allows its social meaning to evaporate. The gestures of a Marlon Brando or a James Dean are personal and idiosyncratic, while a 'Brechtian' actor (for example Peter Lorre or Jack Nicholson) performs rather like a clown or mimic, using diagrammatic gestures which *indicate* rather than reveal. In any case, Brecht's plays, in which the 'heroes' are so often ordinary, tough and unscrupulous, do not encourage the cult of personality. Mother Courage, Asdak and Sweik are boldly outlined on an 'epic' canvas: they are remarkably dynamic social beings, but have no focused 'inner' life.

Brecht rejected the kind of formal unity admired by Lukács. First, Brecht's 'epic' theatre, unlike Aristotle's tragic theatre, is composed of loosely linked episodes of the kind to be found in Shakespeare's history plays and eighteenth-century picaresque novels. There are no artificial constraints of time and place, and no 'well-made' plots. Contemporary inspiration came from the cinema (Charlie Chaplin, Buster Keaton, Eisenstein) and modernist fiction (Joyce and Dos Passos). Secondly, Brecht believed that no model of good form could remain in force indefinitely; there are no 'eternal aesthetic laws'. To capture the living force of reality the writer must be willing to make use of every conceivable formal device, old and new: 'We shall take care not to ascribe realism to a particular historical form of novel belonging to a particular period, Balzac's or Tolstoy's, for instance, so as to set up purely formal and literary criteria of realism.' He considered Lukács' desire to enshrine a particular literary form as the only true model for realism to be a dangerous kind of formalism. Brecht would have been the first to admit that, if his own 'alienation effect' were to become a formula for realism, it would cease to be effective. If we copy other realists' methods, we cease to be realists ourselves: 'Methods wear out, stimuli fail. New problems loom up and demand new techniques. Reality alters; to represent it the means of representation must alter too.' (For further discussion of the Lukács/Brecht debate, and its implications for an analysis of Joyce's *Ulysses*, see chapter 6, section 23, of *Practising Theory and Reading Literature.*) These remarks express clearly Brecht's undogmatic and experimental view of aesthetics. However, there is nothing in the least 'liberal' in his rejection of ortho- doxy; his restless search for new ways of shaking audiences out of their complacent passivity into active engagement was motivated by a dedicated political commitment to unmasking every new disguise used by the deviously protean capitalist system.

THE FRANKFURT SCHOOL: ADORNO AND BENJAMIN

While Brecht and Lukács held conflicting views of realism, the Frankfurt School of Marxist aesthetics rejected realism alto- gether. The Institute for Social Research at Frankfurt practised what it called 'Critical Theory', which was a wide-ranging form of social analysis grounded in Hegelian Marxism and including Freudian elements. The leading figures in philosophy and aesthetics were Max Horkheimer, Theodor Adorno and Herbert Marcuse. Exiled in 1933, the Institute was relocated in New York, but finally returned to Frankfurt in 1950 under Adorno and Horkheimer. They regarded the social system, in Hegelian fashion, as a totality in which all the aspects reflected the same essence. Their analysis of modern culture was influenced by the experience of fascism which had achieved hegemonic domin- ance at every level of social existence in Germany. In America they saw a similar 'one-dimensional' quality in the mass culture and the permeation of every aspect of life by commercialism.

Art and literature have a privileged place in Frankfurt thinking. In an early initiative in Critical Theory, Marcuse proposed the notion of 'affirmative culture', by which he sought to register the dialectical nature of culture as conformist (in its quietist cultivation of inner fulfilment) but also critical (in so far as it bore in its very form the image of an undamaged existence). Marcuse, while always insisting on the negative, transcendent power of 'the aesthetic dimension', retained the revolutionary political commitments of his youth, but the keynote of Frankfurt Marxism was pessimism. For the outstanding exponent of Critical Theory, Adorno, art – with philosophy – was the only theatre of resistance to 'the administered universe' of the twentieth century. Adorno criticised Lukács' view of realism, arguing that literature does not have a direct contact with reality. In Adorno's view, art is set apart from reality; its detachment gives it its special significance and power. Modern- ist writings are particularly distanced from the reality to which they allude, and this distance gives their work the power of criticising reality. While popular art forms are forced to collude with the economic system which shapes them, 'autonomous' works have the power to 'negate' the reality to which they relate. Because modernist texts reflect the alienated inner lives of individuals, Lukács attacked them as 'decadent' embodiments of late capitalist society and evidence of the writers' inability to transcend the atomistic and fragmented worlds in which they were compelled to live. Adorno argues that art cannot simply reflect the social system, but acts within that reality as an irritant which produces an indirect sort of knowledge: 'Art is the negative knowledge of the actual world.' This can be achieved, he believed, by writing 'difficult' experimental texts and not directly polemical or critical works. The masses, argues Hork- heimer, reject the *avant-garde* because it disturbs their unthink- ing and automatic acquiescence in their manipulation by the social system: 'By making down-trodden humans shockingly aware of their own despair, the work of art announces a freedom which makes them fume.'

Literary form is not simply a unified and compressed reflection of the form of society, as it was for Lukács, but a special means of distancing reality and preventing the easy reabsorption of new insights into familiar and consumable packages. Modernists try to disrupt and fragment the picture of modern life rather than master its dehumanising mechanisms. Lukács could see only symptoms of decay in this kind of art and could not recognise its power to *reveal*. Proust's use of *monologue intérieur* does not just reflect an alienated individualism, but both grasps a 'truth' about modern society (the alienation of the individual) and enables us to see that the alienation is part of an objective social reality. In a complex essay on Samuel Beckett's *Endgame* Adorno meditates on the ways in which Beckett uses form to evoke the emptiness of modern culture. Despite the catastrophes and degradations of twentieth-century history, the play suggests, we persist in behaving as if nothing has changed. We persist in our foolish belief in the old truths of the unity and substantiality of the individual or the meaningfulness of language. The play presents characters who possess only the hollow shells of individuality and the fragmented clichés of a language. The absurd discontinuities of discourse, the pared-down characterisation, and plotlessness, all contribute to the aesthetic effect of distancing the reality to which the play alludes, thereby giving us a 'negative' knowledge of modern existence.

Marx believed that he had extracted the 'rational kernel' from the 'mystical shell' of Hegel's dialectic. What survives is the dialectical method of understanding the real processes of human history. The Frankfurt School's work has much of the authentic Hegelian subtlety in dialectical thought. The meaning of dialectic in the tradition of Hegel can be summed up as 'the development which arises from the resolution of contradictions inherent in a particular aspect of reality'. Adorno's *Philosophy of Modern Music*, for example, develops a dialectical account of the composer Schoenberg. The composer's 'atonal' revolution arose in a historical context in which the extreme commercialisation of culture destroys the listener's ability to appreciate the formal unity of a classical work. The commercial exploitation of artistic techniques in cinema, advertising, popular music and so on forces the composer to respond by producing a shattered and fragmented music, in which the very grammar of musical language (tonality) is denied. Each individual note is cut off and cannot be resolved into meaning by the surrounding context. Adorno describes the content of this 'atonal' music in the language of psychoanalysis: the painfully isolated notes express bodily impulses from the unconscious. The new form is related to the individual's loss of conscious control in modern society. By allowing the expression of violent unconscious impulses, Schoenberg's music evades the censor, reason. However, as Fredric Jameson's fine summary shows, the seeds of a new development (the twelve-tone scale) are already latent in this radical atonality:

> For whatever the will toward total freedom, the atonal composer still works in a world of stale tonality and must take his precautions with regard to the past. He must, for example, avoid the kind of consonance or tonal chord which would be likely to reawaken older listening habits, and to reorganise the music into noise or wrong notes. Yet this very danger is enough to awaken in atonality the first principle of a new law or order. For the taboo against accidentally atonal chords carries with it the corollary that the composer should avoid any exaggerated repetition of a single note, for fear such an insistence would ultimately tend to function as a new kind of tonal centre for the ear. It is necessary only to pose the problem of avoiding such repetition in a more formal way for the entire twelve-tone system to show itself upon the horizon.

The dialectic is completed when this new system is related to the new totalitarian organisation of late capitalist imperialism, in which the autonomy of the individual is lost in the massive and monolithic market-system. That is to say, the music is at once a rebellion against a one-dimensional society and also a symptom of an inescapable loss of freedom.

We cannot leave the Frankfurt School without discussing Walter Benjamin. Friend of Adorno but also of Brecht (to whom Adorno was antipathetic by temperament and outlook) and of Gershom Sholem (the great student of Judaic mysticism, who looked askance upon his old companion's conversion to

materialist thought), Benjamin was the most idiosyncratic
Marxist thinker of his generation. His early 'academic' criticism,
devoted to Goethe and to German Baroque drama, is legend-
arily obscure, and much of his cultural journalism is little less so.
He worked for years on his 'Arcades project', a fascinating
exploration of the emerging commercial culture of Paris, 'capital
of the nineteenth century'. He was among the earliest and best
interpreters of Brecht's theatre and a bold, intransigently
materialist theorist of the new means of artistic production, yet
his last essay, the 'Theses on the Philosophy of History',
rendered its Marxist vision in the idiom of messianic theology.
Benjamin's best-known essay, 'The Work of Art in the Age of
Mechanical Reproduction', argues that modern technical
innovations (above all, photography and cinema) have profoundly altered the status of the 'work of art'. Once, artistic
works had an 'aura' deriving from their uniqueness. This was
especially true of the visual arts, but even in the case of literature
this 'aura' survived. The new media totally shatter this quasi-
religious ethos. To a greater and greater extent the *reproduction*
of art objects (by means of photography or radio transmission)
means that they are actually designed for reproducibility; and in
the emergence of cinema we discover 'copies' without an
'original'. Here Benjamin argued, was the technical basis of a
new ethos of artistic production and consumption, one in which
awe and deference would give way to a posture of analysis and
relaxed expertise, in which art, no longer steeped in 'ritual',
would be opened to politics. In fact, it predicts many of the
characteristics of 'Postmodern' cultural forms and attitudes. The
element of wishful thinking in Benjamin's theses was noted by
Adorno at the time, yet the essay remains exemplary for its
attention to the specific historical role of artistic technologies.
Benjamin made the same distinctive emphasis in a companion
essay on the politics of artistic practice, 'The Author as
Producer'.

While new technology might have revolutionary potential,
Benjamin was aware that there was no guarantee of a
revolutionary effect. It was necessary for socialist writers and
artists to realise this potential in their work. Benjamin's views on
the nature of art in its own right were close to Brecht's and
indeed the clearest account of his thoughts was written with

Brecht's plays in mind. Benjamin rejects the idea that revolutionary art is achieved by attending to the correct subject-matter. (In this respect, his views are pitched against the realist orthodoxy of the day.) Instead of being concerned with a work of art's position within the social and economic relations of its time, he asks the question: what is 'the function of a work within the literary production relations of its time'? The artist needs to revolutionise the *artistic* forces of production of his or her time. And this is a matter of *technique,* although the correct technique will arise in response to a complex historical combination of social and technical changes. Paris, the anonymous great city of the Second Empire, is the subject of Baudelaire's and Poe's writings. Their technical innovations are a direct response to the asocial and fragmented conditions of urban existence: 'The original social content of the detective story was the obliteration of the individual's traces in the big-city crowd.' Benjamin writes of a poem by Baudelaire: 'The inner form of these verses is revealed in the fact that in them love itself is recognized as being stigmatized by the big city.'

'STRUCTURALIST' MARXISM: ALTHUSSER, GOLDMANN AND MACHEREY

The intellectual life of Europe during the 1960s was dominated by structuralism. Marxist criticism was not unaffected by this intellectual environment. Both traditions believe that individuals cannot be understood apart from their social existence. Marxists believe that individuals are 'bearers' of positions in the social system and not free agents. Structuralists consider that individual actions and utterances have no meaning apart from the signifying systems which generate them. However, structuralists tend to regard these underlying structures as timeless and self-regulating systems, but Marxists see them as historical, changeable and fraught with contradictions.

Lucien Goldmann, a Romanian theorist based in France, rejected the idea that texts are creations of individual genius and argued that they are based upon 'trans-individual mental structures' belonging to particular groups (or classes). These 'world-views' are perpetually being constructed and dissolved by social groups as they adjust their mental image of the world in response to the changing reality before them. Such mental images usually remain ill-defined and half-realised in the consciousness of social agents, but great writers are able to crystallise world-views in a lucid and coherent form.

Goldmann's celebrated *Le Dieu Caché* (*The Hidden God*) establishes connections between Racine's tragedies, Pascal's philosophy, a French religious movement (Jansenism) and a social group (the *noblesse de la robe*). The Jansenist world-view is tragic: it sees the individual as divided between a hopelessly sinful world and a God who is absent. God has abandoned the world but still imposes an absolute authority upon the believer. The individual is driven into an extreme and tragic solitude. The underlying structure of relationships in Racine's tragedies expresses the Jansenist predicament, which in turn can be related to the decline of the *noblesse de la robe*, a class of court officials who were becoming increasingly isolated and powerless as the absolute monarchy withdrew its financial support. The 'manifest' content of the tragedies appears to have no connection with Jansenism, but at a deeper structural level they share the same form: 'the tragic hero, equidistant from God and from the world, is *radically alone*'. In other words, the expressive relationship between social class and literary text was registered not in 'reflected' content but in a parallelism of form, or 'homology'. By means of the concept of homology, Goldmann was able to think beyond the confines of the dogmatic realist tradition (though he retained his admiration for Lukács' earlier work) and to develop a distinctive variety of Marxist literary and cultural analysis to which he gave the name 'genetic structuralism'.

His later work, especially *Pour une sociologie du roman* (1964), appears to resemble that of the Frankfurt School by focusing on the 'homology' between the structure of the modern novel and the structure of the market economy. He argues that by about 1910 the transition from the 'heroic' age of liberal capitalism to its imperialist phase was well under way. As a consequence the importance of the individual within economic life was drastically reduced. Finally, in the post-1945 period the regulation and management of economic systems by the state and by corporations brought to its fullest development that tendency which Lukács called 'reification' (this refers to the reduction of value to exchange value and the domination of the human world by objects). In the classic novel, objects only had significance in relation to individuals, but, in the novels of Sartre, Kafka and Robbe-Grillet, the world of objects begins to displace the individual. This final stage of Goldmann's writing depended upon a rather crude model of 'superstructure' and 'base', according to which literary structures simply correspond to economic structures. It avoids the pessimism of the Frankfurt School, but lacks their rich dialectical insights.

Louis Althusser, the French Marxist philosopher, has had a major influence on Marxist literary theory especially in France and Britain. His work is clearly related to structuralism and has been claimed for poststructuralism (see also chapter 6, 'Discourse'). He rejects the Hegelian revival within Marxist philosophy, and argues that Marx's real contribution to knowledge stems from his 'break' with Hegel. He criticises Hegel's account of 'totality', according to which the essence of the whole is expressed in all its parts. Althusser avoids terms such as 'social system' and 'order', because they suggest a structure with a centre which determines the form of all its emanations. Instead he talks of the 'social formation', which he regards as a 'decentred' structure. Unlike a living organism this structure has no governing principle, no originating seed, no overall unity. The implications of this view are arresting. The various elements (or 'levels') within the social formation are not treated as reflections of one essential level (the economic level for Marxists): the levels possess a 'relative autonomy', and are ultimately determined by the economic level only 'in the last instance' (this complex formulation derives from Engels). The social formation is a structure in which the various levels exist in complex relations of inner contradiction and mutual conflict; its contradictions are never 'simple' but 'overdetermined' in nature. This structure of contradictions may be dominated at any given stage by one or other of the levels, but which level it is to be is itself 'determined' ultimately by the economic level. For example, as Marx himself observed, in feudal social formations religion is structurally dominant, but this does not mean that religion is the essence or centre of the structure. Its leading role is itself determined by the economic level, though not directly.

Althusser refuses to treat art as simply a form of ideology. In 'A Letter on Art', he locates it somewhere between ideology and scientific knowledge. A great work of literature does not give us a properly conceptual understanding of reality but neither does it merely express the ideology of a particular class. He draws upon Engels' arguments about Balzac (see p.74) and declares that art 'makes us *see*', in a distanced way, 'the ideology from which it is born, in which it bathes, from which it detaches itself as art, and to which it alludes'. Althusser defines ideology as 'a representation of the imaginary relationship of individuals to their real conditions of existence'. The imaginary consciousness helps us to make sense of the world but also masks or represses our real relationship to it. For example, the ideology of 'freedom' promotes the belief in the freedom of all, including labourers, but it masks the real relations of liberal capitalist economy. A dominant system of ideology is accepted as a common-sense view of things by the dominated classes and thus the interests of the dominant class are secured. Art, however, achieves 'a retreat' (a fictional distance deriving from its formal composition) from the very ideology which feeds it. In this way a major literary work can transcend the ideology of the writer.

Pierre Macherey's *A Theory of Literary Production* (1966) was the first extended Althusserian discussion of art and ideology. Rather than treat the text as a 'creation' or a self-contained artifact, he regards it as a 'production' in which disparate materials are worked over and changed in the process. These materials are not 'free implements' to be used consciously to create a controlled and unified work of art. Irrespective of prevailing aesthetic norms and authorial intentions, the text, in working the pre-given materials, is never fully 'aware of what it is doing'. It has, so to speak, an 'unconscious'. When that state of consciousness we call an ideology enters the text it takes on a different form. Ideology is normally lived as if it were totally natural, as if its imaginary and fluid discourse gives a perfect and unified explanation of reality. Once it is worked into a text, all its contradictions and gaps are exposed. The realist writer intends to unify all the elements in the text, but the work that goes on in the textual process inevitably produces certain lapses and omissions which correspond to the incoherence of the ideological discourse it uses: 'for in order to say anything, there are other things *which must not be said*'. The literary critic is not concerned to show how all the parts of the work fit together, or to harmonise and smooth over any apparent contradictions. Like a psychoanalyst, the critic attends to the text's unconscious – to what is unspoken and inevitably repressed.

How would this approach work? Consider Defoe's novel, *Moll Flanders* (of which there is fuller Althusserian and Machereyan discussion in *PTRL*, chapter 6, section 22). In the early eighteenth century, bourgeois ideology smoothed over the contradictions between moral and economic requirements; that is, between on the one hand a providential view of human life which requires the deferment of immediate gratification for a long-term gain, and on the other an economic individualism which drains all value from human relations and fixes it solely in commodities. Set to work in *Moll Flanders* this ideological discourse is represented so that its contradictions are exposed. The operation of literary form on ideology produces this effect of incoherence. The literary use of Moll as narrator itself involves a double perspective. She tells her story prospectively and retro-spectively: she is both a participant who relishes her selfish life as prostitute and thief, and a moraliser who relates her sinful life as a warning to others. The two perspectives are symbolic-ally merged in the episode of Moll's successful business speculation in Virginia where she founds her enterprise upon the ill-gotten gains which were kept secured during her Newgate imprisonment. This economic success is *also* her reward for repenting of her evil life. In this way literary form 'congeals' the fluid discourse of ideology: by giving it formal substance the text shows up the flaws and contradictions in the ideology it uses. The writer does not *intend* this effect since it is produced so to speak 'unconsciously' by the text.

In a later study, written with Etienne Balibar, Macherey departed more radically from the traditional notion of literature which the Frankfurt School defended and Althusser still entertained. The culture of 'the literary' was now rethought as a key practice within the education system, where it served to reproduce class-domination in language.

RECENT DEVELOPMENTS: WILLIAMS,
EAGLETON AND JAMESON

Marxist theory in the United States has been dominated by the Hegelian inheritance of the Frankfurt School (the journal *Telos* is the standard-bearer of this tradition). The revival of Marxist criticism in Britain (in decline since the 1930s) was fuelled by the 1968 'troubles' and by the ensuing influx of continental ideas (*New Left Review* was an important channel). A major theorist emerged in response to the specific conditions at work in each country. Fredric Jameson's *Marxism and Form* (1971) and *The Prison-House of Language* (1972) displayed dialectical skills worthy of a Marxist-Hegelian philosopher. Terry Eagleton's *Criticism and Ideology* (1976) built upon the anti-Hegelian Marxism of Althusser and Macherey, and produced an impressive critique of the British critical tradition and a radical revaluation of the development of the English novel. More recently, Jameson and Eagleton have responded inventively to the challenge of poststructuralism (see pp. 93–9 below, and Chapter 7), and show a remarkable resourcefulness and a willingness to modify their earlier positions.

There was, of course, an outstanding presence already at work in the field: Raymond Williams. Beginning with a critical reassessment of the main English tradition of critical cultural thought (*Culture and Society 1780–1950*, 1958), Williams embarked on a radical theoretical construction of the whole domain of social meaning – 'culture' as 'a whole way of life'. This general perspective was developed in particular studies of drama, the novel, television, and historical semantics as well as further theoretical work. Williams's general project – the study of all forms of signification in their actual conditions of production – was always emphatically historical and materialist; 'cultural materialism' was the name he eventually gave it. Yet it was only in 1977, with the publication of a developed statement of theoretical position, that he began to characterize his work as 'Marxist' (*Marxism and Literature*, 1977). He had long since rejected the Communist orthodoxy of his student days and remained convinced that the outline theory of culture received from Marx was compromised not by its 'materialism' but, quite on the contrary, by its undischarged idealist residues. The air of distant hesitation so imparted to his earlier writings was sometimes construed by a younger generation of Marxists as a sign of theoretical and political insufficiency, and this partly accounts for the fact that Eagleton launched his own theoretical intervention not merely as a rejection of the dominant Leavisian tradition but also as a revolutionary critique of his former mentor, Williams.

Eagleton, like Althusser, argues that criticism must break with its 'ideological prehistory' and become a 'science'. The central problem is to define the relationship between literature and ideology, because in his view texts do not reflect historical reality but rather work upon ideology to produce an *effect* of the 'real'. The text may appear to be free in its relation to reality (it can invent characters and situations at will), but it is not free in its use of ideology. 'Ideology' here refers not to formulated doctrines but to all those systems of representation (aesthetic, religious, judicial and others) which shape the individual's mental picture of lived experience. The meanings and perceptions produced in the text are a reworking of ideology's own working of reality. This means that the text works on reality at two removes. Eagleton goes on to deepen the theory by examining the complex layering of ideology from its most general pre-textual forms to the ideology of the text itself. He rejects Althusser's view that literature can distance itself from ideology; it is a complex reworking of already existing ideological discourses. However, the literary result is not merely a reflection of other ideological discourses but a special *production* of ideology. For this reason criticism is concerned not with just the laws of literary form or the theory of ideology but rather with 'the laws of the production of ideological discourses as literature'.

Eagleton surveys a sequence of novels from George Eliot to D. H. Lawrence in order to demonstrate the interrelations between ideology and literary form. He argues that nineteenth-century bourgeois ideology blended a sterile utilitarianism with a series of organicist concepts of society (mainly deriving from the Romantic humanist tradition). As Victorian capitalism became more 'corporatist' it needed bolstering up by the sympathetic social and aesthetic organicism of the Romantic tradition. Eagleton examines each writer's ideological situation and analyses the contradictions which develop in their thinking and the attempted resolutions of the contradictions in their writings. For example, he argues that Lawrence was influenced by Romantic humanism in his belief that the novel reflects the fluidity of life undogmatically, and that society too is ideally an organic order as against the alien capitalist society of modern England. After the destruction of liberal humanism in the First World War Lawrence developed a dualistic pattern of 'female' and 'male' principles. This antithesis is developed and re-shuffled in the various stages of his work, and finally resolved in the characterisation of Mellors (*Lady Chatterley's Lover*) who combines impersonal 'male' power and 'female' tenderness. This contradictory combination, which takes various forms in the novels, can be related to a 'deep-seated ideological crisis' within contemporary society.

The impact of poststructuralist thought produced a radical change in Eagleton's work in the late 1970s. His attention shifted from the 'scientific' attitude of Althusser towards the revolution-ary thought of Brecht and Benjamin. This shift had the effect of throwing Eagleton back towards the classic Marxist revolution-ary theory of the *Theses on Feuerbach* (1845): 'The question whether objective truth can be attributed to human thinking is not a question of theory but is a *practical* question . . . The philosophers have only *interpreted* the world in various ways; the point is to *change* it.' Eagleton believes that 'deconstructive' theories, as developed by Derrida, Paul de Man and others (see chapter 6), can be used to undermine all certainties, all fixed and absolute forms of knowledge. On the other hand, he criticises deconstruction for its petit-bourgeois denial of 'objectivity' and material 'interests' (especially class interests). This apparently contradictory view can be understood if we note that Eagleton was now espousing Lenin's and not Althusser's view of theory: correct theory 'assumes final shape only in close connection with the practical activity of a truly mass and truly revolutionary movement'. The tasks of Marxist criticism are now set up by politics and not by philosophy: the critic must dismantle received notions of 'literature' and reveal their ideological role in shaping the subjectivity of readers. As a socialist the critic must 'expose the rhetorical structures by which non-socialist works produce politically undesirable effects' and also 'interpret such works where possible "against the grain"', so that they work for socialism.

Eagleton's major book of this phase is *Walter Benjamin or Towards a Revolutionary Criticism* (1981). The odd materialist mysticism of Benjamin is read 'against the grain' to produce a revolutionary criticism. His view of history involves a violent grasping of historical meaning from a past which is always threatened and obscured by reactionary and repressive memory. When the right (political) moment comes, a voice from the past can be seized and appropriated to its 'true' purpose. Brecht's plays, admired by Benjamin, often reread history 'against the grain', breaking down the relentless narratives of history and opening the past to reinscription. For example, Shakespeare's *Coriolanus* and Gay's *Beggar's Opera* are 'rewritten' in order to expose their potential socialist meanings. (Brecht characteristically insisted that we must go beyond mere empathy with Shakespeare's self-regarding 'hero' and must be able to appreciate the tragedy not only of Coriolanus but also 'specifically of the plebs'.) Eagleton applauds Brecht's radical and opportunistic approach to meaning: 'a work may be realist in June and anti-realist in December'. Eagleton frequently alludes to Perry Anderson's *Considerations on Western Marxism* (1976) which shows how the development of Marxist theory always reflects the state of the working-class struggle. Eagleton believes, for example, that the Frankfurt School's highly 'negative' critique of modern culture was a response first to fascist domination in Europe, and then to the pervasive capitalist domination in the United States, but that it was also the result of the School's theoretical and practical divorce from the working-class movement. However, what makes Eagleton's revolutionary criticism distinctively *modern* is his tactical deployment of the Freudian theories of Lacan and the powerful deconstructive philosophy of Jacques Derrida (see chapter 6); his *The Rape of Clarissa* (1982), a re-reading of Richardson's novel inspired politically by both socialism and feminism, exemplifies the force of this revised critical strategy.

Eagleton's work continues to develop and change. *The Ideology of the Aesthetic* (1990) recalls Frankfurtian rather than 'Parisian' antecedents: the culture of 'the aesthetic' in post-Enlightenment

Europe is reviewed dialectically, seen both as a binding agent in the formation of 'normal' bourgeois subjectivity, and as the carrier of irrepressible, disruptive desire.

In America, where the labour movement has been partially corrupted and totally excluded from political power, the appearance of a major Marxist theorist is an important event. On the other hand, if we keep in mind Eagleton's point about the Frankfurt School and American society, it is not without significance that Fredric Jameson's work has been deeply influenced by that School. In *Marxism and Form* (1971) he explores the dialectical aspect of Marxist theories of literature. After a fine sequence of studies (Adorno, Benjamin, Marcuse, Bloch, Lukács and Sartre) he presents the outline of a 'dialectical criticism'.

Jameson believes that in the post-industrial world of monopoly capitalism the only kind of Marxism which has any purchase on the situation is a Marxism which explores the 'great themes of Hegel's philosophy – the relationship of part to whole, the opposition between concrete and abstract, the concept of totality, the dialectic of appearance and essence, the interaction between subject and object'. For dialectical thought there are no fixed and unchanging 'objects'; an 'object' is inextricably bound up with a larger whole, and is also related to a thinking mind which is itself part of a historical situation. Dialectical criticism does not isolate individual literary works for analysis; an individual is always part of a larger structure (a tradition or a movement) or part of a historical situation. The dialectical critic has no pre-set categories to apply to literature and will always be aware that his or her chosen categories (style, character, image, etc.) must be understood ultimately as an aspect of the critic's own historical situation. Jameson shows that Wayne Booth's *Rhetoric of Fiction* (1961: see above, p. 20) is lacking in a proper dialectical self-awareness. Booth adopts the concept of 'point of view' in the novel, a concept which is profoundly modern in its implied relativism and rejection of any fixed or absolute viewpoint or standard of judgement. However, by defending the specific point of view represented by the 'implied author', Booth tries to restore the certainties of the nineteenth-century novel, a move which reflects a nostalgia for a time of greater middle-class stability in an orderly class system.

A Marxist dialectical criticism will always recognise the historical origins of its own concepts and will never allow the concepts to ossify and become insensitive to the pressure of reality. We can never get outside our subjective existence in time, but we *can* try to break through the hardening shell of our ideas 'into a more vivid apprehension of reality itself'.

A dialectical criticism will seek to unmask the inner form of a genre or body of texts and will work from the surface of a work inward to the level where literary form is deeply related to the concrete. Taking Hemingway as his example, Jameson contends that the 'dominant category of experience' in the novels is the process of writing itself. Hemingway discovered that he could produce a certain kind of bare sentence which could do two things well: register movement in nature (things) and suggest the tension of resentments between people. The achieved writing skill is linked conceptually with other human skills which are expressed in relation to the natural world (especially blood sports). The Hemingway cult of *machismo* reflects the American ideal of technical skill but rejects the alienating conditions of industrial society by transposing human skill into the sphere of leisure. Hemingway's laid-bare sentences cannot gain access to the complex fabric of American society and so his novels are directed to the thinned-down reality of foreign cultures in which individuals stand out with the 'cleanness of objects' and can therefore be contained in Hemingway's sentences. In this way Jameson shows how literary form is deeply engaged with a concrete reality.

His *The Political Unconscious* (1981) retains the earlier dialectical conception of theory but also assimilates various conflicting traditions of thought (structuralism, poststructuralism, Freud, Althusser, Adorno) in an impressive and still recognisably Marxist synthesis. Jameson argues that the fragmented and alienated condition of human society implies an original state of Primitive Communism in which both life and perception were 'collective'. When humanity suffered a sort of Blakean Fall, the very human senses themselves established separate spheres of specialisation. A painter treats sight as a specialised sense; his or her paintings are a symptom of alienation. However, they are also a compensation for the loss of a world of original fullness: they provide colour in a colourless world.

All ideologies are 'strategies of containment' which allow society to provide an explanation of itself which suppresses the underlying contradictions of History; it is History itself (the brute reality of economic Necessity) which imposes this strategy of repression. Literary texts work in the same way: the solutions which they offer are merely symptoms of the suppression of History. Jameson cleverly uses A. J. Greimas' structuralist theory (the 'semiotic rectangle') as an analytic tool for his own purposes. Textual strategies of containment present themselves as formal patterns. Greimas' structuralist system provides a complete inventory of possible human relations (sexual, legal, etc.) which, when applied to a text's strategies, will allow the analyst to discover the possibilities which are *not said*. This 'not said' is the repressed History.

Jameson also develops a powerful argument about narrative and interpretation. He believes that narrative is not just a literary form or mode but an essential 'epistemological category'; reality presents itself to the human mind only in the form of stories. Even a scientific theory is a form of story. Further, all narratives require interpretation. Here Jameson is answering the common poststructuralist argument against 'strong' interpretation. Deleuze and Guattari (in *Anti-Oedipus*; see below, p. 143) attack all 'transcendent' interpretation, allowing only 'immanent' interpretation which avoids imposing a strong 'meaning' on a text. Transcendent interpretation tries to master the text and in so doing *impoverishes* its true complexity. Jameson cunningly takes the example of New Criticism (a self-declared immanentist approach), and shows that it is in fact transcendent, its master code being 'humanism'. He concludes that all interpretations are necessarily transcendent and ideological. In the end, all we can do is to use ideological concepts as a means of transcending ideology.

Jameson's 'political unconscious' takes from Freud the essential concept of 'repression', but raises it from the individual to the collective level. The function of ideology is to repress 'revolution'. Not only do the oppressors need this political unconscious but so do the oppressed who would find their existence unbearable if 'revolution' were not repressed. To analyse a novel we need to establish an absent cause (the 'not-revolution'). Jameson proposes a critical method which includes three 'horizons' (a level of immanent analysis, using Greimas for example, a level of social-discourse analysis, and an epochal level of Historical reading). The third horizon of reading is based upon Jameson's complex rethinking of Marxist models of society. Broadly, he accepts Althusser's view of the social totality as a 'decentred structure' in which various levels develop in 'relative autonomy' and work on different time-scales (the coexistence of feudal and capitalist timescales, for example). This complex structure of antagonistic and out-of-key modes of production is the heterogeneous History which is mirrored in the heterogeneity of texts. Jameson is here answering the poststructuralists who would abolish the distinction between text and reality by treating reality itself as just more text. He shows that the textual heterogeneity can be understood only as it relates to social and cultural heterogeneity *outside* the text. In this he preserves a space for a Marxist analysis.

His reading of Joseph Conrad's *Lord Jim* shows that each of the various types of interpretation (impressionistic, Freudian, existential, and so on) which have been applied to the text actually expresses something in the text. Each mode of interpretation in turn reflects a development within modern society which serves the needs of capital. For example, impressionism is typified in the character Stein, the capitalist aesthete, whose passion for butterfly collecting Jameson regards as an allegory of Conrad's own 'passionate choice of impressionism – the vocation to arrest the living raw material of life, and by wrenching it from the historical situation . . . to preserve it beyond time in the imaginary'. This narrative response to History is both ideologically conditioned and utopian; it both represses History and envisages an ideal future.

Jameson's strong, 'epistemological' understanding of narrative illuminates the political motivation of his most important work to date, *Postmodernism, or the Cultural Logic of Late Capitalism* (1991). He maintains that postmodernism is not merely a style but rather the 'cultural dominant' of our time; it redesigns all our artistic and intellectual activities, entails quite distinct patterns of experience, and so conditions, at the deepest levels, what we can know of the contemporary world (see below, chapter 7, pp. 185–6 especially). Jameson's bold synopses of contemporary cultural history bear out his commitment to 'the great themes of Hegel's philosophy'; and his central concern with the crisis of 'cognitive mapping' in late capitalism, with the discovery of forms of narrative and representation through which its reality can be brought into focus, reminds us – in the terms of specifically cultural politics – of the famous Marxian injunction to go beyond interpreting the world to change it.

In the course of this chapter we have referred to 'structuralist' Marxism. The economic writings of Karl Marx themselves have been regarded as essentially structuralist. Before turning to structuralism itself, it is worth emphasising that the differences between Marxist and structuralist theories are much greater than the similarities. For Marxism the ultimate ground of its theories is the material and historical existence of human societies; but for structuralists the final bedrock is the nature of language. While Marxist theories are about the historical changes and conflicts which arise in society and appear indirectly in literary form, structuralism studies the internal working of systems divorced from their historical existence.

SELECTED READING

Basic texts

Adorno, Theodor W., *Prisms* (Neville Spearman, London, 1967).

Adorno, Theodor W. and Horkheimer, Max, *Dialectic of Enlightenment* (Allen Lane, London, 1972).

Adorno, Theodor W., Benjamin, Walter, Bloch, Ernst, Brecht, Bertolt and Lukács, Georg, *Aesthetics and Politics* (New Left Books, London, 1977).

Althusser, Louis, *Lenin and Philosophy and Other Essays*, trans. Ben Brewster (Verso, London, 1971), especially 'Ideology and Ideological State Apparatuses' and 'A Letter on Art'.

Auerbach, Erich, *Mimesis: The Representation of Reality in Western Literature* (1946), trans. W. R. Trask (Princeton University Press, Princeton, NJ, 1953).

Baxandall, Lee and Morawski, Stefan, *Marx and Engels on Literature and Art* (International General, New York, 1973).

Benjamin, Walter, *Illuminations* (Schocken, New York; Cape, London, 1970).

Benjamin, Walter, *Charles Baudelaire: A Lyric Poet in the Era of High Capitalism*, trans. H. Zohn (New Left Books, London, 1973a).

Benjamin, Walter, *Understanding Brecht*, trans. A. Bostock (New Left Books, London, 1973b).

Craig, David (ed.), *Marxists on Literature* (Penguin, Harmondsworth, 1975).

Eagleton, Terry, *Criticism and Ideology* (New Left Books, London, 1976).

Eagleton, Terry, *Walter Benjamin or Towards a Revolutionary Criticism* (New Left Books, London, 1981).

Eagleton, Terry, *The Rape of Clarissa* (Basil Blackwell, Oxford, 1982).

Eagleton, Terry, *Literary Theory: An Introduction* (Basil Blackwell, Oxford, 1983).

Eagleton, Terry, *The Function of Criticism* (Verso, London, 1984).

Eagleton, Terry, *Against the Grain: Essays 1975–1985* (Verso, London, 1986).

Eagleton, Terry, *The Ideology of the Aesthetic* (Basil Blackwell, Oxford, 1990).

Goldmann, Lucien, *The Hidden God* (Routledge & Kegan Paul, London, 1964).

Jameson, Fredric, *Marxism and Form: Twentieth-Century Dialectical Theories of Literature* (Princeton University Press, Princeton, NJ, 1971).

Jameson, Fredric, *The Prison-House of Language: A Critical Account of Structuralism and Russian Formalism*, (Princeton University Press, Princeton, NJ, and London, 1972).

Jameson, Fredric, *The Political Unconscious: Narrative as a Socially Symbolic Act* (Cornell University Press, Ithaca, 1981).

Jameson, Fredric, *The Ideologies of Theory. Vol. 1 Situations of Theory, Vol. 2 The Syntax of History* (Routledge & Kegan Paul, London, 1988).

Jameson, Fredric, *Postmodernism, or the Cultural Logic of Late Capitalism* (Verso, London, 1991).

Lukács, Georg, *The Historical Novel* (1937) (Merlin Press, London, 1962).

Lukács, Georg, *Studies in European Realism* (1950) (Merlin Press, London, 1972).

Lukács, Georg, *The Meaning of Contemporary Realism* (1957) (Merlin Press, London, 1963).

Lukács, Georg, *Writer and Critic and Other Essays* (Merlin Press, London, 1970).

Macherey, Pierre, *A Theory of Literary Production*, trans. G. Wall (Routledge & Kegan Paul, London, Henley and Boston, 1978).

Macherey, Pierre and Balibar, Etienne, 'On Literature as an Ideological Form', in Mulhern (below).

Marcuse, Herbert, *One-Dimensional Man* (Beacon, Boston; Sphere, London, 1964).

Marcuse, Herbert, *Negations* (Allen Lane, London, 1968).
Marcuse, Herbert, *The Aesthetic Dimension* (Macmillan, London, 1979).
Sartre, Jean-Paul, *What is Literature?* (Philosophical Library, New York, 1949).
Willett, John (ed.), *Brecht on Theatre* (Methuen, London, 1964).
Williams, Raymond, *Culture and Society 1780–1950* (Chatto & Windus, London, 1958).
Williams, Raymond, *The Long Revolution* (Chatto & Windus, London, 1961).
Williams, Raymond, *Television: Technology and Cultural Form* (Fontana/ Collins, London, 1974).
Williams, Raymond, *Marxism and Literature* (Oxford University Press, Oxford, 1977).
Williams, Raymond, *Problems in Materialism and Culture* (New Left Books, London, 1980).
Williams, Raymond, *Keywords: A Vocabulary of Culture and Society* (Fontana/Collins, London, 1983).
Williams, Raymond, *Writing in Society* (Verso, London, 1984).

Introductions

Arvon, Henri, *Marxist Aesthetics*, trans. H. Lane (Cornell University Press, Ithaca and London, 1973).
Belsey, Catherine, *Critical Practice* (Methuen, London, 1980).
Bennett, Tony, *Formalism and Marxism* (Routledge, London, 1979).
Dowling, William, C., *Jameson, Althusser, Marx: An Introduction to the Political Unconscious* (Methuen, London; Cornell University Press, Ithaca, 1984).
Eagleton, Terry, *Marxism and Literary Criticism* (Methuen, London, 1976).
Forgacs, David, 'Marxist Literary Theories' in *Modern Literary Theory*, A. Jefferson and D. Robey (eds) (Batsford, London, 2nd edn, 1986).
Laing, Dave, *The Marxist Theory of Art: An Introductory Survey* (Harvester Press, Hassocks, Sussex, 1978).
Lifshitz, Mikhail, *The Philosophy of Art of Karl Marx*, trans. R. B. Winn (Pluto Press, London, 1973; Russian edn, 1933).
Macdonell, Diane, *Theories of Discourse: An Introduction* (Basil Blackwell, Oxford, 1986).

Further reading

Brooker, Peter, *Bertolt Brecht: Dialectics, Poetry, Politics* (Croom Helm, London and New York, 1988).
Frow, John, *Marxism and Literary History* (Basil Blackwell, Oxford, 1986).

Hall, Stuart *et al.* (eds), *Culture, Media, Language: Working Papers in Cultural Studies 1972–79* (Hutchinson, London, 1980).

James, C. Vaughan, *Soviet Socialist Realism: Origins and Theory* (Macmillan, London and Basingstoke, 1973).

Jay, Martin, *The Dialectical Imagination: A History of the Frankfurt School* (Heinemann, London, 1973).

Lunn, Eugene, *Marxism and Modernism* (Verso, London, 1985).

Mulhern, Francis (ed.), *Contemporary Marxist Literary Criticism* (Longman, London and New York, 1992).

Nelson, Cary and Grossberg, Lawrence (eds), *Marxism and the Interpretation of Culture* (Macmillan, London, 1988).

Slaughter, Cliff, *Marxism, Ideology and Literature* (Macmillan, London and Basingstoke, 1980).

Sprinker, Michael, *Imaginary Relations: Aesthetics and Ideology in the Theory of Historical Materialism* (Verso, London, 1987).

Williams, Raymond, *Politics and Letters: Interviews with New Left Review* (Verso, London, 1979).

Wolff, Janet, *The Social Production of Art* (Macmillan, London and Basingstoke, 1981).

Wright, Elizabeth, *Postmodern Brecht: A Re-Presentation* (Routledge, London, 1988).

5 Structuralist theories

New ideas often provoke baffled and anti-intellectual reactions, and this has been especially true of the reception accorded the theories which go under the name of 'structuralism'. Structuralist approaches to literature challenge some of the most cherished beliefs of the ordinary reader. The literary work, we have long felt, is the child of an author's creative life, and expresses the author's essential self. The text is the place where we enter into a spiritual or humanistic communion with an author's thoughts and feelings. Another fundamental assumption which readers often make is that a good book tells the truth about human life – that novels and plays try to 'tell things as they really are'. However, structuralists have tried to persuade us that the author is 'dead' and that literary discourse has no truth function. In a review of a book by Jonathan Culler, John Bayley spoke for the anti-structuralists when he declared 'but the sin of semiotics is to attempt to destroy our sense of truth in fiction . . . In a good story, truth precedes fiction and remains separable from it.' In a 1968 essay, Roland Barthes put the structuralist view very powerfully, and argued that writers only have the power to mix already existing writings, to reassemble or redeploy them; writers cannot use writing to 'express' themselves, but only to draw upon that immense dictionary of language and culture which is 'always already written' (to use a favourite Barthean phrase). It would not be misleading to use the term 'anti-humanist' to describe the spirit of structuralism.

Indeed the word has been used by structuralists themselves to emphasise their opposition to all forms of literary criticism in which the human subject is the source and origin of literary meaning.

THE LINGUISTIC BACKGROUND: SAUSSURE AND BARTHES

The work of the Swiss linguist Ferdinand de Saussure, compiled and published after his death in a single book, *Course in General Linguistics* (1915), has been profoundly influential in shaping contemporary literary theory. Saussure's two key ideas provide new answers to the questions 'What is the object of linguistic investigation?' and 'What is the relationship between words and things?' He makes a fundamental distinction between *langue* and *parole* – between the language *system*, which pre-exists actual examples of language, and the individual *utterance*. *Langue* is the social aspect of language: it is the shared system which we (unconsciously) draw upon as speakers. *Parole* is the individual realisation of the system in actual instances of language. This distinction is essential to all later structuralist theories. The proper object of linguistic study is the system which underlies any particular human signifying practice, not the individual utterance. This means that, if we examine specific poems or myths or economic practices, we do so in order to discover what system of rules – what grammar – is being used. After all, human beings use speech quite differently from parrots: the former evidently have a grasp of a system of rules which enables them to produce an infinite number of well-formed sentences; parrots do not.

Saussure rejected the idea that language is a word-heap gradually accumulated over time and that its primary function is to refer to things in the world. In his view, words are not symbols which correspond to referents, but rather are 'signs' which are made up of two parts (like two sides of a sheet of paper): a mark, either written or spoken, called a 'signifier', and a concept (what is 'thought' when the mark is made), called a 'signified'. The view he is rejecting may be represented thus:

SYMBOL = THING

Saussure's model is as follows:

$$\text{SIGN} = \frac{\text{signifier}}{\text{signified}}$$

'Things' have no place in the model. The elements of language acquire meaning not as the result of some connection between words and things, but only as parts of a system of relations. Consider the sign-system of traffic lights:

red – amber – green

signifier ('red')
signified (stop)

The sign signifies only within the system 'red = stop / green = go / amber = prepare for red or green'. The relation between signifier and signified is arbitrary: there is no natural bond between red and stop, no matter how natural it may *feel*. When the British joined the Common Market they had to accept new electrical colour codings which seemed unnatural (brown not red = live; blue not black = neutral). Each colour in the traffic system signifies not by asserting a positive univocal meaning but by marking a *difference*, a distinction within a system of opposites and contrasts: traffic-light 'red' is precisely 'not-green'; 'green' is 'not-red'.

Language is one among many sign-systems (some believe it is the fundamental system). The science of such systems is called 'semiotics' or 'semiology'. It is usual to regard structuralism and semiotics as belonging to the same theoretical universe. Structuralism, it must be added, is often concerned with systems which do not involve 'signs' as such (kinship relations, for example, thus indicating its equally important origins in anthropology – see the references to Lévi–Strauss below, p.107, p.110–11) but which can be treated in the same way as sign-systems. The American philosopher C. S. Peirce made a useful distinction between three types of sign: the 'iconic' (where the sign *resembles* its referent, e.g. a picture of a ship or a road-sign for falling rocks); the 'indexical' (where the sign is *associated*, possibly causally, with its referent, e.g. smoke as a sign of fire, or clouds as a sign of rain); and the 'symbolic' (where the sign has an *arbitrary* relation to its referent, e.g. language).

The most celebrated modern semiotician is Yury Lotman of the then USSR. He developed the Saussurean and Czech types of structuralism in works such as *The Analysis of the Poetic Text* (1972). One of the major differences between Lotman and the French structuralists is his retention of evaluation in his analyses. Literary works, he believes, have more value because they have a 'higher information load' than non-literary texts. His approach brings together the rigour of structuralist linguistics and the close reading techniques of New Criticism. Maria Corti, Caesare Segre, Umberto Eco (for a brief discussion of him as postmodern novelist, see below, p.178) in Italy and Michael Riffaterre (see above, chapter 3) from France are the leading European exponents of literary semiotics.

The first major developments in structuralist studies were based upon advances in the study of phonemes, the lowest-level elements in the language system. A phoneme is a meaningful sound, one that is recognised or perceived by a language user. Hundreds of different 'sounds' may be made by the speakers of particular languages, but the number of phonemes will be limited. The word 'spin' may be pronounced within a wide range of phonetic difference, so long as the essential phoneme remains recognisable as itself. One must add that the 'essential phoneme' is only a mental *abstraction*: all actually occurring sounds are *variants* of phonemes. We do not recognise sounds as meaningful bits of noise in their own right, but register them as different in some respects from other sounds. Barthes draws attention to this principle in the title of his most celebrated book, S/Z (see below, pp. 133–6), which picks out the two sibilants in Balzac's *Sarrasine* (Sä-rä-zēn), which are differentiated phonemically as *voiced* (z) and *unvoiced* (s). On the other hand there are differences of raw sound at the phonetic (not phonemic) level which are not 'recognised' in English: the /p/ sound in 'pin' is evidently different from the /p/ sound in 'spin', but English speakers do not recognise a difference: the difference is not recognised in the sense that it does not 'distribute' meaning between words in the language. Even if we said 'sbin', we would probably hear it as 'spin'. The essential point about this view of language is that underlying our use of language is a *system*, a pattern of paired opposites, *binary oppositions*. At the level of the phoneme, these include nasalised/non-nasalised, vocalic/non-vocalic, voiced/unvoiced, tense/lax. In a sense, speakers appear to have internalised a set of rules which manifests itself in their evident *competence* in operating language.

We can observe 'structuralism' of this type at work in the anthropology of Mary Douglas (an example used by Jonathan Culler). She examines the abominations of Leviticus, according to which some creatures are clean and some unclean on an apparently random principle. She solves the problem by constructing the equivalent of a phonemic analysis, according to which two rules appear to be in force:

1. 'Cloven-hoofed, cud-chewing ungulates are the model of the proper kind of food for a pastoralist'; animals which only half conform (pig, hare, rock badger) are unclean.
2. Another rule applies if the first is not relevant: each creature should be in the element to which it is biologically adapted. So fish without fins are unclean, and so on.

At a more complex level, the anthropology of Claude Lévi-Strauss develops a 'phonemic' analysis of myths, rites, kinship structures. Instead of asking questions about the origins or causes of the prohibitions, myths or rites, the structuralist looks for the system of differences which underlies a particular human practice.

As these examples from anthropology show, structuralists try to uncover the 'grammar', 'syntax', or 'phonemic' pattern of particular human systems of meaning, whether they be those of kinship, garments, *haute cuisine*, narrative discourse, myths, or totems. The liveliest examples of such analyses can be found in the earlier writings of Roland Barthes, especially in the wide-ranging *Mythologies* (1957) and *Système de la mode* (1967). The theory of these studies is given in *Elements of Semiology* (1967; see below, p. 131).

The principle – that human performances presuppose a received system of differential relations – is applied by Barthes to virtually all social practices; he interprets them as sign-systems which operate on the model of language. Any actual 'speech' (*parole*) presupposes a system (*langue*) which is being used. Barthes recognises that the language system may change, and that changes must be initiated in 'speech'; nevertheless, at any given moment there exists a working system, a set of rules from which all 'speeches' may be derived. To take an example, when Barthes examines the wearing of garments, he sees it not as a matter of personal expression or individual style, but as a 'garment system' which works like a language. He divides the 'language' of garments between 'system' and 'speech' ('syntagm').

System	*Syntagm*
'Set of pieces, parts or details which cannot be worn at the same time on the same part of the body, and whose variation corresponds to a change in the meaning of the clothing: toque-bonnet-hood, etc.'	'Juxtaposition in the same type of dress of different elements: skirt-blouse-jacket.'

To make a garment 'speech', we choose a particular ensemble (syntagm) of pieces each of which could be replaced by other pieces. An ensemble (sports jacket/grey-flannelled trousers/white open-necked shirt) is equivalent to a specific sentence uttered by an individual for a particular purpose; the elements fit together to make a particular kind of utterance and to evoke a meaning or style. No one can actually perform the system itself, but their selection of elements from the sets of garments which make up the system express their *competence* in handling the system. Here is a representation of a culinary example Barthes provides:

System	*Syntagm*
'Set of foodstuffs which have affinities or differences, within which one chooses a dish in view of a certain meaning: the types of entrée, roast or sweet.'	'Real sequence of dishes chosen during meal; menu.'

(a restaurant *à la carte* menu has both levels: entrée and examples).

STRUCTURALIST NARRATOLOGY: PROPP. LÉVI-STRAUSS, GREIMAS, TODOROV AND GENETTE

When we apply the linguistic model to literature, we appear to be sending coals to Newcastle. After all if literature is already linguistic, what is the point of examining it in the light of a linguistic model? Well, for one thing, it would be a mistake to identify 'literature' and 'language'. It is true that literature *uses* language as its medium, but this does not mean that the structure of literature is identical with the structure of language. The units of literary structure do not coincide with those of language. This means that when the Bulgarian narratologist, Tzvetan Todorov (see below, p. 112), advocates a new poetics which will establish a general 'grammar' of literature, he is talking about the underlying rules governing literary practice. On the other hand, structuralists agree that literature has a special relationship with language: it draws attention to the very nature and specific properties of language. In this respect structuralist poetics are closely related to Formalism.

Structuralist narrative theory develops from certain elementary linguistic analogies. Syntax (the rules of sentence construction) is the basic model of narrative rules. Todorov and others talk of 'narrative syntax'. The most elementary syntactic division of the sentence unit is between subject and predicate: 'The knight (subject) slew the dragon with his sword (predicate).' Evidently this sentence could be the core of an episode or even an entire tale. If we substitute a name (Launcelot or Gawain) for 'the knight', or 'axe' for 'sword', we retain the same essential structure. By pursuing this analogy between sentence structure and narrative, Vladimir Propp developed his theory of Russian fairy stories.

Propp's approach can be understood if we compare the 'subject' of a sentence with the typical characters (hero, villain, etc.) and the 'predicate' with the typical actions in such stories. While there is an enormous profusion of details, the whole corpus of tales is constructed upon the same basic set of thirty-one 'functions'. A function is the basic unit of the narrative 'language' and refers to the significant actions which form the narrative. These follow a logical sequence, and although no tale includes them all, in every tale the functions always remain in sequence. The last group of functions is as follows:

25. A difficult task is proposed to the hero.
26. The task is resolved.
27. The hero is recognised.
28. The false hero or villain is exposed.
29. The false hero is given a new appearance.
30. The villain is punished.
31. The hero is married and ascends the throne.

It is not difficult to see that these functions are present not just in Russian fairy tales or even non-Russian tales, but also in comedies, myths, epics, romances and indeed stories in general. However, Propp's functions have a certain archetypal simplicity which requires elaboration when applied to more complex texts. For example, in the Oedipus myth, Oedipus is set the task of solving the riddle of the sphinx; the task is resolved; the hero is recognised; he is married and ascends the throne. However, Oedipus is also the false hero and the villain; he is exposed (he murdered his father on the way to Thebes and married his mother, the queen), and punishes himself. Propp had added seven 'spheres of action' or roles to the thirty-one functions: villain, donor (provider), helper, princess (sought-after person) and her father, dispatcher, hero (seeker or victim), false hero. The tragic myth of Oedipus requires the substitution of 'mother/ queen and husband' for 'princess and her father'. One character can play several roles, or several characters can play the same role. Oedipus is both hero, provider (he averts Thebes' plague by solving the riddle), false hero, and even villain.

Claude Lévi-Strauss, the structuralist anthropologist, analyses the Oedipus myth in a manner which is truly structuralist in its use of the linguistic model. He calls the units of myth 'mythemes' (compare phonemes and morphemes in linguistics). They are organised in binary oppositions (see above, pp.106–7) like the basic linguistic units. The general opposition underlying the Oedipus myth is between two views of the origin of human beings: (1) that they are born from the earth; (2) that they are born from coition. Several mythemes are grouped on one side or the other of the antithesis between (1) the *over*valuation of kinship ties (Oedipus marries his mother; Antigone buries her brother unlawfully); and (2) the *under*valuation of kinship (Oedipus kills his father; Eteocles kills his brother). Lévi-Strauss is not interested in the narrative *sequence*, but in the structural *pattern* which gives the myth its meaning. He looks for the 'phonemic' structure of myth. He believes that this linguistic model will uncover the basic structure of the human mind – the structure which governs the way human beings shape all their institutions, artifacts and forms of knowledge.

A. J. Greimas, in his *Sémantique Structurale* (1966), offers an elegant streamlining of Propp's theory. While Propp focused on a single genre, Greimas aims to arrive at the universal 'grammar' of narrative by applying to it a semantic analysis of sentence structure. In place of Propp's seven 'spheres of action' he proposes three pairs of binary oppositions which include all six roles (*actants*) he requires:

Subject/Object
Sender/Receiver
Helper/Opponent

The pairs describe three basic patterns which perhaps recur in all narrative:

1. Desire, search, or aim (subject/object).
2. Communication (sender/receiver).
3. Auxiliary support or hindrance (helper/opponent).

If we apply these to Sophocles' *Oedipus the King*, we arrive at a more penetrating analysis than when using Propp's categories:

1. O searches for the murderer of Laius. Ironically he searches for himself (he is both subject and object).
2. Apollo's oracle predicts O's sins. Teiresias, Jocasta, the messenger and the herdsman all, knowingly or not, confirm its truth. The play is about O's misunderstanding of the message.
3. Teiresias and Jocasta try to prevent O from discovering the murderer. The messenger and the herdsman unwittingly assist him in the search. O himself obstructs the correct interpretation of the message.

It can be seen at a glance that Greimas' reworking of Propp is in the direction of the 'phonemic' patterning we saw in Lévi-Strauss. In this respect Greimas is more truly 'structuralist' than the Russian Formalist Propp, in that the former thinks in terms of *relations* between entities rather than of the character of entities in themselves. In order to account for the various narrative sequences which are possible he reduces Propp's thirty-one functions to twenty, and groups them into three structures (syntagms): 'contractual', 'performative', and 'disjunctive'. The first, the most interesting, is concerned with the establishing or breaking of contracts or rules. Narratives may employ either of the following structures:

contract (or prohibition) → violation → punishment
lack of contract (disorder) → establishment of contract (order)

The Oedipus narrative has the first structure: he violates the prohibition against patricide and incest, and punishes himself.

The work of Tzvetan Todorov is a summation of Propp, Greimas and others. All the syntactic rules of language are restated in their narrative guise – rules of agency, predication, adjectival and verbal functions, mood and aspect, and so on. The minimal unit of narrative is the 'proposition', which can be either an 'agent' (e.g. a person) or a 'predicate' (e.g. an action). The propositional structure of a narrative can be described in the most abstract and universal fashion. Using Todorov's method, we might have the following propositions:

X is king   X marries Y
Y is X's mother   X kills Z
Z is X's father

These are some of the propositions which make up the narrative of the Oedipus myth. For X read Oedipus; for Y, Jocasta; for Z, Laius. The first three propositions denominate agents, the first and the last two contain predicates (to be a king, to marry, to kill). Predicates may work like adjectives and refer to static states of affairs (to be a king), or they may operate dynamically like verbs to indicate transgressions of law, and are therefore the most dynamic types of proposition. Having established the smallest unit (proposition), Todorov describes two higher levels of organisation: the *sequence* and the *text*. A group of propositions forms a sequence. The basic sequence is made up of five propositions which describe a certain state which is disturbed and then re-established albeit in altered form. The five propositions may be designated thus:

Equilibrium[1] (e.g. Peace)
Force[1] (Enemy invades)
Disequilibrium (War)
Force[2] (Enemy is defeated)
Equilibrium[2] (Peace on new terms)

Finally a succession of sequences forms a text. The sequences may be organised in a variety of ways, by embedding (story within a story, digression, etc.), by linking (a string of sequences), or by alternation (interlacing of sequences), or by a mixture of these. Todorov provides his most vivid examples in a study of Boccaccio's *Decameron* (*Grammaire du Décaméron*, 1969). His attempt to establish the universal syntax of narrative has all the air of a scientific theory. As we shall see, it is precisely against this confidently objective stance that the poststructuralists react.

Gérard Genette developed his complex and powerful theory of discourse in the context of a study of Proust's *À la recherche du temps perdu*. He refines the Russian Formalist distinction between 'story' and 'plot' (see chapter 2) by dividing narrative into three levels: story (*histoire*), discourse (*récit*), and *narration*. For example, in *Aeneid* II Aeneas is the story-teller addressing his audience (*narration*); he presents a verbal *discourse*; and his discourse represents events in which he appears as a character (*story*). These dimensions of narrative are related by three aspects, which Genette derives from the three qualities of the verb: *tense*, *mood*, and *voice*. To take just one example, his distinction between 'mood' and 'voice' neatly clarifies problems which can arise from the familiar notion of 'point-of-view'. We often fail to distinguish between the voice of the narrator and the perspective (mood) of a character. In Dickens's novel *Great Expectations*, Pip presents the perspective of his younger self through the narrative voice of his older self.

Genette's essay on 'Frontiers of narrative' (1966) provided an overview of the problems of narration which has not been bettered. He considers the problem of narrative theory by exploring three binary oppositions. The first, 'diegesis and mimesis' (narrative and representation) occurs in Aristotle's *Poetics* and presupposes a distinction between simple narrative (what the author says in his or her own voice as author) and direct imitation (when the author speaks in the person of a character). Genette shows that the distinction cannot be sustained, since if one *could* have direct imitation involving a pure representation of what someone actually said, it would be like a Dutch painting in which actual objects were included on the canvas. He concludes: 'Literary representation, the *mimesis* of the ancients, is not, therefore, narrative plus "speeches": it is narrative and only narrative.' The second opposition, 'narration and description', presupposes a distinction between an active and a contemplative aspect of narration. The first is to do with actions and events, the second with objects or characters. 'Narration' appears, at first, to be essential, since events and actions are the essence of a story's temporal and dramatic content, while 'description' appears to be ancillary and ornamental. 'The man went over to the table and picked up a knife' is dynamic and profoundly narrativistic. However, having established the distinction, Genette immediately dissolves it by pointing out that the nouns and verbs in the sentence are also descriptive. If we change 'man' to 'boy', or 'table' to 'desk', or 'picked up' to 'grabbed', we have altered the description. Finally, the opposition 'narrative and discourse' distinguishes between a pure telling in which 'no one speaks' and a telling in which we are aware of the person who is speaking. Once again, Genette cancels the opposition by showing that there can never be a pure narrative devoid of 'subjective' coloration. However transparent and unmediated a narrative may appear to be, the signs of a judging mind are rarely absent. Narratives are nearly always impure in this sense, whether the element of 'discourse' enters via the voice of the narrator (Fielding, Cervantes) or a character-narrator (Sterne), or through epistolary discourse (Richardson). Genette believes that narrative reached its highest degree of purity in Hemingway and Hammett, but that with the *nouveau roman* narrative began to be totally swallowed up in the writer's own discourse. In our next chapter we shall see that Genette's theoretical approach, with its positing and cancellation of oppositions, opens the door to the 'deconstructive' philosophy of Jacques Derrida.

If the reader has followed us so far, he or she may well object that structuralist poetics seems to have little to offer the practising critic. (In fact, in chapter 3, sections 7 and 8 of *Practising Theory and Reading Literature* Raman Selden puts into practice the key structuralist concept of 'binary oppositions' in an analysis of Arthur Miller's play *Death of a Salesman*, and other aspects of structuralist narratology in relation to John Updike's short story 'Should Wizard Hit Mommy?') It is perhaps not without significance that fairy stories, myths, and detective stories often feature as examples in structuralist writings. Such studies aim to define the *general principles* of literary structure and not to provide interpretations of individual texts. A fairy story will provide clearer examples of the essential narrative grammar of all stories than will *King Lear* or *Ulysses*. Tzvetan Todorov's lucid 'The Typology of Detective Fiction' (1966) distinguishes the narrative structures of detective fiction into three chronologically evolving types: the 'whodunit', the 'thriller' and the 'suspense novel'. He makes a virtue of the fact that the narrative structures of popular literature can be studied much more systematically than those of 'great' literature, because they readily conform to the rules of popular genres.

METAPHOR AND METONYMY: JAKOBSON AND LODGE

There are some instances when a structuralist theory provides the practical critic with a fertile ground for interpretative applications. This is true of Roman Jakobson's study of 'aphasia' (speech defect) and its implications for poetics. He starts by stating the fundamental distinction between horizontal and vertical dimensions of language, a distinction related to that between *langue* and *parole*. Taking Barthes' garments system as an example, we note that in the vertical dimension we have an inventory of elements that may be substituted for one another: toque-bonnet-hood; in the horizontal dimension, we have elements chosen from the inventory to form an actual sequence (skirt-blouse-jacket). Thus a given sentence may be viewed either vertically or horizontally:

1. Each element is *selected* from a set of possible elements and could be substituted for another in the set.
2. The elements are *combined* in a sequence, which constitutes a *parole*.

This distinction applies at all levels – phoneme, morpheme, word, sentence. Jakobson noticed that aphasic children appeared to lose the ability to operate one or other of these dimensions. One type of aphasia exhibited 'contiguity disorder', the inability to combine elements in a sequence; the other suffered 'similarity disorder', the inability to substitute one element for another. In a word-association test, if you said 'hut', the first type would produce a string of synonyms, antonyms, and other *substitutions*: 'cabin', 'hovel', 'palace', 'den', 'burrow'. The other type would offer elements which *combine* with 'hut', forming potential sequences: 'burnt out', 'is a poor little house'. Jakobson goes on to point out that the two disorders correspond to two figures of speech – metaphor and metonymy. As the foregoing example shows, 'contiguity disorder' results in substitution in the vertical dimension as in metaphor ('den' for 'hut'), while 'similarity disorder' results in the production of parts of sequences for the wholes as in metonymy ('burnt out' for 'hut'). Jakobson suggested that normal speech behaviour also tends towards one or other extreme, and that literary style expresses itself as a leaning towards either the metaphoric or the metonymic. The historical development from romanticism through realism to symbolism can be understood as an alternation of style from the metaphoric to the metonymic back to the metaphoric. David Lodge, in *The Modes of Modern Writing* (1977), applied the theory to modern literature, adding further stages to a cyclical process: modernism and symbolism are essentially metaphoric, while anti-modernism is realistic and metonymic.

An example. In its broad sense, metonymy involves the shift from one element in a sequence to another, or one element in a context to another: we refer to a *cup* of something (meaning its *contents*); the *turf* (for *racing*), a fleet of a hundred *sails* (for *ships*).

Essentially metonymy requires a *context* for its operation; hence Jakobson's linking of realism with metonymy. Realism speaks of its object by offering the reader aspects, parts, and contextual details, in order to evoke a whole. Consider the passage near the opening of Dickens's *Great Expectations*. (Further practical application of metaphor and metonomy in respect of this novel and of Eugene O'Neill's play *The Hairy Ape* may be found in *PTRL*, chapter 3, section 9.) Pip begins by establishing himself as an identity in a landscape. Reflecting on his orphaned condition, he tells us that he can describe his parents through the only visual remains – their graves: 'As I never saw my father or my mother . . . my first fancies regarding what they were like were *unreasonably* [our italics] derived from their tombstones. The shapes of the letters on my father's, gave me an odd idea that he was a square stout man. . . .' This initial act of identification is metonymic in that Pip links two parts of a context: his father and his father's tombstone. However, this is not a 'realistic' metonymy but an 'unrealistic' derivation, 'an odd idea', although suitably childlike (and in that sense psychologically realistic). Proceeding to the immediate setting on the evening of the convict's appearance, the moment of truth in Pip's life, he gives the following description:

> Ours was the marsh country, down by the river, within, as the river wound, twenty miles of the sea. My first most vivid and broad impression of the *identity of things*, [our italics] seems to me to have been gained on a memorable raw afternoon towards evening. At such a time I found out for certain, that this bleak place overgrown with nettles was the churchyard; and that Philip Pirrip, late of this parish, and also Georgiana wife of the above, were dead and buried; and that . . . the dark flat wilderness beyond the churchyard, intersected with dykes and mounds and gates, with scattered cattle feeding on it, was the marshes; and that the low leaden line beyond, was the river; and that the distant savage lair from which the wind was rushing was the sea; and that the small bundle of shivers growing afraid of it all and beginning to cry, was Pip.

Pip's mode of perceiving the 'identity of things' remains metonymic and not metaphoric: churchyard, graves, marshes, river, sea and Pip are conjured up, so to speak, from contextual features. The whole (person, setting) is presented through selected aspects. Pip is evidently more than a 'small bundle of shivers' (he is also a bundle of flesh and bones, thoughts and feelings, social and historical forces), but here his identity is asserted through metonymy, a significant detail offered as his total self at this moment.

In a useful elaboration of Jakobson's theory David Lodge rightly points out that 'context is all-important'. He shows that changing context can change the figures. Here is Lodge's amusing example:

> Those favourite filmic metaphors for sexual intercourse in the pre-permissive cinema, skyrockets and waves pounding on the shore, could be disguised as metonymic background if the consummation were taking place on a beach on Independence Day, but would be perceived as overtly metaphorical if it were taking place on Christmas Eve in a city penthouse.

The example warns us against using Jakobson's theory too inflexibly.

STRUCTURALIST POETICS: JONATHAN CULLER

Jonathan Culler made the first attempt to assimilate French structuralism to an Anglo-American critical perspective in 1975. He accepts the premiss that linguistics affords the best model of knowledge for the humanities and social sciences. However, he prefers Noam Chomsky's distinction between 'competence' and 'performance' to Saussure's between '*langue*' and '*parole*'. The notion of 'competence' has the advantage of being closely associated with the *speaker* of a language; Chomsky showed that the starting point for an understanding of language was the native speaker's ability to produce and comprehend well-formed sentences on the basis of an unconsciously assimilated knowledge of the language system. Culler brings out the significance of this perspective for literary theory: 'the real object of poetics is not the work itself but its intelligibility. One must attempt to explain how it is that works can be understood; the implicit knowledge, the conventions that enable readers to make sense of them, must be formulated. . . .' His main endeavour is to shift the focus from the text to the reader (see chapter 3). He believes that we can determine the rules that govern the interpretation of texts, but not those rules that govern the writing of texts. If we begin by establishing a range of interpretations which seem acceptable to skilled readers, we can then establish what norms and procedures led to the interpretations. To put it simply, skilled readers, when faced with a text, seem to know how to make sense of it – to decide what is a possible interpretation and what is not. There seem to be rules governing the sort of sense one might make of the most apparently bizarre literary text. Culler sees the structure not in the system underlying the text but in the system underlying the reader's act of interpretation. To take a bizarre example, here is a three-line poem:

Night is generally my time for walking;
It was the best of times, it was the worst of times;
Concerning the exact year there is no need to be precise.

When we asked a number of colleagues to read it, a variety of interpretative moves were brought into play. One saw a *thematic* link between the lines ('Night', 'time', 'times', 'year'); another tried to envisage a *situation* (psychological or external); another tried to see the poem in terms of formal patternings (a past tense – 'was' – framed by present tenses – 'is'); another saw the lines as adopting three different attitudes to time: specific, contradictory, and non-specific. One colleague recognised that line two comes from the opening of Dickens's *A Tale of Two Cities*, but still accepted it as a 'quotation' which served a function within the poem. We finally had to reveal that the other lines were also from the openings of Dickens's novels (*The Old Curiosity Shop* and *Our Mutual Friend*). What is significant from a Cullerian point of view is not that the readers were caught out but that they followed recognisable procedures for making sense of the lines. (Raman Selden's practical application of this theory – sometimes described as 'naturalisation' – may be found in chapter 3, section 6 of *PTRL*, where he analyses Christopher Smart's eighteenth-century religious poem 'Jubilate Agno'.)

The main difficulty about Culler's approach surrounds the question of how systematic one can be about the interpretative rules used by readers. He recognises that the procedures of skilled readers will vary with genre and period, but does not allow for the profound ideological differences between readers which may undermine the institutional pressures for conformity in reading practices. It is hard to conceive of a single matrix of rules and conventions which would account for the diversity of interpretations which might be produced in a single period about individual texts. At any rate, we cannot simply take for granted the existence of any entity called a skilled reader, defined as the product of the institutions we term 'literary criticism'.

Structuralism has attracted some literary critics because it promises to introduce a certain rigour and objectivity into the impressionistic realm of literature. This rigour is achieved at a cost. By subordinating *parole* to *langue* the structuralist neglects the specificity of actual texts, and treats them as if they were like the patterns of iron filings produced by an invisible force. The most fruitful applications of the Saussurean model have been those which treat structuralist concepts as *metaphors* – as heuristic devices for analysing texts. Attempts to found a 'scientific' literary structuralism have not produced impressive results. Not only the text but also the author is cancelled as the structuralist places in brackets the actual work and the person who wrote it, in order to isolate the true object of enquiry – the system. In traditional Romantic thought, the author is the thinking and suffering being who precedes the work and whose experience nourishes it; the author is the origin of the text, its creator and progenitor. According to structuralists, writing has no origin. Every individual utterance is preceded by language: in this sense, every text is made up of the 'already written'.

By isolating the system, structuralists also cancel history, since the structures discovered are either universal (the universal structures of the human mind) and therefore timeless, or arbitrary segments of a changing and evolving process. Historical questions characteristically are about *change* and *innovation*, whereas structuralism has to exclude them from consideration in order to isolate a system. Therefore structuralists are interested not in the development of the novel or the transition from feudal to Renaissance literary forms, but in the structure of narrative as such and in the system of aesthetics governing a period. Their approach is necessarily static and ahistorical: they are interested in neither the moment of the text's production (its historical context, its formal links with past writing, etc.) nor the moment of its reception or 'reproduction' (the interpretations imposed on it subsequent to its production – see above, chapter 3, for theories to do with this).

There is no doubt that structuralism represented a major challenge to the dominant New Critical, Leavisite, and generally humanist types of critical practice. They all presupposed a view of language as something capable of *grasping* reality. Language had been thought of as a reflection of either the writer's mind or the world as seen by the writer. In a sense the writer's language was hardly separable from his or her personality; it expressed the author's very being. However, as we have seen, the Saussurean perspective draws attention to the pre-existence of language. In the beginning was the word, and the word created the text. Instead of saying that an author's language reflects reality, the structuralists argue that the structure of language produces 'reality'. This represents a massive 'demystification' of literature. The source of meaning is no longer the writer's or the reader's *experience* but the operations and oppositions which govern language. Meaning is determined no longer by the individual but by the system which governs the individual.

At the heart of structuralism is a *scientific* ambition to discover the codes, the rules, the systems, which underlie all human social and cultural practices. The disciplines of archaeology and geology are frequently invoked as the models of structuralist enterprise. What we see on the surface are the traces of a deeper history; only by excavating beneath the surface will we discover the geological strata or the ground plans which provide the true explanations for what we see above. One can argue that all science is structuralist in this respect: we see the sun move across the sky, but science discovers the true structure of the heavenly bodies' motion.

Readers who already have some knowledge of the subject will recognise that we have presented only a certain classical type of structuralism in this chapter – one whose proponents suggest that definite sets of relations (oppositions, sequences of functions or propositions, syntactical rules) underlie particular practices, and that individual performances derive from structures in the same way as the shape of landscapes derives from the geological strata beneath. A structure is like a centre or point of origin, and replaces other such centres of origins (the individual or history). However, our discussion of Genette showed that the very definition of an opposition within narrative discourse sets up a *play* of meaning which resists a settled or fixed structuration. For example, the opposition between 'description' and 'narration' tends to encourage a 'privileging' of the second term ('description' is ancillary to 'narration'; narrators describe incidentally, as they narrate). But, if we interrogate this now hierarchised pair of terms, we can easily begin to reverse it by showing that 'description' is after all dominant because all narration implies description. In this way we begin to undo the structure which had been centred upon 'narration'. This process of 'deconstruction' which can be set in motion at the very heart of structuralism is one of the major elements in what we call poststructuralism.

SELECTED READING

Basic texts

Barthes, Roland, *Elements of Semiology* (1967), trans. A. Lavers and C. Smith (Jonathan Cape, London, 1967).

Barthes, Roland, *Writing Degree Zero*, trans. A. Lavers and C. Smith (Jonathan Cape, London, 1967).

Barthes, Roland, *Critical Essays*, trans. R. Howard (Northwestern University Press, Evanston, Ill., 1972).

Barthes, Roland, *Selected Writings*, introd. Susan Sontag (Fontana, London, 1983).

Blonsky, Marshall (ed.), *On Signs: A Semiotic Reader* (Basil Blackwell, Oxford, 1985).

Chatman, Seymour, *Story and Discourse: Narrative Structure in Fiction and Film* (Cornell University Press, Ithaca and London, 1978).

de Saussure, Ferdinand, *Course in General Linguistics* (1915), trans. W. Baskin (Fontana/Collins, London, 1974).

Ehrmann, Jacques (ed.), *Structuralism* (Doubleday, Anchor Books, New York, 1970).

Genette, Gérard, *Narrative Discourse* (Basil Blackwell, Oxford, 1980).

Genette, Gérard, *Figures of Literary Discourse*, trans. A. Sheridan (Basil Blackwell, Oxford, 1982), esp. chap. 7, 'Frontiers of narrative'.

Innes, Robert E. (ed.), *Semiotics: An Introductory Reader* (Hutchinson, London, 1986).

Jakobson, Roman, 'Linguistics and Poetics' in *Style in Language*, T. Sebeok (ed.) (MIT Press, Cambridge, Mass., 1960), pp. 350–77.

Jakobson, Roman (with M. Halle), *Fundamentals of Language* (Mouton, The Hague and Paris, 1975).

Lane, Michael (ed.), *Structuralism: A Reader* (Jonathan Cape, London, 1970).

Lévi-Strauss, Claude, *Structural Anthropology*, trans. C. Jacobson and B. G. Schoepf (Allen Lane, London, 1968), esp. chaps 2 and 11.

Lodge, David, *The Modes of Modern Writing: Metaphor, Metonymy, and the Typology of Modern Literature* (Arnold, London, 1977).

Lotman, Yury, *The Analysis of the Poetic Text*, ed. and trans. D. Barton Johnson (Ardis, Ann Arbor, 1976).

Lotman, Yury, *The Structure of the Artistic Text*, trans. R. Vroon, Michigan Slavic Contributions, no. 7 (Michigan University Press, Ann Arbor, 1977).

Propp, Vladimir, *The Morphology of the Folktale* (Texas University Press, Austin and London, 1968).

Todorov, Tzvetan, *The Fantastic: A Structural Approach to a Literary Genre*, trans. R. Howard (Cornell University Press, Ithaca, 1975).

Todorov, Tzvetan, *The Poetics of Prose*, trans. Richard Howard (Cornell University Press, Ithaca, 1977). Includes 'The Typology of Detective Fiction'.

Todorov, Tzvetan, *Literature and Its Theories* (Routledge, London, 1988).

Introductions

Culler, Jonathan, *Structuralist Poetics: Structuralism, Linguistics and the Study of Literature* (Routledge & Kegan Paul, London, 1975).

Harland, R., *Superstructuralism: The Philosophy of Structuralism and Post-Structuralism* (Routledge, London, 1987).

Hawkes, Terence, *Structuralism and Semiotics* (Methuen, London, 1977).

Rimmon-Kenan, Shlomith, 'A Comprehensive Theory of Narrative: Genette's *Figures III* and the Structuralist Study of Fiction', *Poetics and Theory of Literature*, vol. 1 (1976), pp. 33–62.

Robey, David (ed.), *Structuralism: An Introduction* (Clarendon Press, Oxford, 1973).

Scholes, Robert, *Structuralism in Literature: An Introduction* (Yale University Press, New Haven and London, 1974).

Sturrock, John, *Structuralism* (Paladin, London, 1986).

Todorov, Tzvetan, *Introduction to Poetics*, trans. R. Howard (Harvester Press, Brighton, 1981).

Further reading

Connor, Steven, 'Structuralism and Post-structuralism: From the Centre to the Margin' in *Encyclopedia of Literature and Criticism*, Martin Coyle, Peter Garside, Malcolm Kelsall and John Peck (eds), (Routledge, London, 1990).

Culler, Jonathan, *Saussure* (Fontana, London, 1976).

Doubrovsky, Serge, *The New Criticism in France*, trans. D. Coltman (University of Chicago Press, Chicago and London, 1973).

Heath, Stephen, *The Nouveau Roman: A Study in the Practice of Writing* (Elek, London, 1972), chap. 1.

Jackson, Leonard, *The Poverty of Structuralism: Literature and Structuralist Theory* (Longman, London, 1991).

Jameson, Fredric, *The Prison-House of Language: A Critical Account of Structuralism and Russian Formalism* (Princeton University Press, Princeton and London, 1972).

Lodge, David, *Working with Structuralism* (Routledge, London, 1986).

N.B. Most of the significant contemporary theory in this area is of course that which, by definition, constitutes the 'Selected Reading' at the end of the next chapter on '*Post*structuralist theories'.

6 Poststructuralist theories

At some point in the late 1960s, structuralism gave birth to 'poststructuralism'. Some commentators believe that the later developments were already inherent in the earlier phase. One might say that poststructuralism is simply a fuller working-out of the implications of structuralism. But this formulation is not quite satisfactory, because it is evident that poststructuralism tries to deflate the scientific pretensions of structuralism. If structuralism was heroic in its desire to master the world of artificial signs, poststructuralism is comic and anti-heroic in its refusal to take such claims seriously. However, the poststructuralist mockery of structuralism is almost a self-mockery: poststructuralists are structuralists who suddenly see the error of their ways.

It is possible to see the beginnings of a poststructuralist counter-movement even in Saussure's linguistic theory. As we have seen, *langue* is the systematic aspect of language which works as the underpinning structure of *parole*, the individual instance of speech or writing. The sign is also bipartite: signifier and signified are like two sides of a coin. However, Saussure also notices that there is no necessary connection between signifier and signified. Sometimes a language will have one word (signifier) for two concepts (signifieds): in English 'sheep' is the animal and 'mutton' the meat; French has only one word for both signifieds ('mouton'). It is as though the various languages carve up the world of things and ideas into different concepts (signifieds) on the one hand, and different words (signifiers) on the other. As Saussure puts it, 'A linguistic system is a series of differences of sound combined with a series of differences of ideas.' The signifier 'hot' is able to work as part of a sign because it *differs* from 'hat', 'hit', 'hop', 'hog', 'lot', and so on. These 'differences' can be aligned with different signifieds. He concludes with his celebrated remark 'In language there are only differences *without positive terms.*' However, before we jump to the wrong conclusion, he immediately adds that this is only true if we take signifiers and signifieds separately. There is a natural tendency, he assures us, for one signified to seek its own signifier, and to form with it a *positive unit.* Saussure's assertion of a certain stability in signification is to be expected in a 'pre-Freudian' thinker: while the signifier/ signified relationship is arbitrary, speakers in practice require particular signifiers to be securely attached to particular concepts, and therefore they assume that signifier and signified form a unified whole and preserve a certain identity of meaning.

Poststructuralist thought has discovered the essentially *unstable* nature of signification. The sign is not so much a unit with two sides as a momentary 'fix' between two moving layers. Saussure had recognised that signifier and signified are two separate systems, but he did not see how unstable units of meaning can be when the systems come together. Having established language as a total system independent of physical reality, he tried to retain a sense of the sign's coherence, even though his splitting of the sign into two parts threatened to undo it. Poststructuralists have in various ways prised apart the two halves of the sign.

Surely, we might ask, the unity of the sign is confirmed whenever we use a dictionary to find a meaning (signified) of a word (signifier)? In fact, the dictionary confirms only the relentless deferment of meaning: not only do we find for every signifier several signifieds (a 'crib' signifies a manger, a child's bed, a hut, a job, a mine-shaft lining, a plagiarism, a literal translation, discarded cards at cribbage), but each of the signifieds becomes yet another signifier which can be traced in the dictionary with its own array of signifieds ('bed' signifies a place for sleeping, a garden plot, a layer of oysters, a channel of a river, a stratum). The process continues interminably, as the signifiers lead a chameleon-like existence, changing their colours with each new context. Much of the energy of poststructuralism has gone into tracing the insistent activity of the signifier as it forms chains and cross-currents of meaning with other signifiers and defies the orderly requirements of the signified.

DISCOURSE

Structuralists (see chapter 5) attack the idea that language is an instrument for reflecting a pre-existent reality or for expressing a human intention. They believe that 'subjects' are produced by linguistic structures which are 'always already' in place. A subject's utterances belong to the realm of *parole*, which is governed by *langue*, the true object of structuralist analysis. This systematic view of communication excludes all subjective processes by which individuals interact with others and with society. The poststructuralist critics of structuralism introduce the concept of the 'speaking subject' or the 'subject in process'. Instead of viewing language as an impersonal system, they regard it as always articulated with other systems and especially with subjective processes. This conception of language-in-use is summed up in the term 'discourse'.

The Bakhtin School (see chapter 2) were probably the first modern literary theorists to reject the Saussurean notion of language. They insisted that all instances of languages had to be considered in a social context. Every utterance is potentially the site of a struggle: every word that is launched into social space implies a dialogue and therefore a contested interpretation. The relations between signifiers and signifieds are always fraught with interference and conflict. Language cannot be neatly dissociated from social living; it is always contaminated, interleaved, opaquely coloured by layers of semantic deposits resulting from the endless processes of human struggle and interaction.

Later, a parallel movement occurred in linguistic thought. In his celebrated distinction between *histoire* (narrative) and *discours* (discourse) Emile Benveniste tried to preserve the notion of a non-subjectivised region of language. He argued that a purely narrative use of language (characterised in French fiction by the use of the 'past historic' or 'aorist' tense) is quite devoid of intervention by the speaker. This appears to deny Bakhtin's belief that all language-in-use is 'dialogic'. The 'I-you' dimension is excluded in pure narrative, which seems to narrate itself without subjective mediation. The dialogues embedded in a fiction are situated and rendered manageable by the authority of the *histoire* which itself has no apparent subjective origin. As Catherine Belsey puts it, 'classic realism proposes a model in which author and reader are subjects who are the source of shared meanings, the origin of which is mysteriously extra-discursive' (*Critical Practice*, 1980). As has been demonstrated by Gérard Genette (see chapter 5, 'Structuralist Narratology') and many others, the *histoire/discours* distinction does not hold water. Take the first sentence of the first chapter of George Eliot's *Middlemarch*: 'Miss Brooke had that kind of beauty which seems to be thrown into relief by poor dress.' At the level of *histoire* we are being told that Miss Brooke had a certain kind of beauty, and the impersonal syntax of the sentence seems to give it objectivity and truth. The locution 'that kind', however, immediately introduces a 'discursive' level: it refers to something which readers are expected to recognise and confirm. Roland Barthes would have said that George Eliot is here using the 'cultural code' (see the section on Barthes below). This underlines the fact that not only is the author endorsing a certain culturally specific assumption but that the 'I-you' relationship between author and reader is being invoked. Poststructuralists would agree that narrative can never escape the discursive level. The slogan 'there is only discourse' requires careful explication, but it sums up effectively the thrust of this chapter.

Poststructuralist thought often takes the form of a critique of empiricism (the dominant philosophical mode in Britain at least from the mid-seventeenth century onwards). It saw the subject as the source of all knowledge: the human mind receives impressions from without which it sifts and organises into a knowledge of the world, which is expressed in the apparently transparent medium of language. The 'subject' grasps the 'object' and puts it into words. This model has been challenged by a theory of 'discursive formations', which refuses to separate subject and object into separate domains. Knowledges are always formed from discourses which pre-exist the subject's experiences. Even the subject itself is not an autonomous or unified identity, but is always 'in process' (see below on Kristeva and Lacan). There has been a parallel shift in the history and philosophy of science. T. S. Kuhn (see chapter 3) and Paul Feyerabend have challenged the belief in the steady progression of knowledge in the sciences, and have shown that science 'progresses' in a series of jumps and breaks, in a *discontinuous* movement from one discursive formation (or 'paradigm') to another. Individual scientists are not subjects apprehending objects through the blank mirror of the senses (and their technical extensions). They conduct and write up their research within the conceptual limits of particular scientific discourses, which are historically situated in relation to their society and culture.

The work of Michel Foucault (see below) has gone much further than this in mapping the discursive formations which, often in the name of science, have enabled institutions to wield power and domination by defining and excluding the mad, the sick, the criminal, the poor and the deviant. For Foucault discourse is always inseparable from power, because discourse is the governing and ordering medium of every institution. Discourse determines what it is possible to say, what are the criteria of 'truth', who is allowed to speak with authority, and where such speech can be spoken. For example, to take a degree in English literature we must study in or correspond with a validated institution. Only recognised teachers of the institution are allowed to determine the ways in which subjects are studied. In a given period only certain kinds of speaking and writing are recognised as valid. Marxist critics of Foucault have regarded his theory of discursive formations as unduly pessimistic and have suggested ways of theorising discourse in terms of ideological formations which allow more readily for the possibility of resistance and subversion of dominant discourses (see below, 'New Historicism').

Louis Althusser (see chapter 4, '"Structuralist" Marxism') made an important contribution to discourse theory in his 'Ideology and Ideological State Apparatuses' (1969). He argues that we are all 'subjects' of ideology which operates by summoning us to take our places in the social structure. This summoning (or 'interpellation') works through the discursive formations materially linked with 'state apparatuses' (religious, legal, educational, and so on). The 'imaginary' consciousness which ideology induces gives us a representation of the way individuals relate to their 'real conditions of existence', but being merely an undisrupted and harmonious 'image' it actually represses the real relations between individuals and the social structure. By translating 'discourse' into 'ideology' Althusser gives a political charge to the theory by introducing a domination-subordination model. He adopts for his own purposes the psychoanalytic terminology of Jacques Lacan (see below) who questions the humanist notion of a substantial and unified subjectivity (an illusion derived from the pre-Oedipal 'imaginary' phase of childhood). However, Althusser's model of the subject's formation is more static. Lacan conceives the subject as a permanently unstable entity, split between the conscious life of the 'ego' and the unconscious life of 'desire'. Colin MacCabe has suggested that a more Lacanian model of interpellation can be invisaged:

> A Marxist reading of the division of the subject in the place of the Other would theorise the individual's assumption of the place produced for him or her by the complex of discursive formations and would insist that these places would be constantly threatened and undermined by their constitutive instability in the field of language and desire. ('On Discourse', 1981)

The work of Michel Pêcheux, which goes some way to providing a more elaborate account of the operation of ideological discourses in relation to subjectivity, will be discussed in the section on 'New Historicism', where Foucault's pessimism about the possibility of resistance to the discursive power of ideologies is countered by the arguments of Cultural Materialism.

ROLAND BARTHES: THE PLURAL TEXT

Barthes was undoubtedly the most entertaining, witty and daring of the French theorists of the 1960s and 1970s. His career took several turns, but preserved a central theme: the conventionality of all forms of representation. He defines literature (in an early essay) as 'a message of the signification of things and not their meaning (by "signification" I refer to the process which produces the meaning and not this meaning itself)'. He echoes Roman Jakobson's definition of the 'poetic' as the 'set to the message', but Barthes stresses the *process* of signification, which appears less and less predictable as his work proceeds. The worst sin a writer can commit is to pretend that language is a natural, transparent medium through which the reader grasps a solid and unified 'truth' or 'reality'. The virtuous writer recognises the artifice of all writing and proceeds to make play with it. Bourgeois ideology, Barthes' *bête noire*, promotes the sinful view that reading is natural and language transparent; it insists on regarding the signifier as the sober partner of the signified, thus in authoritarian manner repressing all discourse into a meaning. *Avant-garde* writers allow the unconscious of language to rise to the surface: they allow the signifiers to generate meaning at will and to undermine the censorship of the signified and its repressive insistence on one meaning.

If anything marks a poststructuralist phase in Barthes it is his abandoning of scientific aspirations. In *Elements of Semiology* (1967; see above, chapter 5), he believed that structuralist method could explain all the sign-systems of human culture. However, in the very same text, he recognised that structuralist discourse itself could become the object of explanation. The semiological investigator regards his or her own language as a 'second-order' discourse which operates in Olympian fashion upon the 'first-order' object-language. The second-order language is called a metalanguage. In realising that any metalanguage could be put in the position of a first-order language and be interrogated by another metalanguage, Barthes glimpsed an infinite regress (an 'aporia'), which destroys the authority of all metalanguages. This means that, when we read as critics, we can never step outside discourse and adopt a position invulnerable to a subsequent interrogative reading. All discourses, including critical interpretations, are equally *fictive*; none stand apart in the place of Truth.

What might be called Barthes' poststructuralist period is best represented by his short essay 'The Death of the Author' (1968). He rejects the traditional view that the author is the origin of the text, the source of its meaning, and the only authority for interpretation. At first, this sounds like a restatement of the familiar New Critical dogma about the literary work's independence (autonomy) from its historical and biographical background. The New Critics believed that the unity of a text lay not in its author's intention but in its structure (for discussion of the 'intentional fallacy', see above, chapter 1, p. 16). This self-contained unity, nevertheless, has subterranean connections with its author, because, in their view, it represents a complex verbal enactment (a 'verbal icon') corresponding to the author's intuitions about the world. Barthes' formula is utterly radical in its dismissal of such humanistic notions. His author is stripped of all metaphysical status and reduced to a location (a crossroad), where language, that infinite storehouse of citations, repetitions, echoes and references, crosses and recrosses. The reader is thus free to enter the text from any direction; there is no correct route. The death of the author is already inherent in structuralism, which treats individual utterances (*paroles*) as the products of impersonal systems (*langues*). What is new in Barthes is the idea that readers are free to open and close the text's signifying process without respect for the signified. They are free to take their pleasure of the text, to follow at will the defiles of the signifier as it slips and slides evading the grasp of the signified. Readers are also sites of language's empire, but they are free to connect the text with systems of meaning and ignore the author's 'intention'. The central character in Dennis Potter's *Blackeyes* (1987) is a photographic model who possesses the openness of a sign awaiting the mark of the observer's inscribing gaze. Blackeyes expresses the 'sensuality of the passive. Her perfectly formed oval of a face was a blank upon which male desire could be projected. Her luminous large, jet-like eyes said nothing, and so said everything. She was pliable. She was there to be invented, in any posture, any words, over and over again, in ejaculatory longing.' She is a poststructuralist text totally at the mercy of the reader's pleasure. (Other, earlier, examples of 'free' characters who are available for an observer's inscription – note, they are all female – might be: Widow Wadman in *Tristram Shandy*, where Sterne leaves a blank page for the reader to fill in his (?) own ideal description of the most 'concupiscible' woman in the world in place of Sterne's characterisation; Tess, in Hardy's novel, who is often regarded as composed of images set up by the male gaze she is constantly subject to; and Sarah Woodruff in John Fowles's *The French Lieutenant's Woman*, whom the author considers an 'enigma' he cannot know.)

In *The Pleasure of the Text* (1975a) Barthes explores this reckless abandon of the reader. He begins by distinguishing between two senses of 'pleasure':

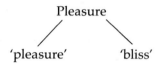

Within Pleasure there is 'bliss' (*jouissance*) and its diluted form, 'pleasure'. The general pleasure of the text is whatever *exceeds* a single transparent meaning. As we read, we see a connection, an echo, or a reference, and this disruption of the text's innocent, linear flow gives pleasure. Pleasure involves the production of a *join* (seam, fault, or flaw) between two surfaces: the place where naked flesh meets a garment is the focus of erotic pleasure. In texts the effect is to bring something unorthodox or perverse into connection with naked language. Reading the realistic novel we create another 'pleasure' by allowing our attention to wander, or by skipping: 'it is the very rhythm of what is read and what is not read that creates the pleasure of the great narratives'. This is especially true of reading erotic writing (though Barthes insists that pornography has no texts of bliss because it tries too hard to give us the ultimate truth). The more limited reading of pleasure is a comfortable practice which conforms to cultural habits. The text of bliss 'unsettles the reader's historical, cultural, psychological assumptions, . . . brings a crisis to his relation with language'. It is clear that such a text does not conform to the sort of easily enjoyed pleasure demanded in the market economy. Indeed, Barthes considers that 'bliss' is very close to boredom: if readers resist the ecstatic collapse of cultural assumptions, they will inevitably find only boredom in the modernist text. How many blissful readers of Joyce's *Finnegans Wake* have there been?

Barthes' *S/Z* (1970) is an impressive poststructuralist performance. He begins by alluding to the vain ambitions of structuralist narratologists who try 'to see all the world's stories . . . within a single structure'. The attempt to uncover *the* structure is vain, because each text possesses a 'difference'. This difference is not a sort of uniqueness, but the result of textuality itself. Each text refers back differently to the infinite sea of the 'already written'. Some writing tries to discourage the reader from freely reconnecting text and this 'already written' by insisting on specific meaning and reference. A realistic novel offers a 'closed' text with a limited meaning. Other texts encourage the reader to *produce* meanings. The 'I' which reads is 'already itself a plurality of other texts' and is allowed by the *avant-garde* text the maximum liberty to produce meanings by putting what is read in touch with this plurality. The first type of text allows the reader only to be a *consumer* of a fixed meaning, while the second turns the reader into a *producer*. The first type of text is called 'readerly' (*lisible*), the second 'writerly' (*scriptible*). The first is made to be read (consumed), the second to be written (produced). The writerly text exists only in theory, though Barthes' description of it suggests the texts of modernism: 'this ideal text is a galaxy of signifiers, not a structure of signifieds; it has no beginning; . . . we gain access to it by several entrances, none of which can be authoritatively declared to be the main one; the codes it mobilizes extend as far as the eye can reach.'

What are the 'codes'? (For a further examination of the Barthesian 'codes' in practice, see chapter 5, section 16, of *Practising Theory and Reading Literature*, on Edgar Allan Poe's novella *The Fall of the House of Usher*.) As the quotation above makes clear, they are not the structuralist systems of meaning we might expect. Whatever systems (Marxist, formalist, structuralist, psychoanalytic) we choose to apply to the text can only activate one or more of the virtually infinite 'voices' of the text. As the reader adopts different viewpoints the text's meaning is produced in a multitude of fragments which have no inherent unity. *S/Z* is a reading of Balzac's short novella, *Sarrasine*, which Barthes divides into 561 lexias (reading units). The lexias are read in sequence through the grid of five codes:

Hermeneutic
Semic
Symbolic

Proairetic
Cultural

The hermeneutic code concerns the *enigma* which arises whenever discourse commences. Who is this about? What is happening? What is the obstacle? Who committed the murder? How will the hero's purpose be achieved? A detective story is sometimes called a 'whodunit', thus drawing attention to the special importance of enigma to this genre. In *Sarrasine* the enigma surrounds La Zambinella. Before the question 'Who is she?' is finally answered ('she' is a castrato dressed as a woman), the discourse is spun out with one delaying answer after another: 'she' is a 'woman' ('snare'), 'a creature outside nature' ('ambiguity'), 'no one knows' (a 'jammed answer'). The code of 'semes' concerns the connotations often evoked in characterisation or description. An early account of La Zambinella, for example, sparks off the semes 'femininity', 'wealth', and 'ghostliness'. The symbolic code concerns the polarities and antitheses which allow multivalence and 'reversibility'. It marks out the patterns of sexual and psychoanalytic relations people may enter. For example, when we are introduced to Sarrasine, he is presented in the symbolic relation of 'father and son' ('he was the only son of a lawyer . . .'). The absence of the mother (she is unmentioned) is significant, and when the son decides to become an artist he is no longer 'favoured' by the father but 'accursed' (symbolic antithesis). This symbolic coding of the narrative is developed later when we read of the warm-hearted sculptor Bouchardon who enters the absent place of the mother and effects a reconciliation between father and son. The proairetic code (or code of actions) concerns the basic sequential logic of action and behaviour. Barthes marks such a sequence between lexias 95 and 101: the narrator's girl-friend touches the old castrato and reacts by breaking out in a cold sweat; when his relatives react in alarm, she makes for a side room and throws herself upon a couch in fright. Barthes marks the sequence as five stages of the coded action 'to touch': (1) touching; (2) reaction; (3) general reaction; (4) to flee; (5) to hide. They form a sequence which the reader, unconsciously operating the code, perceives as 'natural' or 'realistic'. Finally, the cultural code embraces all references to the common fund of 'knowledge' (physical, medical, psychological, literary, and so on) produced by society. Sarrasine first reveals his genius 'in one of those works in which future talent struggles with the effervescence of youth' (lexia 174). 'One of those' is a regular formula for signalling this code (see above, p. 128, in relation to George Eliot). Barthes ingeniously notes a double cultural reference: 'Code of ages and code of Art (talent as discipline, youth as effervescence).'

Why did Barthes choose to study a realistic novella and not an *avant-garde* text of *jouissance*? The cutting-up of the discourse and the dispersal of its meanings across the musical score of codes seem to deny the text its classic status as realistic story. The novella is exposed as a 'limit text' for realism. The elements of ambivalence destroy the unity of representation which we expect in such writing. The theme of castration, the confusion of sexual roles, and the mysteries surrounding the origins of capitalist wealth all invite an anti-representational reading. It is as if the principles of poststructuralism were already inscribed in this so-called realist text. (For more on 'the signifier' and semiotics in relation to a specific literary text, see Raman Selden's own 'Barthesian' reading of Nathaniel Hawthorne's *The Scarlet Letter* in chapter 4, section 10 of *PTRL*; for further Barthesian application of the notion of the 'writerly' text, see chapter 5, section 15 there, on Wallace Stevens's poem 'A High-toned Old Christian Woman'.)

PSYCHOANALYTIC THEORIES

The relationship between psychoanalysis and literary criticism spans much of the twentieth century. Fundamentally concerned with the articulation of sexuality in language, it has moved through three main emphases in its pursuit of the literary 'unconscious': on the author (and its corollary, 'character'), on the reader and on the text. It starts with Sigmund Freud's analysis of the literary work as a symptom of the artist, where the relationship between author and text is analogous to dreamers and their 'text' (literature = 'fantasy'); is modified by post-Freudians like Norman Holland (see above, pp. 64–5) in a pschyoanalytic reader-response criticism where the reader's 'transactive' relation to the text is foregrounded; and is contested by Carl Jung's 'archetypal' criticism in which, *contra* Freud, the literary work is not a focus for the writer's or reader's personal psychology but a representation of the relationship between the personal and the collective unconscious, the images, myths, symbols, 'archetypes' of past cultures. More recently, psychoanalytic criticism has been remodelled in the context of poststructuralism by the work of Jacques Lacan and his followers, in which the coupling of a dynamic notion of 'desire' with a model of structural linguistics has been influentially innovative. This is especially the case in feminist psychoanalytical criticism (see below, chapter 8, pp. 222–30), which, as Elizabeth Wright has said, is concerned with:

> the interaction of literature, culture and sexual identity, emphasising the way that configurations of gender are located in history. The feminist psychoanalytic enquiry has perhaps the potential for becoming the most radical form of psychoanalytic criticism, since it is crucially concerned with the very construction of subjectivity.

JACQUES LACAN: LANGUAGE AND THE UNCONSCIOUS

Western thought has for a long time assumed the necessity of a unified 'subject'. To *know* anything presupposes a unified consciousness which does the knowing. Such a consciousness is rather like a focused lens without which nothing can be seen as a distinct object. The medium through which this unified subject perceives objects and truth is *syntax*. An orderly syntax makes for an orderly mind. However, reason has never had things all its own way; it has always been threatened by the subversive noise of pleasure (wine, sex, song), of laughter, and of poetry. Puritan rationalists such as Plato always keep a sharp eye on these dangerous influences. They can all be summed up in the one concept – 'desire'. Disruption can go beyond the merely literary to the social level. Poetic language shows how dominant social discourses can be undermined by the creation of new 'subject positions'. This implies that far from being a mere blank which awaits its social or sexual role, the subject is *'in process' and is capable of being other than it is.*

The psychoanalytic writings of Lacan have given critics a new theory of the 'subject'. Marxist, formalist and structuralist critics have dismissed 'subjective' criticisms as Romantic and reactionary, but Lacanian criticism has developed a 'materialist' analysis of the 'speaking subject' which has been more acceptable. According to the linguist Emile Benveniste, 'I', 'he', 'she', and so on, are merely subject positions which language lays down. When I speak, I refer to myself as 'I' and to the person I address as 'you'. When 'you' reply, the persons are reversed and 'I' becomes 'you', and so on. We can communicate only if we accept this strange reversibility of persons. Therefore, the ego which uses the word 'I' is not identical with this 'I'. When I say 'Tomorrow I graduate', the 'I' in the statement is known as the 'subject of the enunciation', and the ego which makes the statement is the 'subject of the enunciating'. Poststructuralist thought enters the gap between these two subjects, while Romantic thought simply elides them.

Lacan considers that human subjects enter a pre-existing system of signifiers which take on meanings only within a language system. The entry into language enables us to find a subject position within a relational system (male/female, father/ mother/daughter). This process and the stages which precede it are governed by the unconscious.

According to Freud, during the earliest phases of infanthood the libidinal drives have no definite sexual object but play around the various erotogenic zones of the body (oral, anal, 'phallic'). Before gender or identity are established there is only the rule of the 'pleasure principle'. The 'reality principle' eventually supervenes in the form of the father who threatens the male child's Oedipal desire for the mother with the punishment of 'castration'. The repression of desire makes it possible for the male child to identify with the place of the father and with a 'masculine' role. The Oedipal voyage of the female is much less straightforward, and Freud's endemic sexism has been attacked by some feminist critics (see chapter 8). This phase introduces morality, law, and religion, symbolised as 'patriarchal law', and induces the development of a 'superego' in the child. However, the repressed desire does not go away and remains in the unconscious, thus producing a radically *split* subject. Indeed, this force of desire *is* the unconscious.

Lacan's distinction between the 'imaginary' and the 'symbolic' corresponds to Kristeva's between 'semiotic' and 'symbolic' (see below, p. 222). This 'imaginary' is a state in which there is no clear distinction between subject and object: no central self exists to set object apart from subject. In the prelinguistic 'mirror phase' the child, from within this 'imaginary' state of being, starts to project a certain unity into the fragmented self-image in the mirror (there does not have to be an actual mirror); he or she produces a 'fictional' ideal, an 'ego'. This specular (speculum = mirror) image is still partly imaginary (it is not clear whether it is the child or another), but also partly differentiated as 'another'. The imaginary tendency continues even after the formation of the ego, because the myth of a unified selfhood depends upon this ability to identify with objects in the world as 'others'. Nevertheless, the child must also learn to differentiate itself from others if it is to become a subject in its own right. With the father's prohibition the child is thrown headlong into the 'symbolic' world of differences (male/female, father/son, present/absent, and so on). Indeed, the 'phallus' (not the penis but its 'symbol') is, in Lacan's system, the privileged signifier, which helps all signifiers achieve a unity with their signifieds. In the symbolic domain phallus is king. As we shall see, feminist critics have had a good deal to say about this.

Neither the imaginary nor the symbolic can fully comprehend the Real, which remains out there somewhere beyond their reach. Our instinctive *needs* are shaped by the discourse in which we express our *demand* for satisfaction. However, discourse's moulding of needs leaves not satisfaction but *desire*, which runs on in the chain of signifiers. When 'I' express my desire in words, 'I' am always subverted by that unconscious which presses on with its own sideways game. This unconscious works on in metaphoric and metonymic substitutions and displacements which elude consciousness, but reveals itself in dreams, jokes and art.

Lacan restates Freud's theories in the language of Saussure. Essentially, unconscious processes are identified with the unstable *signifier*. As we have seen, Saussure's attempts to solder up the gap between the separate systems of signifiers and signifieds was in vain. For example, when a subject enters the symbolic order and accepts a *position* as 'son' or 'daughter', a certain linking of signifier and signified is made possible. However, 'I' am never where I think; 'I' stand at the axis of signifier and signified, a split being, never able to give my position a full presence. In Lacan's version of the sign, the signified 'slides' beneath a signifier which 'floats'. Freud considered dreams the main outlet for repressed desires. His theory of dreams is reinterpreted as a textual theory. The unconscious hides meaning in symbolic images which need to be deciphered. Dream images undergo 'condensation' (several images combine) and 'displacement' (significance shifts from one image to a contiguous one). Lacan calls the first process 'metaphor' and the second 'metonymy' (see Jakobson, chapter 5). In other words, he believes that the garbled and enigmatic dream work follows the laws of the signifier. Freud's 'defence mechanisms' too are treated as figures of speech (irony, ellipsis, and so on). Any kind of psychic distortion is restated as a quirk of the signifier rather than some mysterious prelinguistic urge. For Lacan there never were any undistorted signifiers. His psychoanalysis is the scientific rhetoric of the unconscious. (For a Freudian, and then more specifically Lacanian, reading of Shakespeare's *Hamlet* see *PTRL*, chapter 4, section 11.)

Lacan's Freudianism has encouraged modern criticism to abandon faith in language's power to refer to things and to express ideas or feelings. Modernist literature often resembles dreams in its avoidance of a governing narrative position and its free play of meaning. Lacan himself wrote a much discussed analysis of Poe's 'The Purloined Letter', a story containing two episodes. In the first, the Minister perceives that the Queen is anxious about a letter she has left lying exposed on a table unnoticed by the King who has entered her boudoir unexpectedly. The Minister replaces the letter with a similar one. The Queen cannot intervene for fear that the King will be alerted. In the second episode, following the Prefect of police's failure to find the letter in the Minister's house, Dupin (a detective) immediately sees it openly thrust in a card-rack on the Minister's mantlepiece. He returns, distracts the Minister, and replaces the letter with a similar one. Lacan points out that the letter's contents are never revealed. The story's development is shaped not by the character of individuals or the contents of the letter but by the *position* of the letter in relation to the trio of persons in each episode. These relations to the letter are defined by Lacan according to three kinds of 'glance': the first sees nothing (the King's and the Prefect's); the second sees that the first glance sees nothing but thinks its secret safe (the Queen's and, in the second episode, the Minister's); the third sees that the first two glances leave the 'hidden' letter exposed (the Minister's and Dupin's). The letter, then, acts like a signifier by producing subject positions for the characters in the narrative. Lacan considers that in this the story illustrates the psychoanalytic theory that the symbolic order is 'constitutive for the subject'; the subject receives a 'decisive orientation' from the 'itinerary of a signifier'. He treats the story as an allegory of psychoanalysis, but also considers psychoanalysis as a model of fiction. The repetition of the structure of scene one in scene two is governed by the effects of a pure signifier (the letter); the characters move into their places as the unconscious prompts.

(For a fuller account not only of Lacan's essay but also of Derrida's critical reading of Lacan's reading, see Barbara Johnson's essay in Robert Young's *Untying the Text*, 1981. In a brilliant demonstration of poststructuralist thought she introduces a further displacement of meaning into the potentially endless sequence: Poe > Lacan > Derrida > Johnson.)

JULIA KRISTEVA: LANGUAGE AND REVOLUTION

Kristeva's most important work on literary meaning is *La révolution du langage poétique* (1974). Unlike that of Barthes her theory is based upon a particular system of ideas: psychoanalysis. The book attempts to explore the process by which what is ordered and rationally accepted is continually being threatened by the 'heterogeneous' and the 'irrational'.

Kristeva gives us a complex psychological account of the relationship between the 'normal' and the 'poetic'. Human beings are from the beginning a space across which physical and psychic impulses flow rhythmically. This indefinite flux of impulses is gradually regulated by the constraints of family and society (potty-training, gender-identification, separation of public and private, and so on). At the earliest, pre-Oedipal stage, the flow of impulses centres on the mother, and allows not the formulation of a personality but only a rough demarcation of parts of the body and their relations. A disorganised prelinguistic flux of movements, gestures, sounds and rhythms lays a foundation of semiotic material which remains active beneath the mature linguistic performance of the adult. She calls this material 'semiotic' because it works like an unorganised signifying process. We become aware of this activity in dreams in which images are processed in 'illogical' ways (for Freud's theory, see Lacan, above).

In the poetry of Mallarmé and Lautréamont these primary processes of rhythm and sound pattern are liberated from the unconscious (according to Lacan, they *are* the unconscious). Kristeva relates the use of sound in poetry to primary sexual impulses. The opposition *Mama* and *Papa* sets nasal *m* against plosive *p*. The *m* transmits maternal 'orality', while the *p* relates to male 'anality'.

As the semiotic becomes regulated, the beaten pathways become the logic, coherent syntax and rationality of the adult, which Kristeva calls the 'symbolic'. The symbolic works with the substance of the semiotic and achieves a certain mastery over it, but can never produce its own signifying substance. The symbolic places subjects in their positions and makes it possible for them to have identities. Kristeva adopts Lacan's Freudian explanation of the emergence of this phase.

The word 'revolution' in Kristeva's title is not simply metaphoric. The possibility of radical social change is, in her view, bound up with the disruption of authoritarian discourses. Poetic language introduces the subversive openness of the semiotic 'across' society's 'closed' symbolic order: 'What the theory of the unconscious seeks, poetic language practices, within and against the social order.' Sometimes she considers that modernist poetry actually prefigures a social revolution which in the distant future will come about when society has evolved a more complex form. However, at other times she fears that bourgeois ideology will simply recuperate this poetic revolution by treating it as a safety valve for the repressed impulses it denies in society. Kristeva's view of the revolutionary potential of women writers in society is just as ambivalent (see chapter 8).

DELEUZE AND GUATTARI: SCHIZOANALYSIS

Gilles Deleuze and Félix Guattari, in *Anti-Oedipus: Capitalism and Schizophrenia* (1972) and *Kafka: Pour une littérature mineure* (1975) offer at once a radical critique of psychoanalysis – drawing on, but going beyond, Lacan – and a close textual method for the reading of texts which they term 'schizoanalysis'. Their attack on psychoanalysis primarily targets its representation of desire as based in lack or need, which Deleuze and Guattari see as a capitalist device that deforms the unconscious: the Oedipus complex, hijacked as an internalised set of power relations, is the result of repression by capitalism within the family. Schizoanalysis would, conversely, *construct* an unconscious in which desire constitutes an untramelled 'flow' – an energy which is not contained by Oedipal 'anxiety' but is a positive source of new beginnings: 'schizoanalysis' means the liberation of desire. Where paranoiac unconscious desire 'territorializes' – in terms of nation, family, church, school, etc. – a schizophrenic one 'deterritorializes', offering a subversion of these (capitalist) totalities. In this sense, as Elizabeth Wright has said, Deleuze and Guattari's '"material psychiatry" becomes a political factor in its attempts to release the libidinal flow from what they see as oppression rather than repression'.

The relationship of schizophrenia to literature is that the latter too can subvert, and free itself from, the system. But the author/ text also needs a 'desire-liberating reader', a 'schizoanalyst', to activate its potentially revolutionary discourses. Deleuze and Guattari's analysis of Kafka, whom they find particularly suited to their project (his work, in a favourite concept of theirs, is a 'rhizome' – 'a fertile tuber that sprouts unexpected plants out of concealment' [Wright]), is a bravura close, textual, entirely anti-New-Critical, out-deconstructing-deconstruction analysis of his work, which exposes the 'gaps' and tensions in the text, the continuously fluid combinations of images, and the subversion of 'normal' notions of representation, symbol and text within both psychoanalytic and other literary-critical discourse. In regarding the work not as 'text' but as essentially uncoded, the practice of the 'revolutionary' schizoanalytic reader/writer will 'deterritorialize' any given representation: in the case of Kafka hence accounting for his 'revolutionary' force by exposing the unconscious discourses of desire as more powerful than those of family and state. Nevertheless, as for Kristeva, the paradox of Deleuze and Guattari's promotion of schizoanalysis is that the domain of literature and literary criticism can only ever be a displacement (and defusing?) of their revolutionary *political* potential.

JACQUES DERRIDA: DECONSTRUCTION

Derrida's paper 'Structure, Sign, and Play in the Discourse of the Human Sciences', given at a symposium at Johns Hopkins University in 1966, virtually inaugurated a new critical movement in the United States. Its argument put in question the basic metaphysical assumptions of Western philosophy since Plato. The notion of 'structure', he argues, even in 'structuralist' theory has always presupposed a 'centre' of meaning of some sort. This 'centre' governs the structure but is itself not subject to structural analysis (to find the structure of the centre would be to find another centre). People desire a centre because it guarantees *being as presence*. For example, we think of our mental and physical life as centred on an 'I'; this personality is the principle of unity which underlies the structure of all that goes on in this space. Freud's theories completely undermine this metaphysical certainty by revealing a division in the self between conscious and unconscious. Western thought has developed innumerable terms which operate as centring principles: being, essence, substance, truth, form, beginning, end, purpose, consciousness, man, God, and so on. It is important to note that Derrida does not assert the possibility of thinking outside such terms; any attempt to undo a particular concept is to become caught up in the terms which the concept depends on. For example, if we try to undo the centring concept of 'consciousness' by asserting the disruptive counterforce of the 'unconscious', we are in danger of introducing a new centre, because we cannot choose but enter the conceptual system (conscious/unconscious) we are trying to dislodge. All we *can* do is to refuse to allow either pole in a system (body/soul, good/bad, serious/unserious) to become the centre and guarantor of presence.

This desire for a centre is called 'logocentrism' in Derrida's classic work, *Of Grammatology*. 'Logos' (Greek for 'word') is a term which in the New Testament carries the greatest possible concentration of presence: 'In the beginning was the Word.' Being the origin of all things, the 'Word' underwrites the full presence of the world; everything is the effect of this one cause. Even though the Bible is written, God's word is essentially *spoken*. A spoken word emitted from a living body appears to be closer to an originating thought than a written word. Derrida argues that this privileging of speech over writing (he calls it 'phonocentrism') is a classic feature of logocentrism.

What prevents the sign from being a full presence? Derrida invents the term *'différance'* to convey the divided nature of the sign. In French the 'a' in *'différance'* is not heard, and so we hear only *'différence'*. The ambiguity is perceptible only in writing: the verb *'différer'* means both 'to differ' and 'to defer'. To 'differ' is a spatial concept: the sign emerges from a system of differences which are spaced out within the system. To 'defer' is temporal: signifiers enforce an endless postponement of 'presence'. Phonocentric thought ignores *'différance'* and insists upon the self-presence of the spoken word.

Phonocentrism treats writing as a contaminated form of speech. Speech seems nearer to originating thought. When we hear speech we attribute to it a 'presence' which we take to be lacking in writing. The speech of the great actor, orator, or politician is thought to possess 'presence'; it incarnates, so to speak, the speaker's soul. Writing seems relatively impure and obtrudes its own system in physical marks which have a relative permanence; writing can be repeated (printed, reprinted, and so on) and this repetition invites interpretation and reinterpretation. Even when a speech is subjected to interpretation it is usually in written form. Writing does not need the writer's presence, but speech always implies an immediate presence. The sounds made by a speaker evaporate in the air and leave no trace (unless recorded), and therefore do not appear to contaminate the originating thought as in writing. Philosophers have often expressed their dislike of writing; they fear that it will destroy the authority of philosophic Truth. This Truth depends upon pure thought (logic, ideas, propositions) which risk contamination when written. Francis Bacon believed that one of the main obstacles to scientific advance was the love of eloquence: 'men began to hunt more after words than matter; and more after . . . tropes and figures, than after the weight of matter, . . . soundness of argument.' However, as the word 'eloquence' suggests, the qualities in writing to which he objected are those originally developed by orators. Thus, those very features of elaboration in writing which threaten to cloud the purity of thought were originally cultivated for speech.

This coupling of 'writing' and 'speech' is an example of what Derrida calls a 'violent hierarchy'. Speech has full presence, while writing is secondary and threatens to contaminate speech with its materiality. Western philosophy has supported this ranking in order to preserve presence. But, as the Bacon example shows, the hierarchy can easily be undone and reversed. We begin to see that both speech and writing share certain writerly features: both are signifying processes which lack presence. To complete the reversal of the hierarchy, we can now say that speech is a species of writing. This reversal is the first stage of a Derridean 'deconstruction'.

Derrida uses the term 'supplement' to convey the unstable relationship between couplets such as speech/writing. For Rousseau writing is merely a supplement to speech; it adds something inessential. In French, *'suppléer'* also means 'to substitute' (to take the place of), and Derrida shows that writing not only supplements but also takes the place of speech, because speech is always already written. All human activity involves this supplementarity (addition-substitution). When we say that 'nature' preceded 'civilisation', we are asserting another violent hierarchy in which a pure presence lauds itself over a mere supplement. However, if we look closely, we find that nature is always already contaminated with civilisation; there is no 'original' nature, only a myth which we desire to promote.

Consider another example. Milton's *Paradise Lost* may be said to rest on the distinction between good and evil. Good has the original fullness of being. It originated with God. Evil is a second comer, a supplement, which contaminates his original unity of being. However, if we look more closely, we begin to see reversal taking place. For example, if we seek a time when good was without evil, we find ourselves caught in an abysmal regression. Was it before the Fall? Before Satan's? What caused

Satan's fall? Pride. Who created pride? God, who created angels and humans free to sin. We never reach an original moment of pure goodness. We may reverse the hierarchy and say that there are no 'good' acts by humans until after the Fall. Adam's first act of sacrifice is an expression of love for the fallen Eve. This 'goodness' comes only after evil. God's prohibition itself presupposes evil. In *Areopagitica* Milton opposed the licensing of books because he believed that we can be virtuous only if we are given the opportunity to struggle against evil: 'that which purifies us is trial, and trial is by what is contrary'. Thus, good comes *after* evil. There are many critical and theological strategies which can sort out this mess, but there remains a basis for deconstruction. Such a reading begins by noting the hierarchy, proceeds to reverse it, and finally resists the assertion of a new hierarchy by displacing the second term from a position of superiority too. Blake believed that Milton was on Satan's side in his great epic, and Shelley thought that Satan was morally superior to God. They simply reverse the hierarchy, substituting evil for good. A deconstructive reading would go on to recognise that the couplet cannot be hierarchised in either direction without 'violence'. Evil is both addition *and* substitution. Deconstruction can begin when we locate the moment when a text *transgresses the laws it appears to set up for itself*. At this point texts go to pieces, so to speak. (In chapter 4, section 12 of *PTRL*, Raman Selden offers an example of the Derridean deconstructive method in action in relation to Wordsworth's poem 'Afterthought', and in chapter 5, section 14, to his 'To H. C., Six Years Old'.)

In 'Signature Event Context' Derrida gives writing three characteristics:

1. A written sign is a mark which can be repeated in the absence not only of the subject who emitted it in a specific context but also of a specific addressee.
2. The written sign can break its 'real context' and can be read in a different context regardless of what its writer intended. Any chain of signs can be 'grafted' into a discourse in another context (as in a quotation).
3. The written sign is subject to 'spacing' (*espacement*) in two senses: first, it is separated from other signs in a particular

chain; secondly, it is separated from 'present reference' (that is, it can refer only to something not actually present in it).

These characteristics appear to distinguish writing from speech. Writing involves a certain irresponsibility, because if signs are repeatable out of context, then what authority can they possess? Derrida proceeds to deconstruct the hierarchy by, for example, pointing out that when we interpret oral signs, we have to recognise certain stable and identical forms (signifiers), whatever accent, tone, or distortion may be involved in the utterance. It appears that we have to exclude the accidental phonic (sound) substance and recover a pure form. This form is the repeatable signifier, which we had thought characteristic of writing. Once again, we conclude that speech is a species of writing.

J. L. Austin's theory of 'speech acts' was developed to supersede the old logical-positivist view of language which assumed that the only meaningful statements are those which describe a state of affairs in the world. All other sorts of statements are not real ones but 'pseudo-statements'. Austin uses the term 'constative' to cover the first (referential statements), and 'performative' to cover those utterances which actually perform the actions they describe ('I swear to tell the whole truth and nothing but the truth' *performs* an oath). Derrida acknowledges that this makes a break with logocentric thought by recognising that speech does not have to represent something to have a meaning. However, Austin also distinguishes between degrees of linguistic force. To make a merely linguistic utterance (say, to speak an English sentence) is a *locutionary* act. A speech act which has *illocutionary* force involves performing the act (to promise, to swear, to argue, to affirm, and so on). A speech act has *perlocutionary* force if it brings about an effect (*I persuade* you by arguing; I *convince* you by swearing; and so on). Austin requires that speech acts must have contexts. An oath can occur only in a court within the appropriate judicial framework or in other situations in which oaths are conventionally performed. Derrida questions this by suggesting that the repeatability ('iterability') of the speech act is more fundamental than its attachment to a context.

Austin remarks in passing that to be performative a statement must be spoken 'seriously' and not be a joke or used in a play or poem. An oath in a Hollywood court scene is 'parasitic' upon a real-life oath. John Searle's reply to Derrida, 'Reiterating the Differences', defends Austin's view and argues that a 'serious' discourse is logically prior to fictional, 'parasitic' citations of it. Derrida probes this and neatly demonstrates that a 'serious' performative cannot occur unless it is a repeatable sign-sequence (what Barthes called the 'always-already-written'). A real courtroom oath is just a special case of the game people play in films and books. What Austin's pure performative and the impure, parasitic versions have in common is that they involve repetition and citation, which are typical of the 'written'.

After his 1966 paper Derrida became an academic celebrity in the United States. Deconstruction had a major influence upon humanities departments, and Derrida took up a teaching position at Yale University.

The power of the deconstructive movement can be gauged by the fact that many other major intellectual traditions have been forced into radical reassessments. For example, a *rapprochement* between deconstructive philosophy and modern Marxism is impressively undertaken by Michael Ryan in his *Marxism and Deconstruction* (1982), in which he shows how both have encouraged 'plurality' rather than 'authoritarian unity', criticism rather than obedience, 'difference' rather than 'identity' and a general scepticism about absolute or totalising systems.

AMERICAN DECONSTRUCTION: DE MAN, WHITE, BLOOM, HARTMAN AND MILLER

American critics flirted with a number of alien presences in their attempts to throw off the long-cherished formalism of the New Critics. The scientific 'myth criticism' of Northrop Frye, the Hegelian Marxism of Lukács, the phenomenology of Poulet and the rigours of French structuralism each had its day. It is something of a surprise that Derrida won over many of America's most powerful critics. Several of them are Romantic specialists. Romantic poets are intensely concerned with experiences of timeless illumination ('epiphanies') which occur at certain privileged moments in their lives. They try to recapture these 'spots of time' in their poetry, and to saturate their words with this absolute presence. However, they also lament the loss of 'presence': 'there hath passed away a glory from the earth'. It is not therefore surprising that Paul de Man and others have found Romantic poetry an open invitation to deconstruction. Indeed de Man argues that the Romantics actually deconstruct their own writing by showing that the presence they desire is always absent, always in the past or future.

De Man's *Blindness and Insight* (1971) and *Allegories of Reading* (1979) are impressively rigorous works of deconstruction. Their debt to Derrida is evident, but de Man develops his own terminology. The first book circles around the paradox that critics only achieve insight through a certain blindness. They adopt a method or theory which is quite at odds with the insights it produces: 'All these critics [Lukács, Blanchot, Poulet] seem curiously doomed to say something different from what they meant to say.' The insights could be gained only because the critics were 'In the grip of this peculiar blindness'. For example, the American New Critics based their practice upon the Coleridgean notion of organic form, according to which a poem has a formal unity analogous to that of natural form. However, instead of discovering in poetry the unity and coherence of the natural world, they reveal multi-faceted and ambiguous meanings: 'This unitarian criticism finally becomes a criticism of ambiguity.' This ambiguous poetic language seems to contradict their idea of an object-like totality.

De Man believes that this insight-in-blindness is facilitated by an unconscious slide from one kind of unity to another. The unity which the New Critics so frequently discover is not in the text but in the act of interpretation. Their desire for total understanding initiates the 'hermeneutic circle' of interpretation. Each element in a text is understood in terms of the whole, and the whole is understood as a totality made up of all the elements. This interpretative movement is part of a complex process which produces literary 'form'. Mistaking this 'circle' of interpretation for the text's unity helps them sustain a blindness which produces insight into poetry's divided and multiple meaning (the elements do not form a unity). Criticism must be ignorant of the insight it produces.

Derrida's questioning of the distinction between speech and writing is paralleled by his interrogation of those between 'philosophy' and 'literature', and between the 'literal' and the 'figurative'. Philosophy can only be philosophical if it ignores or denies its own textuality: it believes it stands at a remove from such contamination. 'Literature' is regarded by philosophy as mere fiction, as a discourse in the grip of 'figures of speech'. By reversing the hierarchy philosophy/literature Derrida places philosophy *sous rature* or 'under erasure' (p̶h̶i̶l̶o̶s̶o̶p̶h̶y̶) – philosophy is itself governed by rhetoric and yet is preserved as a distinct form of 'writing' (we still see 'philosophy' under the mark of erasure). Reading philosophy as literature does not prevent us from reading literature as philosophy; Derrida refuses to assert a new hierarchy (literature/philosophy), although some Derrideans are guilty of this partial deconstruction. Similarly, we discover that 'literal' language is in fact 'figurative' language whose figuration has been forgotten. However, the concept of the 'literal' is not thereby eliminated but only deconstructed. It remains in effect, but 'under erasure'.

In *Allegories of Reading* de Man develops a 'rhetorical' type of deconstruction already begun in *Blindness and Insight*. 'Rhetoric' is the classical term for the art of persuasion. De Man is concerned with the theory of 'tropes' which accompanies rhetorical treatises. 'Figures of speech' (tropes) allow writers to say one thing but mean something else: to substitute one sign for another (metaphor), to displace meaning from one sign in a chain to another (metonymy), and so on. Tropes pervade language, exerting a force which destabilises logic, and thereby denies the possibility of a straightforwardly literal or referential use of language. To the question 'Tea or coffee?' I reply 'What's the difference?' My rhetorical question (meaning 'It makes no difference which I choose') contradicts the logic of my question's 'literal' meaning ('What is the difference between tea and coffee?'). De Man shows that, just as critical insights result from critical blindness, so passages of explicit critical reflection or thematic statement in literary texts seem to depend on the suppression of the implications of the rhetoric used in such passages. De Man grounds his theory in close readings of specific texts (an 'applied' version of such, on Emily Dickinson's poem 'A Thought Went Up my Mind Today', appears in *PTRL*, chapter 4, section 12), and considers that it is the effects of language and rhetoric that prevent a direct representation of the real. He follows Nietzsche in believing that language is essentially figurative and not referential or expressive; there is no original unrhetorical language. This means that 'reference' is always contaminated with figurality.

De Man applies these arguments to criticism itself. Reading is always necessarily 'misreading', because 'tropes' inevitably intervene between critical and literary texts. Critical writing conforms essentially to the literary figure we call 'allegory'; it is a sequence of signs which stands at a distance from another sequence of signs, and seeks to stand in its place. Criticism is thus returned, like philosophy, to the common textuality of 'literature'. What is the point of this 'misreading'? De Man thinks that some misreadings are correct and others incorrect. A correct misreading tries to include and not repress the inevitable misreadings which all language produces. At the centre of this argument is the belief that literary texts are *self-deconstructing*: 'a literary text simultaneously asserts and denies the authority of its own rhetorical mode'. The deconstructor appears to have little to do except to collude with the text's own processes. If he or she succeeds, a correct misreading can be achieved.

De Man's refined critical procedure does not involve an actual denial of language's referential function (reference is merely placed 'under erasure'). However, since texts never seem to emerge from their textuality, there may be something in Terry Eagleton's view that American (and especially de Man's) deconstruction perpetuates by another means New Criticism's dissolution of history. While the New Critics cocooned the text in 'form' to protect it from history, the deconstructors swallow up history in an expanded empire of literature, 'viewing famines, revolutions, soccer matches and sherry trifle as yet more undecidable "text"'. Deconstruction cannot in theory establish a hierarchy text/history, but in practice it sees only text as far as the eye can reach.

The rhetorical type of poststructuralism has taken various forms. In historiography (the theory of history) Hayden White has attempted a radical deconstruction of the writings of well-known historians. In *Tropics of Discourse* (1978) he argues that historians believe their narratives to be objective, but because it involves structure their narration cannot escape textuality: 'Our discourse always tends to slip away from our data towards the structures of consciousness with which we are trying to grasp them.' Whenever a new discipline arises it must establish the adequacy of its own language to the objects in its field of study. However, this is done not by logical argument but by a '*pre*figurative move that is more tropical than logical'. When historians order the material of their study, they render it manageable by the silent application of what Kenneth Burke called the 'Four Master Tropes': metaphor, metonymy, synecdoche, and irony. Historical thinking is not possible except in terms of tropes. White agrees with Piaget in thinking that this figurative consciousness may be part of normal psychological development. He goes on to examine the writings of major thinkers (Freud, Marx, E. P. Thompson and others) and shows that their 'objective knowledge' or 'concrete historical reality' is always shaped by the master tropes.

In literary criticism Harold Bloom has made spectacular use of tropes. Despite being a Yale professor, he is less radically 'textual' than de Man or Hartman (see below), and still treats literature as a special field of study. However, his combination of the theory of tropes, Freudian psychology and cabbalistic mysticism is a daring one. He argues that since Milton, the first truly 'subjective' poet, poets have suffered an awareness of their 'belatedness': coming late in poetic history they fear that their poetic fathers have already used up all the available inspiration. They experience an Oedipal hatred of the father, a desperate desire to deny paternity. The suppression of their aggressive feelings gives rise to various defensive strategies. No poem stands on its own, but always in relation to another. In order to write belatedly, poets must enter a psychic struggle, to create an imaginative space. This involves 'misreading' their masters in order to produce a new interpretation. This 'poetic misprision' creates the required space in which they can communicate their own authentic inspiration. Without this aggressive wrenching of predecessors' meaning, tradition would stifle all creativity.

Cabbalistic writings (Jewish rabbinical texts which reveal hidden meanings in the Bible) are classic examples of *revisionary* texts. Bloom believes that Isaac Luria's sixteenth-century version of cabbalistic mysticism is an exemplary model of the way poets revise earlier poets in post-Renaissance poetry. He develops from Luria the three stages of revision: *limitation* (taking a new look), *substitution* (replacing one form by another) and *representation* (restoring a meaning). When a 'strong' poet writes, he repeatedly passes through the three stages in a dialectical manner, as he grapples with the strong poets of the past (we intentionally leave Bloom's masculine idiom exposed).

In *A Map of Misreading* (1975) he charts how meaning is produced in 'Post-Enlightenment images, by the language strong poets use in defence against, and response to, the language of prior strong poets'. The 'tropes' and 'defenses' are interchangeable forms of 'revisionary ratios'. Strong poets cope with the 'anxiety of influence' by adopting separately or successively six psychic defences. These appear in their poetry as tropes which allow a poet to 'swerve' from a father's poems. The six tropes are irony, synecdoche, metonymy, hyperbole/litotes, metaphor and metalepsis. Bloom uses six classical words to describe the six kinds of relationship between the texts of fathers and sons (revisionary ratios): *clinamen, tessera, kenosis, daemonisation, askesis* and *apophrades*. *Clinamen* is the 'swerve' a poet makes in order to justify a new poetic direction (a direction which, it is implied, the master would or should have taken). This involves a deliberate misinterpretation of an earlier poet. *Tessera* is 'fragment': a poet treats the materials of a precursor poem as if they were in pieces, and required the finishing touch of the successor. *Clinamen* (revisionary ratio) has the rhetorical form of 'irony' (the figure of speech, not of thought), and is the psychic defence called 'reaction-formation'. Irony says one thing and means something different (sometimes the opposite). The other ratios are similarly expressed as both trope and psychic defence (*tessera* = synecdoche = 'turning against the Self', and so on). Unlike de Man and White, Bloom does not privilege rhetoric in his readings. It would be more accurate to call his method 'psychocritical'.

Bloom pays particular attention to the Romantic 'crisis-poems' of Wordsworth, Shelley, Keats and Tennyson. Each poet struggles to misread his predecessors creatively. Each poem passes through the stages of revision and each stage works through the pairs of revisionary ratios. Shelley's 'Ode to the

West Wind', for example, struggles with Wordsworth's 'Immortality' ode as follows: stanzas I-II, *clinamen/tessera*; IV, *kenosis/daemonisation*; V, *askesis/apophrades*. It is necessary to study Part III of *A Map of Misreading* to grasp the full working of Bloom's method.

Geoffrey Hartman, having emerged from New Criticism, plunged into deconstruction and left behind him a scattered trail of fragmentary texts (collected in *Beyond Formalism*, 1970, *The Fate of Reading*, 1975, and *Criticism in the Wilderness*, 1980). Like de Man he regards criticism as inside rather than outside literature. He has used this licence to justify his seemingly random pillaging of other texts (literary, philosophical, popular) to spin out his own discourse. For example, at one point he writes about the harshness and strangeness of Christ's parables, which were smoothed over by the 'older hermeneutics' which 'tended to be incorporative or reconciling, like Donne's "spider love that transubstantiates all"'. Donne's phrase is drawn in by association. 'Transubstantiation' is used metaphorically in a poem about love, but Hartman activates its religious connotations; his 'incorporative' picks up the incarnational connotations of 'transubstantiation'. He randomly suppresses or ignores the poisonous implication (in Donne's period) of 'spider'. His critical writings are frequently interrupted and complicated by such imperfectly digested references. The imperfection reflects Hartman's view that critical reading should aim not to produce consistent meaning but to reveal 'contradictions and equivocations' in order to make fiction 'interpretable by making it less readable'. Since criticism is inside literature, it must be equally unreadable.

He rebels against the scholarly common-sense criticism of the Arnoldian tradition ('sweetness and light'). More generally he adopts a poststructuralist rejection of science's 'ambition to master . . . its subject (text, psyche) by technocratic, predictive, authoritarian formulas'. However, he also questions the speculative and abstract 'sky-flying' of the philosopher-critic, who flies too high to keep in touch with actual texts. His own brand of mildly speculative and densely textual criticism is an attempt at reconciliation. He both admires and fears Derrida's radical theory. He welcomes criticism's newly found creativity, but hesitates before the yawning abyss of indeterminacy, which threatens it with chaos. As Vincent Leitch has written, 'he emerges as a voyeur of the border, who watches or imagines crossover and warns of dangers'. And yet, one cannot help thinking that Hartman's philosophical doubts are lulled by the lure of textual pleasure. Consider the following extract from his discussion of Derrida's *Glas*, which incorporates passages from Genet's *Journal du voleur* (*The Thief's Journal*):

> *Glas*, then, is Derrida's own *Journal du voleur*, and reveals the vol-onto-theology of writing. Writing is always theft or bricolage of the logos. The theft redistributes the logos by a new principle of equity . . . as the volatile seed of flowers. Property, even in the form of the *nom propre*, is *non-propre*, and writing is an act of crossing the line of the text, of making it indeterminate, or revealing the *midi* as the *mi-dit*.

During the 1960s J. Hillis Miller was deeply influenced by the Geneva School's 'phenomenological' criticism (see chapter 3). His work since 1970 has centred on the deconstruction of fiction (especially in *Fiction and Repetition: Seven English Novels*, 1982). This phase was inaugurated with a fine paper on Dickens given in 1970, in which he takes up Jakobson's theory of metaphor and metonymy (see chapter 5). He begins by showing how the realism of *Sketches by Boz* is not a mimetic effect but a figurative one. Looking at Monmouth Street, Boz sees 'things, human artifacts, streets, buildings, vehicles, old clothes in shops'. These things metonymically signify something which is absent: he infers from the things 'the life that is lived among them'. However, Miller's account does not end with this relatively structuralist analysis of realism. He shows how the metonymic dead men's clothes come to life in Boz's mind as he imagines their absent wearers: 'waistcoats have almost burst with anxiety to put themselves on'. This metonymic 'reciprocity' between a person and his surroundings (house, possessions, and so on) 'is the basis for the metaphorical substitutions so frequent in Dickens' fiction'. Metonymy asserts an *association* between clothes and wearer, while metaphor suggests a *similarity* between them. First, clothes and wearer are linked by context, and secondly, as context fades, we allow clothes to substitute for wearer. Miller perceives a further self-conscious fictionality in

Dickens's fondness for theatrical metaphor. He frequently describes the behaviour of individuals as an imitation of theatrical styles or of works of art (one character goes through 'an admirable bit of serious pantomime', speaks in 'a stage whisper', and appears later 'like the ghost of Queen Anne in the tent scene in Richard'). There is an endless deferment of presence: everyone imitates or repeats someone else's behaviour, real or fictional. The metonymic process encourages a literal reading (this *is* London), while at the same time it acknowledges its own figurality. We discover that metonymy is as much a fiction as metaphor. Miller in effect deconstructs Jakobson's original opposition between 'realistic' metonymy and 'poetic' metaphor. A 'correct interpretation' of them sees the 'figurative as figurative'. Both 'invite misinterpretation which takes as substantial what are in fact only linguistic fictions'. Poetry, however metaphorical, is liable to be 'read literally', and realistic writing, however metonymic, is open to 'a correct figurative reading which sees it as fiction rather than *mimesis*'. It can be argued that Miller here falls into the vice of incomplete reversal of a metaphysical hierarchy (literal/figurative). By talking about a 'correct interpretation' and a 'misinterpretation' he exposes himself to the anti-deconstructive arguments of Gerald Graff (*Literature Against Itself*, 1979), who objects that Miller 'forecloses the very possibility of language's referring to the world' and therefore implies that every text (not just Dickens's) calls its own assumptions into question.

Barbara Johnson's *The Critical Difference* (1980) contains subtle and lucid deconstructive readings of literature and criticism. She shows that both literary and critical texts set up 'a network of differences into which the reader is lured with a promise of comprehension'. For example, in *S/Z* Barthes identifies and dismantles the masculine/feminine 'difference' in Balzac's *Sarrasine* (see above, pp. 133–6). By cutting up the novella into lexias Barthes appears to resist any total reading of the text's meaning in terms of sexuality. Johnson shows that Barthes' reading nevertheless privileges 'castration', and, further, that his distinction between the 'readerly' and the 'writerly' text corresponds to Balzac's distinction between the ideal woman (Zambinella as conceived by Sarrasine) and the castrato (Zambinella in actuality). Thus Zambinella resembles both the perfect unity of the readerly text and the fragmented and undecidable writerly text. Barthes' method of reading evidently favours 'castration' (cutting up). Sarrasine's image of Zambinella is based upon narcissism: her perfection (perfect woman) is the symmetrical counterpart of Sarrasine's masculine self-image. That is, Sarrasine loves 'the image of the lack of what he thinks he himself possesses'. Oddly enough, the castrato is 'simultaneously outside the difference between the sexes as well as representing the literalization of its illusory symmetry'. In this way Zambinella destroys Sarrasine's reassuring masculinity by showing that it is based on castration. Johnson's essential point about Barthes' reading of Balzac is that Barthes actually spells out the fact of castration where Balzac leaves it unspoken. In this way Barthes reduces a 'difference' to an 'identity'. Johnson makes this point not as a criticism of Barthes but as an illustration of the inevitable blindness of critical insight (to use de Man's terms).

DISCOURSE AND POWER: MICHEL FOUCAULT

There is another strand in poststructuralist thought which believes that the world is more than a galaxy of texts, and that some theories of textuality ignore the fact that discourse is involved in *power*. They reduce political and economic forces, and ideological and social control, to aspects of signifying processes. When a Hitler or a Stalin seems to dictate to an entire nation by wielding the power of discourse, it is absurd to treat the effect as simply occurring within discourse. It is evident that real power is exercised through discourse, and that this power has real effects.

The father of this line of thought is the German philosopher Nietzsche, who said that people first decide what they want and then fit the facts to their aim: 'Ultimately, man finds in things nothing but what he himself has imported into them.' All knowledge is an expression of the 'Will to Power'. This means that we cannot speak of any absolute truths or of objective knowledge. People recognise a particular piece of philosophy or scientific theory as 'true' only if it fits the descriptions of truth laid down by the intellectual or political authorities of the day, by the members of the ruling elite, or by the prevailing ideologues of knowledge.

Like other poststructuralists Foucault regards discourse as a central human activity, but not as a universal, 'general text', a vast sea of signification. He is interested in the historical dimension of discursive *change*. What it is possible to say will change from one era to another. In science a theory is not recognised in its own period if it does not conform to the power consensus of the institutions and official organs of science. Mendel's genetic theories fell on deaf ears in the 1860s; they were promulgated in a 'void' and had to wait until the twentieth century for acceptance. It is not enough to speak the truth; one must be 'in the truth'.

In his early work on 'madness' Foucault found it difficult to find examples of 'mad' discourse (except in literature: de Sade, Artaud). He deduced that the rules and procedures which determine what is considered normal or rational successfully silence what they exclude. Individuals working within particular discursive practices cannot think or speak without obeying the unspoken 'archive' of rules and constraints; otherwise they risk being condemned to madness or silence (Foucault's relevance to feminism and to postcolonial theory is apparent here). This discursive mastery works not just by exclusion, but also by 'rarefaction' (each practice narrows its content and meaning by thinking only in terms of 'author' and 'discipline'). Finally, there are the social constraints, especially the formative power of the education system, which defines what is rational and scholarly.

Foucault's books, especially *Madness and Civilization* (1961), *The Birth of the Clinic* (1963), *The Order of Things* (1966), *Discipline and Punish* (1975) and *The History of Sexuality* (1976), show that various forms of 'knowledge' about sex, crime, psychiatry and medicine have arisen and been replaced. He concentrates on the fundamental shifts occurring between epochs. He offers no period generalisations, but traces the overlapping series of discontinuous fields. History is this disconnected range of discursive practices. Each practice is a set of rules and procedures governing writing and thinking in a particular field. These rules govern by exclusion and regulation. Taken together the fields form a culture's 'archive', its 'positive Unconscious'.

Although the policing of knowledge is often associated with individual names (Aristotle, Plato, Aquinas, Locke, and so on), the set of structural rules which inform the various fields of knowledge is quite beyond any individual consciousness. The regulation of specific disciplines involves very refined rules for running institutions, training initiates and transmitting knowledge. The Will-to-Knowledge exhibited in this regulation is an impersonal force. We can never know our own era's archive because it is the Unconscious from which we speak. We can understand an earlier archive only because we are utterly different and remote from it. For example, when we read the literature of the Renaissance, we often notice the richness and exuberance of its verbal play. In *The Order of Things* Foucault shows that in this period *resemblance* played a central role in the structure of all knowledges. Everything echoed everything else; nothing stood on its own. We see this vividly in the poetry of John Donne, whose mind never rests on an object but moves back and forth from spiritual to physical, human to divine, and universal to individual. In his *Devotions* he describes in cosmic terms the symptoms of the fever that almost killed him, linking the microcosm (man) and the macrocosm (universe): his tremblings are 'earthquakes', his faintings are 'eclipses' and his feverish breath 'blazing stars'. From our modern standpoint we can see the various kinds of correspondence which shape Renaissance discourses, but the writers themselves saw and thought *through* them and therefore could not see them as we see them.

Following Nietzsche Foucault denies that we can ever possess an objective knowledge of history. Historical writing will always become entangled in tropes; it can never be a science. Jeffrey Mehlman's *Revolution and Repetition* (1979) shows how Marx's *Eighteenth Brumaire* presents the 'revolution' of Louis Napoleon as a 'farcical repetition' of his uncle's revolution. Marx's historical account, according to Mehlman, acknowledges the impossibility of knowledge; there is only the absurd trope of 'repetition'. However, Foucault does not treat the strategies writers use to make sense of history as merely textual play. Such discourses are produced within a real world of power struggle. In politics, art, and science, power is gained through discourse: discourse is 'a violence that we do to things'. Claims to objectivity made on behalf of specific discourses are always spurious: there are no absolutely 'true' discourses, only more or less powerful ones. (Some account of the work of Foucault's most significant American disciple, Edward Said, will be found in the section on 'Postcolonialism', pp. 190–3 below.)

NEW HISTORICISM

During the 1980s the dominance of deconstruction in the United States was challenged by a new theory and practice of literary history. While most poststructuralists are sceptical about attempts to recover historical 'truth', the New Historicists believe that Foucault's work opens the way to a new and non-truth-oriented form of historicist study of texts. A parallel development has occurred in Britain, but the influence of Foucault is there enriched by Marxist and feminist accents.

Throughout the nineteenth century there ran side by side two contradictory approaches to literary history. One presented it as a series of isolated monuments, achievements of individual genius. The other was 'historicist', and saw literary history as part of a larger cultural history. Historicism was the offspring of Hegelian idealism, and, later, of the evolutionary naturalism of Herbert Spencer. Several major 'historicists' studied literature in the context of social, political and cultural history. They saw a nation's literary history as an expression of its evolving 'spirit'. Thomas Carlyle summed up their view when he wrote: 'The history of a nation's poetry is the essence of its history, political, scientific, religious' (*Edinburgh Review*, 53, no. 105, 1831).

In 1943 E. M. W. Tillyard published an extremely influential historicist account of the culture of Shakespeare's period – *The Elizabethan World Picture*. He argued, in Hegelian fashion, that the literature of the period expressed the spirit of the age, which centred on ideas of divine order, the chain of being and the correspondences between earthly and heavenly existences. For Tillyard Elizabethan culture was a seamlessly unified system of meanings, which could not be disturbed by unorthodox or dissenting voices. He believed that the Elizabethans regarded 'disorder' as completely outside the divinely ordained norm, and that deviant figures such as Christopher Marlowe never seriously challenged the settled world-view of the age. This idealist mode of historical thought is captured by J. G. Farrell in *The Singapore Grip* (1979), in which Walter Blackett, chairman of the imperialistic merchant house of Blackett and Webb, tries vainly to understand the collapse of Malaya and of his enterprise during the Second World War:

> Certainly, it was not easy to see a common principle in the great mass of events occurring at any moment far and near. . . . He believed that each individual event in a historical moment was subtly modified by an intangible mechanism which he could only think of as 'the spirit of the time'. If a Japanese bomber had opened its bomb doors over Singapore in the year 1920 no bomb would have struck the city. Its bombs would have been lodged in a transparent roof that covered Singapore like a bubble. . . . The spirit of these times, unfortunately, allowed the bombs of an Asiatic nation to fall on a British city.

The New Historicists, like Tillyard, try to establish the interconnections between the literature and the general culture of a period. However, in every other respect they depart from Tillyard's approach. The poststructuralist intellectual revolution of the 1960s and 1970s challenges the older historicism on several grounds and establishes a new set of assumptions:

1. There are two meanings of the word 'history': (a) 'the events of the past' and (b) 'telling a story about the events of the past'. Poststructualist thought makes it clear that history is always 'narrated', and that therefore the first sense is untenable. The past can never be available to us in pure form, but always in the form of 'representations'; after poststructuralism, history becomes textualised.

2. Historical periods are not unified entities. There is no single 'history', only discontinuous and contradictory 'histories'. There was no single Elizabethan world-view. The idea of a uniform and harmonious culture is a myth imposed on history and propagated by the ruling classes in their own interests.

3. Historians can no longer claim that their study of the past is detached and objective. We cannot transcend our own historical situation. The past is not something which confronts us as if it were a physical object, but is something

we construct from already written texts of all kinds which we construe in line with our particular historical concerns.
4. The relations between literature and history must be rethought. There is no stable and fixed 'history' which can be treated as the 'background' against which literature can be foregrounded. All history (histories) is 'foreground'. 'History' is always a matter of telling a story about the past, using other texts as our intertexts. 'Non-literary' texts produced by lawyers, popular writers, theologians, scientists and historians should not be treated as belonging to a different order of textuality. Literary works should not be regarded as sublime and transcendent expressions of the 'human spirit', but as texts among other texts. We cannot now accept that a privileged 'inner' world of 'great authors' is to be set against the background of an 'outer' world of ordinary history.

The New Historicists in America and their counterparts in Britain, the 'cultural materialists' (the term was borrowed from Raymond Williams by Jonathan Dollimore), have produced a substantial body of work on Renaissance literature and society. The two key influences on their work are Michel Foucault and Louis Althusser, according to whom human 'experience' is shaped by social institutions and specifically by ideological discourses. Both conceive ideology as actively constituted through social struggle, and both show how at another level dominant ideologies sustain and keep social divisions in place. Althusser's theory (see 'Discourse' above, and chapter 4) abandons the orthodox interpretation of ideology as 'false consciousness' in favour of a theory which situates ideology firmly within material institutions (political, juridical, educational, religious, and so on), and conceives ideology as a body of discursive practices which, when dominant, sustain individuals in their places as 'subjects' (subjects them). Every individual is 'interpellated' (or 'hailed') as a subject by a number of ideological discourses, which together serve the interests of the ruling classes. Foucault (see previous section) also emphasises that discourses are always rooted in social institutions. He shows that social and political power works through discourse. For example, certain dichotomies are imposed as definitive of human existence and are operated in ways which have direct effects on society's organisation. Discourses are produced in which concepts of madness, criminality, sexual abnormality, and so on are defined in relation to concepts of sanity, justice and sexual normality. Such discursive formations massively determine and constrain the forms of knowledge, the types of 'normality' and the nature of 'subjectivity' which prevail in particular periods. For example, Foucauldians talk about the emergence of the 'soul' or the 'privatisation of the body' as 'events' produced by the bourgeois culture which arose during the seventeenth century. The discursive practices have no universal validity but are historically dominant ways of controlling and preserving social relations of exploitation.

These ideas have revolutionised the study of romantic and especially Renaissance literature. The New Historicists Stephen Greenblatt, Louis Montrose, Jonathan Goldberg, Stephen Orgel and Leonard Tennenhouse explore the ways in which Elizabethan literary texts (especially drama, masque and pastoral) act out the concerns of the Tudor monarchy, reproducing and renewing the powerful discourses which sustain the system. They see the monarchy as the central axis governing the power structure. While some Americans have dissented from this rather 'functionalist' version of Foucault, American New Historicists have been widely associated with a pessimistic understanding of discursive power in literary representations of the Elizabethan and Jacobean social order. They suggest that, even though many of Shakespeare's plays give voice to subversive ideas, such questionings of the prevalent social order are always 'contained' within the terms of the discourses which hold that social order in place. Falstaff's resistance to monarchic order, for example, is in the end a valuable negative model for Hal, who is thereby enabled more effectively to reject Falstaff's disorderly challenge to normality and to assume kingly power. Greenblatt often thinks of subversion as an expression of an inward necessity: we define our identities always in relation to what we are not, and therefore what we are not (our Falstaffs) must be demonised and objectified as 'others'. The mad, the unruly and the alien are internalised 'others' which help us to consolidate our identities: their existence is allowed only as evidence of the rightness of established power. Greenblatt concludes pessimistically in his 'Epilogue' to *Renaissance Self-Fashioning* (1980): 'In all my texts and documents, there were, so far as I could tell, no moments of pure, unfettered subjectivity; indeed, the human subject itself began to seem remarkably unfree, the ideological product of the relations of power in a particular society.' Such a view, in the context of contemporary American society, is an expression of the 'politics' of cultural despair.

British 'cultural materialists', under the influence of Althusser and Mikhail Bakhtin (see chapters 4 and 2, respectively and 'Discourse' above), have developed a less pessimistic and more politically radical type of historicism, and have challenged the 'functionalism' of Greenblatt. They see Foucault as implying a more precarious and unstable structure of power, and they often aim to derive from his work a history of 'resistances' to dominant ideologies. Jonathan Dollimore, Alan Sinfield, Catherine Belsey, Francis Barker and others have adopted some of the theoretical refinements to be found in Raymond Williams's *Marxism and Literature* (1977, see p. 91), especially his distinction between 'residual', 'dominant' and 'emergent' aspects of culture. By replacing the Tillyardian concept of a single spirit of the age with Williams's more dynamic model of culture, they have freed a space for the exploration of the complex totality of Renaissance society including its subversive and marginalised elements. They assert that every history of subjection also contains a history of resistance, and that resistance is not just a symptom of and justification for subjection but is the true mark of an ineradicable 'difference' (see Derrida above) which always prevents power from closing the door on change. A further important concern of Dollimore and others is with the 'appropriations' of Renaissance cultural representations which occurred at the time and subsequently. (See *PTRL*, chapter 4, section 13, for a fuller discussion of – more particularly British – New Historicism as applied to Shakespeare's *Measure For Measure*.) The meanings of literary texts are never entirely fixed by some universal criterion, but are always in play, and subject to specific (often politically radical) appropriations, including those of the cultural materialists themselves. Catherine Belsey has used the more neutral term 'cultural history' to describe her lively and political view of the task ahead. She urges the new history to adopt the perspective of 'change, cultural difference and the relativity of truth', and to give priority to the 'production of alternative knowledges' and 'alternative subject positions'.

Some of the theoretical tools which Belsey's programme requires have been developed in Michel Pêcheux's *Language, Semantics and Ideology* (1975). He combines Althusserian Marxism, modern linguistics and psychoanalysis in an attempt to develop a new theory of discourse and ideology. Althusser had described the process of 'interpellation' by which subjects identify with the discourses embedded in particular ideological state apparatuses. Pêcheux recognises the need to develop the theory in ways which allow for the subject's possible *resistance* to the discursive formations which transmit ideological positions. It may be true that religious ideology works by interpellating individuals as God's subjects. However, we also need terms to describe the negative or subversive response of atheists and new religionists. Pêcheux solves this problem by proposing three types of subject:

1. The 'good subject', who 'freely' accepts the image of self which is projected by the discourse in question in an act of total 'identification' ('At last I have found my true self').
2. The 'bad subject', who refuses the identity offered by discourse in an act of 'counter-identification' ('Sorry, I don't believe any of that').
3. The subject who adopts a 'third modality' by transforming the subject position which is offered in an act of 'disidentification' ('I don't believe in that sort of god').

American New Historicists tend to see power structures as permitting only identification and counter-identification. British exponents belong to a politically more radical tradition, and they are much more interested in the possibility of subjects not only refusing offered subject positions but actually producing new ones.

The work of Mikhail Bakhtin (see chapter 2) has been used by some New Historicists as a way of escaping the apparent structural closure of Foucault's historical theory. Michael Bristol's *Carnival and Theater: Plebeian Culture and the Structure of*

Authority in Renaissance England (1985) uses Bakhtin's concept of 'Carnival' in order to introduce a more open model of cultural production. He argues that Greenblatt and Dollimore fail to recognise the vitality and power of popular culture in the Elizabethan period. Bakhtin regards 'Carnival' as a 'second culture', which was opposed to the official culture, and which was carried on by the common people throughout the middle ages and well into the early modern period. Bakhtin's idea that Carnival inserts into official structures 'an indeterminacy, a certain semantic open-endedness' could well provide one way of describing how subjects might respond to dominant discourses through the modalities of 'counter-identification' or even 'disidentification'. Bristol summarises the potentially subversive mode of Carnival as follows: 'By bringing privileged symbols and officially authorised concepts into a crudely familiar relationship with common everyday experience, Carnival achieves a transformation downward or "uncrowning" of de jure relations of dependency, expropriation and social discipline.' Of course some Foucauldians would reply that Carnival is also an officially permitted and carefully controlled expression of subversion which by its ritualised form only confirms the power of the authority it mocks.

As we have seen, the term 'New Historicism' covers a wide range of approaches to the study of literature and history. As might be expected these new approaches have questioned the received canon of literary works in orthodox literary histories, often in conjunction with feminist or postcolonialist criticism. Recently this challenge has been made in the area of American Studies in works by Sacvan Bercovitch, Myra Jehlen, Philip Fisher and Henry Louis Gates, Jr (see below, chapter 7, p. 192, for a brief discussion of Gates). In discussing the canon of nineteenth-century American literature, New Historicists such as Jane Tomkins and Cathy Davidson have drawn attention to popular and genre fiction. The sentimental novel, for example, says Tomkins, 'offers a critique of American society far more devastating than any delivered by better-known critics such as Hawthorne and Melville'. At the same time, however, it has been argued that in much New Historicist criticism, challenges to the canon have involved 'less the detection of its "others" . . . than a repeated challenging of the familiar privileged texts which, while throwing them into a new perspective, leaves the canon itself pretty much intact'. Once more, British cultural materialism is thought to present a more decisive challenge, opening up postwar British popular culture and society to a politicised analysis in areas where New Historicist techniques are enlisted by Cultural Studies. The British tradition has tried to differentiate itself from what it sees as a limited American reading of Foucault. However, in the work of Jonathan Goldberg and others, there is a rich fusion of radical currents of historicist thought which suggests the possibility of converging Anglo-American streams. The development of the new literary history has also meant that the former dominance of deconstruction in the United States can no longer be assumed, and a great deal of interesting new work (by Jonathan Culler, Cynthia Chase, Christopher Norris and others) recognises that deconstruction must respond to the challenge of the Foucauldian and Althusserian types of new history.

Structuralist critics set out to master the text and to open its secrets. Poststructuralists believe that this desire is vain because there are unconscious, or linguistic, or historical forces which cannot be mastered. The signifier floats away from the signified, *jouissance* dissolves meaning, the semiotic disrupts the symbolic, *différance* inserts a gap between signifier and signified, and power disorganises established knowledge. Poststructuralists ask questions rather than give answers; they seize upon the differences between what the text says and what it thinks it says. They set the text to work against itself, and refuse to force it to mean one thing only. They deny the separateness of 'literature', and deconstruct non-literary discourses by reading them as themselves rhetorical texts. We may be irritated by the poststructuralists' failure to arrive at conclusions, but they are only being consistent in their attempts to avoid logocentrism. However, as they often admit, their desire to resist assertions is itself doomed to failure because only by saying nothing could they prevent us from thinking that they mean something. Even to summarise their views itself implies their failure. Nevertheless, Foucault and the New Historicists initiate a new kind of intertextual historical theory which is inevitably an interventionist one since it assists in remaking the past. In cultural materialism a commitment to transgressive and oppositional voices becomes more explicit. As such, while it draws upon poststructuralism, it questions the claims of some versions of it to liberate an innocent free play of meanings.

SELECTED READING

Basic texts

Barthes, Roland, *S/Z* (1970), trans. R. Miller (Hill & Wang, New York; Jonathan Cape, London, 1975a).

Barthes, Roland, *The Pleasure of the Text*, trans. R. Miller (Hill & Wang, New York, 1975b).

Barthes, Roland, 'The Death of the Author' in *Image-Music-Text*, trans. S. Heath (Hill & Wang, New York; Fontana, London, 1977).

Bloom, Harold, *The Anxiety of Influence: A Theory of Poetry* (Oxford University Press, New York and London, 1973).

Bloom, Harold, *A Map of Misreading* (Oxford University Press, New York, Toronto, Melbourne, 1975).

Deleuze, Gilles and Guattari, Félix, *Anti-Oedipus: Capitalism and Schizophrenia* (1972) (Viking Press, New York, 1977).

Deleuze, Gilles and Guattari, Félix, *Kafka: Pour une littérature mineure* (Les Editions de Minuit, Paris, 1975).

de Man, Paul, *Blindness and Insight: Essays in the Rhetoric of Contemporary Criticism* (Oxford University Press, New York, 1971).

de Man, Paul, *Allegories of Reading: Figural Language in Rousseau, Nietzsche, Rilke, and Proust* (Yale University Press, New Haven, 1979).

de Man, Paul, *The Rhetoric of Romanticism* (Columbia University Press, New York, 1984).

de Man, Paul, *The Resistance to Theory* (1986) (Manchester University Press, Manchester, 1987).

Derrida, Jacques, *Of Grammatology*, trans. G. C. Spivak (Johns Hopkins University Press, Baltimore, 1976). The translator's preface is useful.

Derrida, Jacques, 'Signature Event Context', *Glyph*, vol. 1 (1977), 172–97.

Derrida, Jacques, *Writing and Difference*, trans. Alan Bass (Routledge, London, 1978).

Derrida, Jacques, *The Post-Card: From Socrates to Freud and Beyond*, trans. Alan Bass (Chicago University Press, Chicago, 1987).

Foucault, Michel, *Language, Counter-Memory, Practice, Selected Essays and Interviews*, ed. D. F. Bouchard (Basil Blackwell, Oxford; Cornell University Press, Ithaca, 1977).

Foucault, Michel, *The Foucault Reader*, ed. Paul Rabinov (Penguin, Harmondsworth, 1986).

Harari, Josué V. (ed.), *Textual Strategies: Perspectives in Post-Structuralist Criticism* (Cornell University Press, Ithaca, 1979).

Hartman, Geoffrey H., *Criticism in the Wilderness* (Johns Hopkins University Press, Baltimore and London, 1980).

Hartman, Geoffrey, *Saving the Text: Literature/Derrida/Philosophy* (Johns Hopkins University Press, Baltimore, 1981).

Hartman, Geoffrey, *Easy Pieces* (Columbia University Press, New York, 1985).

Johnson, Barbara, *The Critical Difference: Essays in the Contemporary Rhetoric of Reading* (Johns Hopkins University Press, Baltimore and London, 1980).

Kristeva, Julia, *The Kristeva Reader*, ed. Toril Moi (Basil Blackwell, Oxford, 1986).

Lacan, Jacques, *Ecrits: A Selection*, trans. A. Sheridan (Tavistock, London, 1977).

Laplanche, Jean and Pontalis, Jean-Baptiste, *The Language of Psycho-Analysis*, trans. D. Nicholson-Smith (Hogarth Press, London, 1973).

Miller, J. Hillis, *Fiction and Repetition: Seven English Novels* (Harvard University Press, Cambridge, Mass., 1982).

Miller, J. Hillis, *The Ethics of Reading: Kant, de Man, Eliot, Trollope, James and Benjamin* (Columbia University Press, New York, 1987).

Miller, J. Hillis, *Victorian Subjects* (Harvester Wheatsheaf, Hemel Hempstead, 1990a).

Miller, J. Hillis, *Tropes, Parables and Performatives: Essays on Twentieth-Century Literature* (Harvester Wheatsheaf, Hemel Hempstead, 1990b).

Ryan, Michael, *Marxism and Deconstruction: A Critical Articulation* (Johns Hopkins University Press, Baltimore and London, 1982).

Young, Robert (ed.), *Untying the Text: A Post-Structuralist Reader* (Routledge & Kegan Paul, Boston, London and Henley, 1981).

Introductions

Allen, Graham, *Harold Bloom* (Harvester Wheatsheaf, Hemel Hempstead, forthcoming 1993).

Atkins, G. Douglas, *Geoffrey Hartman* (Routledge, London, 1990).

Bercovitch, Sacvan (ed.), *Reconstructing American Literary History* (Harvard University Press, Cambridge, Mass., 1986).

Bercovitch, Sacvan and Jehlen, Myra (eds), *Ideology and Classic American Literature* (Cambridge University Press, Cambridge, 1986).

Bogue, Ronald, *Deleuze and Guattari* (Routledge, London, 1989).

Culler, Jonathan, *Barthes* (Fontana, London, 1983).

Dollimore, Jonathan and Sinfield, Alan (eds), *Political Shakespeare: New Essays in Cultural Materialism* (Manchester University Press, Manchester, 1985), 'Introduction'.

Easthope, Anthony, *British Post-Structuralism: Since 1968* (Routledge, London, 1991).

Fisher, Philip (ed.), *The New American Studies* (California University Press, Berkeley, 1991).

Goldberg, Jonathan, 'The Politics of Renaissance Literature: A Review Essay', *ELH*, vol. 49 (1982), 514–42.

Greenblatt, Stephen, *Renaissance Self-Fashioning: from More to Shakespeare* (University of Chicago Press, Chicago, 1980).

Greenblatt, Stephen, *Representing the English Renaissance* (California University Press, Berkeley, 1991a).

Greenblatt, Stephen, *Shakespearean Negotiations: The Circulation of Social Energy in Renaissance England* (California University Press, Berkeley, 1991b).

Howard, Jean E., 'The New Historicism in Renaissance Studies', *English Literary Renaissance*, vol. 16 (1986), 13–43.

Howard, Jean E. and O'Connor, Marion F. (eds), *Shakespeare Reproduced: The Text in History and Ideology* (Methuen, New York, 1987).

Jefferson, Ann, 'Structuralism and Post-structuralism' in *Modern Literary Theory: A Comparative Introduction*, A. Jefferson and D. Robey (eds) (Batsford, London, 2nd edn, 1986), pp. 104–11.

Lechte, John, *Julia Kristeva* (Routledge, London, 1990).

Leitch, Vincent B., *Deconstructive Criticism: An Advanced Introduction* (Hutchinson, London, Melbourne, 1983).

Mapp, Nigel, 'Deconstruction' in *Encyclopaedia of Literature and Criticism*, Martin Coyle, Peter Garside, Malcolm Kelsall and John Peck (eds) (Routledge, London, 1990).

Norris, Christopher, *Derrida* (Fontana, London, 1987).

Norris, Christopher, *Deconstruction: Theory and Practice* (Routledge, London, 2nd edn, 1991).

Rylance, Rick, *Roland Barthes* (Harvester Wheatsheaf, Hemel Hempstead, forthcoming 1993).

Sarup, Madan, *An Introductory Guide to Post-Structuralism and Postmodernism* (Harvester Wheatsheaf, Hemel Hempstead, 1988).

Sarup, Madan, *Jacques Lacan* (Harvester Wheatsheaf, Hemel Hempstead, 1992).

Sturrock, J. (ed.), *Structuralism and Since: From Lévi-Strauss to Derrida* (Oxford University Press, Oxford, 1979).

Veeser, H. Aram (ed.), *The New Historicism* (Routledge, London, 1989).

Wayne, Don E., 'New Historicism' in *Encyclopaedia of Literature and Criticism*, Martin Coyle, Peter Garside, Malcolm Kelsall and John Peck (eds) (Routledge, London, 1990).

White, Hayden, *Tropics of Discourse: Essays in Cultural Criticism* (Johns Hopkins University Press, Baltimore, 1978).

Wilson, Richard and Sutton, Richard (eds), *New Historicism and Renaissance Drama* (Longman, London, 1991).

Wiseman, Mary, *Ecstasies of Roland Barthes* (Routledge, London, 1989).

Wright, Elizabeth, *Psychoanalytic Criticism: Theory in Practice* (Methuen, London and New York, 1984).

Wright, Elizabeth, 'Psychoanalytic Criticism' in *Encyclopaedia of Literature and Criticism*, Martin Coyle, Peter Garside, Malcolm Kelsall and John Peck (eds) (Routledge, London, 1990).

Further reading

Aers, Lesley and Wheale, Nigel, *Shakespeare and the Changing Curriculum* (Routledge, London, 1991).

Atkins, G. Douglas, *Reading Deconstruction: Deconstructive Reading* (University Press of Kentucky, Lexington, 1983).

Belsey, Catherine, *Critical Practice* (Routledge, London, 1980).

Belsey, Catherine, *The Subject of Tragedy: Identity and Difference in Renaissance Drama* (Methuen, London, 1985).

Bristol, Michael, *Carnival and Theater: Plebeian Culture and the Structure of Authority in Renaissance England* (Methuen, London, 1985).

Coward, Rosalind and Ellis, John, *Language and Materialism: Developments in Semiology and the Theory of the Subject* (Routledge & Kegan Paul, London, 1977).

Culler, Jonathan, *On Deconstruction: Theory and Criticism after Structuralism* (Routledge & Kegan Paul, London, 1983).

Davis, Robert Con (ed.), *The Fiction of the Father: Lacanian Readings of the Text* (University of Massachusetts Press, Amherst, 1981).

de Bolla, Peter, *Harold Bloom: Towards Historical Rhetorics* (Routledge, London, 1988).

Dews, Peter, *Logics of Disintegration: Post-Structuralist Thought and the Claims of Critical Theory* (New Left Books, London, 1987).

Drakakis, John (ed.), *Shakespearean Tragedy* (Longman, London, 1991).

During, Simon, *Foucault and Literature: Towards a Genealogy of Writing* (Routledge, London, 1992).

Felman, Shoshana (ed.), *Literature and Psychoanalysis: The Question of Reading – Otherwise* (Johns Hopkins University Press, Baltimore, 1982).

Healy, Thomas, *New Latitudes: Theory and English Renaissance Literature* (Arnold, London, 1992).

Lavers, Annette, *Roland Barthes: Structuralism and After* (Methuen, London, 1982).

Lentricchia, Frank, *After the New Criticism* (Athlone Press, London, 1980). Favours Foucault and Said.

MacCabe, Colin, *The Talking Cure: Essays in Psychoanalysis and Language* (Macmillan, London and Basingstoke, 1981).

MacCannell, Juliet Flower, *Figuring Lacan: Criticism and the Cultural Unconscious* (Routledge, London, 1986).

Michaels, Walter Benn and Pease, Donald (eds), *The American Renaissance Reconsidered* (Johns Hopkins University Press, Baltimore, 1985).

Mitchell, Juliet and Rose, Jacqueline (eds and trans), *Femininity and Sexuality: Jacques Lacan, the Ecole Freudienne* (Macmillan, London, 1982).

Norris, Christopher, *The Deconstructive Turn: Essays in the Rhetoric of Philosophy* (Methuen, London and New York, 1983).

Pêcheux, Michel, *Language, Semantics and Ideology* (1975), trans. H. Nagpal (St. Martin's Press, New York, 1982).

Salusinsky, Imre, *Criticism in Society* (Methuen, New York and London, 1987). Interviews with Derrida, Hartman, Said and others.

Silverman, Hugh J. (ed.), *Derrida and Deconstruction* (Routledge, New York, 1989).

Sinfield, Alan, *Literature, Politics and Culture in Postwar Britain* (Basil Blackwell, Oxford, 1989).

Taylor, Mark C. (ed.), *Deconstruction in Context: Literature and Philosophy* (Chicago University Press, Chicago, 1986).

Tompkins, Jane, *Sensational Designs: The Cultural Work of American Fiction, 1790–1860* (Oxford University Press, London and New York, 1985).

A debate on cultural materialism, between Catherine Belsey and Alan Sinfield and Jonathan Dollimore, appears in *Textual Practice*, vol. 3 (1989), 159–72, and vol. 4 (1990), 91–100.

7 Postmodernist and postcolonialist theories

POSTMODERNISM

During the last twenty years and more, critics and cultural historians have debated the term 'postmodernism'. Some see it as simply the continuation and development of modernist ideas, others have seen in postmodern art a radical break with classical modernism, while others again view past literature and culture retrospectively through postmodern eyes, identifying texts and authors (de Sade, Borges, the Ezra Pound of *The Cantos*) as 'already' postmodern. Yet another argument, associated principally with the philosopher and social theorist Jürgen Habermas, claims that the project of modernity – which here designates the philosophical, social and political values of reason, equality and justice derived from the Enlightenment – is as yet unfulfilled and should not be relinquished. This position also relates to the debate over the continuing relevance (or redundancy) of Marxism, as well as that of modernist art works. Where the project of modernity is defended (with or without an accompanying defence of artistic modernism), this is in the face of the leading contentions of postmodernism that: first, the 'grand narratives' of historical progress initiated by the Enlightenment are discredited; and second, any political grounding of these ideas in 'history' or 'reality' is no longer possible, since both have become 'textualised' in the world of images and simulations which characterise the contemporary age of mass consumption and advanced technologies.

These latter positions comprise the two major 'narratives' of what constitutes postmodernism, and which other comment-ators concur with or refuse to varying degrees. They have raised broad philosophical, aesthetic and ideological questions of interest to a range of academic disciplines (philosophy, social and political theory, sociology, art history, architecture, and urban, media and cultural studies) and forms of cultural production (architecture, film and video, pop and rock music) as well as literary theory and criticism, and they may connect also with what has been said above (see chapter 6) on the relations between structuralism and poststructuralism. Despite the diversity of trends within each movement there is no doubt that poststructuralist thought is to some extent a body of reflections upon the same issues which concern commentators on post-modern literature and culture such as Ihab Hassan, Fredric Jameson and Linda Hutcheon. We will make no attempt to elaborate the differences of interpretation, but rather will try to bring into view those aspects of postmodernism which resemble poststructuralist thinking.

Peter Brooker offers the following succinct account of the development of the term postmodernism:

Since the first uses of the term in the late 1950s and early 1960s, 'postmodernism' has acquired an amoebic range of attributions and meanings, in academic debate and in journalism. In general terms it can be said to describe a mood or condition of radical indeterminacy, and a tone of self-conscious, parodic scepticism towards previous certainties in personal, intellectual and political life. Thus in its two most influential arguments, associated with J-F Lyotard and Jean Baudrillard [see below], it is felt that the 'grand narratives' of human progress and liberation, rooted in Enlightenment thought, have lost credibility; and that a culture of detached media images has come to suffocate and out clone the 'real world', ousting old-fashioned worries about the relationship of the image to the real. This wide and double crisis of legitimacy and representation has thrown everything in the air. And, not surprisingly, the term 'postmodern-ism' itself has become airborne. Loosened from the fixed categories and hierarchies which held art and culture still, yet full of a lack of confidence in rational thought and consensus, it goes slaloming across the forms, media and discourses it means to survey. It is difficult, consequently, to pin down.

What is more, 'postmodernism' is used both as a descriptive and an evaluative term, and not always of the same phenomena. The trio of terms postmodern, postmodernity and postmodernism are thus all used as a way of periodising (usually post-war) developments in capitalist economies and societies; to describe developments across or within the arts (which do not necessarily synchronise with the first set of developments or with each other); but also to signal an attitude or position on these developments. And these can settle anywhere from fervid evangelicalism or faddish knowingness to resignation or resistance. Furthermore, as a relational term, *post-modernism* is seen either as a continuation of, or break with, dominant features in modernism or the avant garde, about which there is also naturally much debate.

Whatever else, these earlier terms are inescapable in any discussion of postmodernism . . . The first thing we ought to appreciate, then, is that modernism has been culturally specific; or rather, that the term has been employed far more regularly in discussions of Anglo-American than of European art movements. In England and America, modernism came to designate a particular set of authors: T. S. Eliot, Ezra Pound, Joyce, Woolf, Faulkner, Wallace Stevens, ringed by minor, that is to say, awkward and hence marginalised, figures such as W. C. Williams, Wyndham Lewis, Gertrude Stein, H. D. and others. In the face of the experience of modernity (technological and economic change, political dissent, the fractured subjective experience of the modern metropolis), the arch-modernist Eliot sought to inscribe both this anomie and a new unity of consciousness and culture through the overarching controls of myth and tradition [see chapter 1, above]. This radical conservation then hardened through its representative figures into the hegemony of a self-incorporated modernism. By 1950 (the beginning of the decade which was to announce postmodernism) Eliot was, said F. R. Leavis, 'a public institution'.

. . . Anglo-American modernism was a cultural **construction**, around selective aesthetic and ideological values, and . . . needs to be distinguished from the historical avant garde: an unquestionably diverse set of movements (in Futurism, Dada, Cubism and Surrealism) which nevertheless shared an opposition to the institution of art and sought, under anarchist or communist or fascist inspiration, to establish a new productive engagement between art and the world. It is **this** tendency, the avant garde assault on artistic autonomy; a dehierarchisation of received relations between high and popular culture; an intermingling of genres and media, which it is argued has rematerialised as a feature of postmodern culture, made general now by the information explosion, global TV and film networks, the ubiquities of rock and pop and fashion styles. Art and literature (themselves conceptually unstable) are integrated into the world of social praxis, free at last of the prison-house of high culture. The price, say some, is that the political project of the historical avant garde has receded; for art is free now only to join the circulation of commodities, a further product and prop of a triumphant consumer capitalism. Across its spinning glassy surfaces of free choice and rapid turnover, single-minded political strategies can gain no hold. Yet another position would see postmodernism as straddling cultural and intellectual systems; a transitional mentality and condition, hooked to the fixities it unravels, by turns and by degrees complicit in, and critical of, them.

(from 'Postmodern Postpoetry' in *Contemporary Poetry Meets Modern Theory*, A. Easthope and J. Thompson (eds) (Harvester Wheatsheaf, Hemel Hempstead, 1991).

Several theorists draw attention to the way in which postmodern critics reject the elitism, sophisticated formal experimentation and tragic sense of alienation to be found in the modernist writers. Ihab Hassan, for example, contrasts modernist 'dehumanisation of Art' with the postmodernist sense of the 'dehumanisation of the Planet, and the End of Man'. While Joyce is 'omnipotent' in his impersonal mastery of art, Beckett is 'impotent' in his minimalist representations of endgames. Modernists remain tragically heroic, while postmodernists express exhaustion and 'display the resources of the void'. Hassan, in *Paracriticisms* (1975), provides suggestive lists of postmodernist footnotes on modernism. They include the following: 'Anti-elitism, anti-authoritarianism. Diffusion of the ego. Participation. Art becomes communal, optional, anarchic. Acceptance . . . At the same time, Irony becomes radical, self-consuming play, entropy of meaning.' As opposed to modernist experimentation, postmodernists produce 'Open, discontinuous, improvisational, indeterminate, or aleatory structures'. They also reject the traditional aesthetics of 'Beauty' and of 'uniqueness'. Echoing a famous essay by Susan Sontag, Hassan adds that they are 'Against interpretation'. (All these positions, as we have seen in chapter 6, are to be found in the various poststructuralist theorists.) If there is a summarising idea it is the theme of the absent centre. The postmodern experience is widely held to stem from a profound sense of *ontological uncertainty*. Human shock in the face of the unimaginable (pollution, holocaust, the death of the 'subject') results in a loss of fixed points of reference. Neither the world nor the self any longer possesses unity, coherence, meaning. They are radically 'decentred'.

This does not mean that postmodern fiction is all as lugubrious as Beckett's. As some theorists have seen, the decentring of language itself has produced a great deal of playful, self-reflexive and self-parodying fiction. Jorge Luis Borges is the master of this manner, and his writings parallel the poststructuralist verbal exuberance of Roland Barthes or J. Hillis Miller. The American authors John Barth and Ishmael Reed, for example, and the European writers Italo Calvino, Umberto Eco, Salman Rushdie and John Fowles are also invariably discussed as postmodernist. In some of these cases, and especially that of Eco, there is an explicit connection between critical theory and fiction. For Eco (semiotician, novelist and journalist), postmodernism is defined by its intertextuality and knowingness, and by its relation to the past – which postmodernism revisits at any historical moment with irony. His best-selling 'novel', *The Name of the Rose* (1980), is at once an example of the interpenetration of previously separated categories of fiction and non-fiction, and vertiginously historical: a detective thriller which mixes gothic suspense with chronicle and scholarship, intersects the medieval with the modern, and has a Chinese-box-like narrative structure, to produce a self-reflexively comic mystery about the suppression and recuperation of the 'carnivalesque' power of the comic itself. (Other examples of self-reflexive postmodernist metafiction where there is a convergence between fiction and theory are John Fowles's novels *The Magus, The French Lieutenant's Woman* and *Mantissa*.) Just as the poststructuralists deny the distinctions between the traditional orders of discourse (criticism, literature, philosophy, politics), leaving an amorphous universe – a 'general text' – so postmodernist writers break down every conceivable boundary of discourse by fusing forms and confusing different realms. Linda Hutcheon's work on contemporary fiction, for instance, has pursued the parodic and still critical mode that postmodernist literature can adopt in this broad textual universe: at once complicit *and* subversive. The self and history, she argues, are not lost in postmodernist fiction (which she terms 'historiographic metafiction'); they are but newly problematised. The self-conscious problematisation of the making of fiction and history is a prime characteristic of this for Hutcheon, in which intertextuality neither simply repudiates the past or ironises it, nor reproduces it as nostalgia. Rather, its use of irony and paradox signal a critical distance within the world of representations, raising questions not about *the* truth but *whose* truth, and about the ideological and discursive construction of the past. Hutcheon can retain a political function for this kind of fiction (*contra* many cultural commentators who see postmodernism generally and postmodernist fiction in particular as, by definition, apolitical) in so far as it both inscribes itself and also intervenes in a given discursive set. Patricia Waugh, in *Metafiction* (1984) and more recently in *Feminine Fictions: Revisiting the Postmodern* (1989), also explores these issues – in the latter case in relation to feminism and the potential for the representation of a new social subject in contemporary fiction.

The two most influential theories of postmodernism sketched above, however – concerning the dominance of the sign and loss of the real, and a scepticism towards the 'grand narratives' of human history and progress – are those advanced respectively by the French philosophers Jean Baudrillard and Jean-François Lyotard.

JEAN BAUDRILLARD: THE LOSS OF THE REAL

Baudrillard's early work questioned the tenets of both Marxism and structuralism. Having argued for the dominance in modern capitalist societies of consumption over production and of the signifier over the signified, Baudrillard has turned his attention in recent years to a critique of technology in the era of media reproduction, and has repudiated all models which distinguish between surface and depth.

Baudrillard's reworking of the themes of poststructuralism and of the French Situationists in the late 1970s and during the 1980s signalled a 'retreat from politics' by intellectuals of the left, and brought Baudrillard cult status. His increasingly apocalyptic and hyperbolic statements in this post-1970s period include the sensationalist messages of 'the loss of the real' and of the appearance of the culture of 'hyperreality', in which models determine yet undermine the real.

Baudrillard's influential book *Simulations* (first translated into English in 1983) is concerned with the depthless world of the 'simulacra'. In the epoch of 'simulation' reality is gone for good and we are left only with appearance. According to Baudrillard, there is no longer a 'real' external world to which signs can refer; there has been an 'implosion of image and reality'. This implosion, according to Neville Wakefield, leads 'into the simulated non-space of hyperreality. The "real" is now defined in terms of the media in which it moves.' It is the image-creating postmodern communication technologies – especially television – which proliferate self-generating, self-mirroring, depthless images. Experience everywhere, now superficial, achieves its final 'utopian' form in the instantaneous abundance and banality of the 'cultureless' society of the United States, quintessentially in Disneyland.

Baudrillard's later writings through the 1980s (for example, *Fatal Strategies, America, Cool Memories,* and the essays 'The Year 2000 Has Already Happened' and 'The Anorexic Ruins') are increasingly nihilistic. He sees postmodernity repeatedly in terms of the disappearance of meaning, of inertia, exhaustion and endings, whether of history or subjectivity. (Other contemporary writings, notably those of Francis Fukuyama, bear similarly on this theme of the 'end of history' following the fall of Communism.) For Baudrillard, everything is 'obscenely' on display, moving endlessly, transparently and literally superficially across a surface where there is no control or stabilising depth. His most provocative recent proposal has been that the Gulf War was not a real but a television war, a media event or spectacle: 'It is unreal, war without the symptoms of war.' He sees in this episode the operation of a 'logic of deterrence', from hot to cold war, and so to fighting over 'the corpse of war'. War is caught up in the process of postmodern simulation: 'TV is our strategic site, a gigantic simulator' which creates war's virtual reality. This view was attacked for its irresponsible sophistry by Christopher Norris, one of Baudrillard's most serious critics. His riposte appeared as the leading chapter in the volume *Uncritical Theory: Postmodernism, Intellectuals and the Gulf War* (1992). Here as elsewhere Norris argues, via the philosophical tradition of Frege, Donald Davidson and Habermas, for an alternative to the structuralist paradigm and the consequent scepticism of post-structuralism and postmodernism. Aside from a refutation of Baudrillard's exclusive world of signs, through an appeal to the common-sensical assurance that inequality, oppression, unemployment, urban decay, destruction and death in war are manifestly real forms of social experience, Norris proposes that presuppositions of truth and right reason are present in human discourse and conduct at all levels, and that these provide a basis for morality and political judgement. Other commentators read Baudrillard's later work with less patience: as simply flippant or, worse, insensitive and offensive; at the very least, as woefully under-theorised and politically without hope.

Baudrillard's writings have come to avoid the specifics of particular social, cultural or artistic forms, while pronouncing on them in a mode that can blend elegant *aperçu* with unfounded hyperbole; but what emerges, for society, theory and art, is the option to recombine, repeat, relaunch the scattered pieces of a (lost) past. Its implicit aesthetic is therefore that of pastiche (Baudrillard often seems engaged in self-pastiche), a notion developed by Fredric Jameson (see below). It most closely relates to the literature of the 'new wave' science-fiction writer J. G. Ballard or the cyberpunk fiction of William Gibson, Bruce Sterling and others (for Jameson 'the supreme literary expression' of postmodernism or late capitalism), as well as to a generation of feature films from *Blade Runner* to the *Terminator* series and *Universal Soldier*. In these fictions, in a parallel scenario to Baudrillard's view that humankind should surrender to the triumphant world of objects, human subjects and subjectivity are involved in a (mostly) losing battle with invasive postmodern technologies. Perhaps the most profitable way to read Baudrillard now is as an example of such 'speculative fiction'. His thoughts along these lines (in *Fatal Strategies*, 1983) provide a melancholy extreme against which to judge these other contemporary speculations and fictionalised anxieties about the end-of-millennium composition and fate of human agency.

JEAN-FRANÇOIS LYOTARD: THE END OF THE GRAND NARRATIVES

For fifteen years a member of a revolutionary Marxist group, Jean-François Lyotard in the 1960s began to question Marxism and to start his 'post-Marxist' investigations in philosophy, language and the arts. In *Discours, figure* (1971) he distinguished between the *seen*, the visual and three-dimensional (the 'figural'), and the *read*, the textual and two-dimensional (the 'discursive'). Lyotard finds here two regimes and sets of laws which the textualising structuralist and semiotic paradigms had ignored, rendering the spatial and visual realm of things too automatically or immediately into the flatness of text. In *Economie libidinale* (1974) Lyotard extended this critique to Marxism, advocating an alternative philosophy of desire, intensities and energetics indebted to Nietzsche. In its assumption that history is available to consciousness, Marxism is seen as emptying history of its materiality, filling the void thus created with a totalising narrative. Discursive consciousness is seen as submerging the figural world and its associated nexus of desire (in a theory close to that of Deleuze and Guattari: see above, chapter 6). This repression represents the mark of the 'modern', consequent upon the procedures of rationality and trailing the models of justice and civilisation which characterise modernity. Thomas Docherty has summarised this position:

> Capital, masculinism and so on – all the forms of a dominant ideological thought which characterises the modern world – depend upon the erasure of figurality and its premature transliteration into the form of discursivity. Modernity itself is based upon the foreclosure of the figure, of the depth of a reality, of the materiality of a historicity which is resistant to the categories of our understanding, but which we force or forge into the shapes of our discursive mental world.

As Docherty adds, what in modernity passes for understanding (the particular discursive mode of rational thinking) is, in this view, 'itself really a mastery or domination, not an understanding at all'.

Lyotard believes therefore that there is a level – the figural, marked by the flow and intensities of desire and its libidinal effects – which is plural, heterogenous and forced into unitary meaning by totalising reason. He is led to a valorisation of difference, of contrary repressed impulses, open to the multiple and incommensurable. This he then develops beyond a philosophy of vitalism to a philosophy of language and justice in texts of the 1980s (*Just Gaming*, 1985 and *The Differend*, 1983). Art which participates in this postmodern awareness of difference and heterogeneity will therefore critique and destabilise the closures of modernity. It will explore the 'unsayable' and 'invisible'.

Lyotard's *The Postmodern Condition* (1979), however, has proved the major focus for debates on cultural postmodernism. Drawing first on Nietzsche's critique that the totalising claims of reason, to argue for a social ethics based upon itself, are without moral or philosophical grounds (or 'legitimation'), and second on Wittgenstein, Lyotard argues that the criteria regulating the 'truth claims' of knowledge derive from discrete, context-dependent 'language games', not absolute rules or standards. In its 'modern' phase, for example, science sought legitimation from one of two narrative types: that of human liberation associated with the Enlightenment and the revolutionary tradition, or that of the prospective unity of all knowledge associated with Hegelianism.

According to Lyotard, neither of these legitimating 'meta-narratives' or '*grands récits*' now has credibility. In this critique, echoing the pessimism of the Frankfurt School though Lyotard's focus is more narrowly upon forms of modern and postmodern knowledge, the Enlightenment project is seen as having produced a range of social and political disasters: from modern warfare, Auschwitz and the Gulag to nuclear threat and severe ecological crisis. The results of modernisation have been bureaucracy, oppression and misery as the Enlightenment narrative of liberation and equality has ground into its opposite. Jürgen Habermas, as indicated above, has resisted this view and maintains that a commitment to the operation of an intersubjective 'communicative reason' will make the goals of justice and democracy realisable. In Lyotard's view the 'truth claims' and assumed consensus of such a universalising history are repressive and untenable. Deprived of this grounding, 'postmodern' science pursues the technical and commercial aims of optimal performance: a change reinforced by new, computerised technologies which make information a political quantity. But yet this technocratic order is at odds with an internal experimental drive which questions the paradigms of 'normal science'. What Lyotard calls the activity of 'paralogism' – exercised in illogical or contradictory reasoning – produces a breakthrough into the unknown of new knowledge. There thus emerges a new source of legitimation, invested in more modest *'petits récits'* and indebted to the radical *avant-garde* imperative to experiment and 'make it new'.

The postmodern aesthetic that emerges from Lyotard's work, therefore (most conveniently examined in the appendix to *The Postmodern Condition*: 'Answering the Question: What is Postmodernism?'), can be thought of as an investigative aesthetic of the 'sublime'. It should be noted moreover that this does not sequentially *follow* modernism so much as comprise its founding conditions. Here Lyotard departs from Baudrillard, Jameson and other postmodern commentators who see a decisive break between the modern and postmodern periods. For Lyotard, the postmodern is not an epoch, and less a periodising concept than a mode. 'The postmodern is undoubtedly part of the modern', as Lyotard puts it: 'it would be that which, in the modern, puts forward the unpresentable in presentation itself'. Similarly, the 'figural' and 'discursive' are not to be thought of as sequential or as exclusively identified with the postmodern and modern; the postmodern and figural can appear within the modern and discursive. This then presents a way of identifying postmodern writers and tendencies in the strictly 'modern' period (the Joyce of *Finnegans Wake*, for example) and for recovering distinctions between forms of more closed and terroristic, and more open and experimental, modernism (between high modernism and the radical *avant-garde*, for example, or between T. S. Eliot, William Carlos Williams and Gertrude Stein).

In addition, the postmodern mode proceeds without predetermined criteria or rules, which are discovered rather than assumed. By analogy this will also apply in the political arena, and to a working-through, there, to notions of 'postmodern' justice. It is here, however, in the consideration of social and political complexities that Lyotard's thought is found by some to be at its weakest or most ambiguous. Thus Lyotard, along with deconstruction generally, can be said to have authorised a consciously decentred postmodernism and micro-politics, keyed to social heterogeneity, the local, provisional and pragmatic; its political or ethical judgements undecided in advance. On the other hand, his views appear to sponsor a romantic anarchism, high on rhetoric and low on concrete social transformation. (Jameson's foreword to *The Postmodern Condition* issues warnings along these lines; others have noted Lyotard's failure to identify macro-structures of inequality and injustice, particularly concerning gender.)

POSTMODERNISM AND MARXISM: JAMESON AND EAGLETON

Two significant articles on postmodernism from within the Anglo-American tradition, which responded to the positions presented by Baudrillard and Lyotard and to the challenge postmodernism offers to Marxism in particular, were published in *New Left Review* by Fredric Jameson in 1984 and Terry Eagleton in 1985 (for further treatment of both critics, see chapter 4 above). Jameson has consistently explored questions of social, economic and cultural change raised by postmodernism, and thus its relation to the changing nature of capitalism and the place of Marxism within it. The title of his 1984 essay, now itself a key document in debates on postmodernism and reproduced as the title-essay of his later volume, *Postmodernism, or the Cultural Logic of Late Capitalism* (1991), highlights the symbiotic relationship between postmodernism and what Jameson sees as the expansion and consolidation of capitalist hegemony. Jameson believes that postmodernism is not merely one period style among others but the dominant style which takes its particular significance from the context of late capitalist society. He sees a profound connection between the 'electronic and nuclear-powered' technology of the multinational global

economy and the depthless, fragmented and randomly heterogeneous images of postmodernist culture. This culture has
effaced the frontier (strongly defended by modernist art)
between high culture and mass culture. Jameson points to the
postmodern fascination with the 'whole "degraded" landscape
of schlock and kitsch, of TV series and *Readers' Digest* culture, of
advertising and motels, of the late show and the grade-B
Hollywood film' and of pulp fiction. The commercial culture is
no longer 'quoted' and parodied in Joycean fashion, but
incorporated directly into postmodern art. Andy Warhol's work
reveals the total interpenetration of aesthetic and commodity
production. Jameson suggests that 'pastiche' is the characteristic
mode of this culture: the 'disappearance of the subject' (see
Barthes above, chapter 6) deprives the artist of an individual
style and leaves the mimicry of past styles without purpose or
irony. Jameson summarises his view of recent 'nostalgia' art as
follows: 'The approach to the present by way of the art language
of the simulacrum, or of the pastiche of the stereotypical past,
endows present reality and the openness of present history with
the spell and distance of a glossy mirage.' Postmodernist art can
no longer represent a real past but only our ideas and
stereotypes about the past in the form of 'pop' history.

The central problem of Jameson's position (and of other
political theorists and critics of the left) is squaring his
acceptance of postmodernism as our cultural 'condition' with a
commitment to Marxism. While he would accept Baudrillard's
view of present society as a society of the simulacrum, free of
reference to reality, and even Lyotard's of Marxism as a now
vestigial metanarrative, he wishes to retain a distinction
between surface and depth within a dialectical materialism
which sees itself as still able to affect social and cultural
transformation.

Eagleton, in his article, pursues further the idea of the
convergence of art and commodity in late capitalism. Marx's
analysis of money and exchange value included the concept of
'commodity fetishism'. This refers to the mystifying process by
which human labour is transposed into its products: the value
which labour time bestows upon products is seen as an
independent and objective property of the products themselves.
This inability to see products for what they are is at the root of

social alienation and exploitation. Eagleton treats 'fetishism' as an aesthetic category: the process of commodity fetishism is an *imaginary* one which insists on the independent reality of the fictively conceived commodity, and the alienated human mind accepts the objective independence of its own imaginary creation. In view of this profound 'unreality' of both art and commodity, Eagleton asserts the 'historical truth that the very autonomy and brute self-identity of the postmodernist artefact is the effect of its thorough *integration* into an economic system where such autonomy, in the form of the commodity fetish, is the order of the day'.

Linda Hutcheon (see above) believes both Jameson and Eagleton to imply that postmodernist intertextuality merely reproduces the past as nostalgia, rather than revealing the past as she sees it, as always ideologically and discursively constructed. In *The Politics of Postmodernism* (1989), Hutcheon replies to Eagleton – 'a Marxist critic who has accused postmodern fiction of being ahistorical' – by way of an analysis of Eagleton's own historical novel, *Saints and Sinners* (1987). She argues that 'it works towards a critical return to history and politics *through* – not despite – metafictional self-consciousness and parodic intertextuality. This is the postmodernist paradox, a "use and abuse" of history'. Other Marxist critics who see an intensification of capitalism, an extension of privilege and disadvantage on a global scale, and the continued relevance of class politics follow Eagleton in being antagonistic towards theories of postmodernism, and are critical, too, of Jameson's apparent acceptance of those features identified by Baudrillard and Lyotard. Some have modified their cultural politics into updated forms of Marxism which take account of changes in society's economic infrastructure: the changed nature of work and class consciousness; the influence of new technologies and the so-called social movements (the women's movement, and gay and lesbian, black, ecology and peace movements), and their effects upon contemporary mentalities and forms of cultural expression.

It is evident that there are as many 'postmodernisms' as theorists. However, there is little doubt that the *Weltanschauung* we have described overlaps the world-view implied by most poststructuralist thinkers and critics. The questioning of all 'depth models', the decentring of the world and the self, the rejection of elitist aesthetics and experimental formalisms, the disruption of all discursive boundaries, the obliteration of the frontiers between high and low culture and between art and commodity, and the resistance to meaning and interpretation are all also themes of poststructuralism.

POSTCOLONIALISM

A further movement which draws on the more radical implica-tions of poststructuralism is the study of colonial discourse, or what is usually termed 'postcolonial criticism' – although we should offer a caveat about settling too neatly on a name for this internally diverse cluster of writers and writings. Analysis of the cultural dimension of colonialism/imperialism is as old as the struggle against it; such work has been a staple of anti-colonial movements everywhere. It entered the agenda of metropolitan intellectuals and academics as a reflex of a new consciousness attendant on Indian independence (1947) and as part of a general leftist reorientation to the 'Third-World' struggles (above all in Algeria) from the 1950s onwards. Frantz Fanon's *The Wretched of the Earth* (1961) was and remains an inspirational key text (it had an important preface by the metropolitan 'convert', Jean-Paul Sartre). Thereafter, 'postcolonial criticism' overtook the troublesome ideological category of 'Common-wealth literature' to emerge in the 1980s as a set of concerns marked by the indeterminacies and decentredness otherwise associated, philosophically, with poststructuralism and particu-larly deconstruction (see above, chapter 6).

The appearance of postcolonial criticism has therefore over-lapped with the debates on postmodernism, though it brings, too, an awareness of power relations between Western and 'Third-World' cultures which the more playful and parodic, or aestheticising, postmodernism has neglected or been slow to develop. From a postcolonial perspective, Western values and traditions of thought and literature, including versions of postmodernism, are guilty of a repressive ethnocentrism. Models of Western thought (derived, for example, from Artistotle, Descartes, Kant, Marx, Nietzsche and Freud) or of literature (Homer, Dante, Flaubert, T. S. Eliot) have dominated world culture, marginalising or excluding non-Western traditions and forms of cultural life and expression.

Jacques Derrida has described Western metaphysics as 'the white mythology which reassembles and reflects the culture of the West: the white man takes his own mythology, Indo-European mythology, his own *logos*, that is, the *mythos* of this idiom, for the universal form of that he must still wish to call Reason', and the methods of deconstruction have proved a major inspiration for postcolonial critics. Some of the other theoretical arguments discussed elsewhere in this book – derived, for example, from Bakhtin's dialogics, Gramsci's concept of hegemony and Foucault's writings on power and knowledge – have also been relevant to post- or anti-colonial ways of thinking and reading, and Lyotard's 'postmodern' critique of the universalising historical narratives and strategies of Western rationality has clearly been influential too. The fact that these models find their source in Western intellectual traditions, however, makes them somewhat problematical. In Lyotard's case, for example, there is ironically a totalising thrust to his 'war on totality' and to his 'incredulity towards master narratives' and, for some, an arrogance all too characteristic of the blindnesses of Western *avant-gardist* paradigms.

Linda Hutcheon attempts to clarify some of these matters by drawing a distinction between respective aims and political agendas. Thus, postmodernism and poststructuralism direct their critique at the unified humanist subject, while postcolonialism seeks to undermine the imperialist subject. The first, she says, must 'be put on hold' in order for postcolonial and feminist discourses 'first to assert and affirm a denied or alienated subjectivity'. But this is to commit non-Western cultures (as it commits women) to a form of subjectivity and a (repressed) narrative of individual and national self-legitimation characterising Western liberal-humanism. The danger, evidently, is that 'colonial subjects' are confirmed in their subjection to Western ideological modes, which are themselves confirmed at the same time in their controlling centrality. This is the perspective of 'Orientalism' explored and exposed by Edward Said (*Orientalism*, 1978), a principal influence upon postcolonial criticism, whose work is motivated by his political commitment to the

Palestinian cause. Foucault's most distinguished American disciple, Said is attracted to his mentor's Nietzschean version of poststructuralism because it allows him to link the theory of discourse with real social and political struggles. By challenging Western discourse, Said follows the logic of Foucault's theories: no discourse is fixed for all time; it is both a cause and an effect. It not only wields power but also stimulates opposition.

EDWARD SAID

'Orientalism', Edward Said points out, occupies three overlapping domains. It designates firstly the 4000-year history of and cultural relations between Europe and Asia; secondly the scientific discipline producing specialists in Oriental languages and culture from the early nineteenth century; and thirdly the long-term images, stereotypes and general ideology about 'the Orient' as the 'Other', constructed by generations of Western scholars, which produce myths about the laziness, deceit and irrationality of orientals, as well as their reproduction and rebuttal in current debates on the Arab-Islamic world and its exchanges, particularly, with the United States. 'Orientalism' depends, in all these aspects, on a culturally constructed distinction between 'the Occident' and 'the Orient' (a fact less of nature than of 'imaginative geography', as Said terms it) and is inescapably political, as is its study. This then raises the crucial issue for postcolonialism of the position of the critic; as Said puts it in 'Orientalism Reconsidered' (1986), of 'how knowledge that is non-dominative and non-coercive can be produced in a setting that is deeply inscribed with the politics, the considerations, the positions and the strategies of power'. Said rejects any assumption of a 'free' point outside the object of analysis, and rejects too the assumptions of Western historicism which has homogenised world history from a privileged and supposedly culminating Eurocentricity. Said's work draws upon Marxism (Gramsci), Adorno's 'negative dialectics', and more markedly, as we have noted, on Foucault's analysis of discourse as power, to elucidate the function of cultural representations in the construction and maintenance of 'First'/'Third-World' relations. Analysis, he says, must be understood 'as in the fullest sense being *against* the grain, deconstructive, utopian'. He calls for a critical 'decentred consciousness' and for interdisciplinary work committed to the collective libertarian aim of dismantling systems of domination. At the same time he warns against the obstacle to this goal of 'possessive exclusivism'; the danger that anti-dominant critiques will demarcate separatist areas of resistance and struggle. The critic's credentials do not reside in the presumed authenticity of ethnic or sexual identity or experience, or in any purity of method, but elsewhere. Where and what this elsewhere is, is the major problem of postcolonial criticism, and of other differently directed forms of radical 'ideology critique'. Said's own *Orientalism* has been criticised in this respect for its under-theorised and unproblematic appeal to humanist values; but while the stronger echoes of deconstruction in Said's later writing help to answer this charge, deconstruction in itself does not ground the kinds of political practice and change Said wishes to see.

In the title essay of *The World, the Text and the Critic* (1983), Said explores the 'worldliness' of texts. He rejects the view that speech is in the world and texts are removed from the world, possessing only a nebulous existence in the minds of critics. He believes that recent criticism overstates the 'limitlessness' of interpretation because it cuts the connections between text and actuality. The case of Oscar Wilde suggests to Said that all attempts to divorce text from actuality are doomed to failure. Wilde tried to create an ideal world of style in which he would sum up all existence in an epigram. However, writing finally brought him into conflict with the 'normal' world. An incriminating letter signed by Wilde became a key document in the Crown's case against him. Texts are profoundly 'worldly': their use and effects are bound up with 'ownership, authority, power and the imposition of force'.

What of the power of the critic? Said argues that when we write a critical essay, we may enter one or more of several relations with text and audience. The essay may stand *between* literary text and reader, or on the side of one of them. Said puts an interesting question concerning the real historical context of the essay: 'What is the quality of the essay's speech, toward, away from, into the *actuality*, the arena of non-textual historical vitality and presence that is taking place simultaneously with the essay itself?' Because poststructuralist thought excludes the 'non-textual', Said's words (actuality, non-textual, presence) are a challenge to it. He goes on to direct this question of context towards the more familiar monolithic meaning of a past text, but must always write within the 'archive' of the present. Said, for example, can only speak of Wilde in terms which are sanctioned now by a prevailing discourse, which in turn is produced impersonally from the archive of the present. He claims no authority for what he says, but nevertheless tries to produce *powerful* discourse.

A particularly influential figure in the context of African-American criticism is Henry Gates, Jr, whose collection of essays *Black Literature and Literary Theory* (1984) was a ground-breaking work, and whose later books *Figures in Black: Words, Signs and the 'Racial' Self* (1987) and *The Signifying Monkey: A Theory of Afro-American Literary Criticism* (1988) offer an innovative, deconstruction-influenced analysis of black literature. Incorporating insights from Bakhtin, Foucault, Lacan, Derrida and Bloom, but inflecting them with racial 'difference', Gates draws attention to the necessarily 'comparative' nature of the analysis of black texts because of their 'complex double formal antecedents, the Western and the black'; engages in close reading of the *language* of the text; and explores the relations between African and African-American vernacular traditions and black literature – for example, showing in *The Signifying Monkey* how signifying and pastiche are prototypical literary and vernacular tropes. His work develops a critical approach, within such traditions, which releases the black voice to speak for itself. In the British context, Homi Bhabha deploys a more specifically poststructuralist repertoire (Foucault, Derrida and a latterday version of psychoanalysis) for his explorations of 'colonial discourse'. His work also exemplifies the feedback effect of 'Third-World' interests on already-established metropolitan agendas. The collection *Nation and Narration* (1990) explores the making, remaking and unmaking of national identities in familiar critical canons and in great novels and novelists from both old and new metropoles (England, France, the United States and Australia, as well as Latin America, Asia and Africa), tracing the complex discursive webs of race, ethnicity, gender and class that compose them. Contemporary British 'national culture' is specifically addressed in the work of Paul Gilroy (*There Ain't No Black in the Union Jack*, 1987).

GAYATRI SPIVAK

A leading postcolonial critic who closely follows the lessons of deconstruction and whose work raises once more the difficult politics of this enterprise is Gayatri Chakravorty Spivak, also translator and author of the important translator's preface to Derrida's *Of Grammatology* (1976). In addition to a defiantly unassimilated 'ethics' of deconstruction, Spivak draws, too, on Marxism and feminism, and this stringently 'anti-foundationalist', hybridised eclecticism is itself significant, since she aims not to synthesise these sources but to preserve their discontinuities – the ways they bring each other to crisis. She realises she appears as 'an anomaly': sometimes regarded as a 'Third-World Woman' and thus as a convenient marginal or awkward special guest, the eminent but 'visiting' American Professor; sometimes as the Bengali middle-class exile; sometimes as a success story in the star system of American academic life. She cannot be simply or singly positioned, or 'centred', biographically, professionally or theoretically; and yet she *is*, and much of her thought and writing attends scrupulously to this process, to the conditions and rationale of the ways she herself is named by her others, as an 'other', or as the same. This gives rise to a patient, seemingly backward-moving or suspended procedure of questioning and statement which elicits the taken-for-granted in the positioning of the subject, and the naming, or 'worlding' in her term, of 'The Third World' under that very description. Spivak's methods, in other words, are above all deconstructive. Like Derrida she is interested in 'how truth is constructed rather than in exposing error', and as she confirms: 'Deconstruction can only speak in the language of the thing it criticises . . . The only things one really deconstructs are things into which one is intimately mired.' This makes it very different from ideology critique; as she puts it on another occasion, deconstructive investigation allows you to look at 'the ways in which you are complicit with what you are so carefully and cleanly opposing'.

Postcolonial criticism in general draws attention to questions of identity for individual human subjects, including the critics themselves, in relation to broader national histories and destinies; and Spivak's work is of special interest because she has made the unsynchronised and contradictory factors of ethnicity, class and gender that compose such identities her own 'subject'. She traces this 'predicament of the postcolonial intellectual' in a neo-colonised world in her own case as well as in the texts of the Western or Indian traditions she examines. What seems to join these aspects of her work is the strategy of 'negotiating with the structures of violence' imposed by Western liberalism: to intervene, question and change the system from within. This can mean showing both how a label like 'Third-World' or 'Third-World Woman' expresses the desire of peoples in the 'First World' for a manageable other, and how a master text of English literature needs an 'other' to construct itself, but does not know or acknowledge this need. A striking example of the latter analysis appears in Spivak's discussion of the novels *Jane Eyre*, *Wide Sargasso Sea* and *Frankenstein* in the essay 'Three Women's Texts and a Critique of Imperialism'. Spivak sees in *Jane Eyre* – otherwise a classic text for Anglo-American feminism – 'an allegory of the general epistemic violence of imperialism'; and in her central observation she reads the last section of Jean Rhys's *Wide Sargasso Sea*, where Rochester's creole bride Antoinette is brought to England and imprisoned there as the renamed Bertha, as an enactment of the unwritten narrative of *Jane Eyre*. 'Rhys makes Antoinette see her *self* as her Other, Brontë's Bertha . . . In this fictive England she must play out her role, act out the transformation of her "self" into that fictive Other, set fire to the house and kill herself, so that Jane Eyre can become the feminist individualist heroine of British fiction.'

One problem with this is that the figure of 'the subaltern' in Spivak's writings (a category for the colonised non-elite, borrowed from Gramsci, and represented fictionally by Antoinette/Bertha) cannot speak. That is to say, the oppressed and silenced cannot, by definition, speak or achieve self-legitimation without ceasing to be that named subject under neo-colonialism. But if the oppressed subalterns cannot be spoken for by Western intellectuals – because this would not alter the most important fact of their position – nor speak for themselves, there can apparently be no non- or anti-colonial discourse. Deconstructive postcolonialism is brought to an impasse having achieved its political limit, complicit at last with the systems it opposes but in which it is 'intimately mired'. One might see this as a consequence of accepting deconstruction's notion of 'textuality', although Spivak insists that this means, in Derrida, more a weave of constituting traces and conditions than simply an endless verbal textuality. Even so, the post-colonial critic is held within textuality, committed to the 'deconstructive problematisation of the positionality of the subject of investigation'. At one moment at least, however, in a discussion of 'New Historicism' (see above, chapter 6), Spivak appears to accept that there is 'something else' identifying reality beyond the production of signs. This has to do with the 'production narrative' of capitalism for which Marxism offers a global account. Yet Spivak calls for a moratorium on global solutions and instructively describes Marxism as 'a critical philosophy' without a positive politics. 'The mode of production narrative in Marx,' she says, 'is not a master narrative and the idea of class is not an inflexible idea'. Marx's texts can be read, that is to say, in other ways than in the fundamentalist interpretations of the Marxist tradition. This is to read Marx through Derrida perhaps, but together with her opposition to liberal/individual feminism and her decisive anti-sexism, it offers a purchase on questions of capitalist power and patriarchy which extends the deconstruction of privileged Western intellectual subject positions.

A further related development can be seen in recent debates on the literary canon and syllabuses in schools, colleges and universities. Great Britain first experienced a challenge to literary orthodoxy of this kind in the 1970s under the influence, principally, of Althusserian Marxism; but its most recent manifestation, under the newer pressures of postcolonialism, has occurred in the United States. The call for a reshaping of the literary canon so as to feature black women writers, for example, as in *US Chronicle of Higher Education* in 1985, can be seen against this background, as can the debates on 'multiculturalism' and 'political correctness'. In this context, questions arise as to the redundancy or intrinsic and eternal merits of the Western literary and intellectual traditions. For example, Gayatri Spivak reports telling students at Stanford that 'your solution to enlarge the curriculum is in fact a continuation of the neocolonial production of knowledge although in practice I am with you because on the other side are real racists. The fact that this battle should be won does not mean at all that winning it does not keep a Euroamerican centrism alive.' Indeed, from the perspective of 'subaltern' peoples, debates on the literary canon in American higher education may seem a further luxury of 'First-World' domination, but nevertheless developments in this realm will learn from and contribute to the study of colonial and 'Third-World' discourse. The false, self-serving universalism of metropolitan culture has always been a leading theme of writing in this area. Poststructuralist critiques of Enlightenment reason (in science, historical thought, ethics, etc.) have both reinforced and been reinforced by this vein of critique. In all cases, it is insisted, in the face of *bien pensant* academic pluralists, that what is at stake is not the extension of study into 'new' areas, but a reconstruction in which the 'old' heartlands of the cultural canon are 'made strange', exposed to the provisionality and contradiction that the narratives of national/ethnic/racial identity may displace or repress but cannot abolish.

A key problem remains in the actual naming of this criticism as 'postcolonial', for the prefix 'post-' raises questions similar to those arising from its attachment to the term 'modernism'. Does 'post-' signal a break into a phase and consciousness of newly constructed independence and autonomy 'beyond' and 'after' colonialism, or does it imply a continuation and intensification of the system, better understood as neo-colonialism? The second understanding authorises the strategies of the 'post-colonial' critic (inside, but critical of, neo-colonialism) adopted by Gayatri Spivak. This is not an anti-colonialist or anti-imperialist criticism, however, of the kind that can be attributed to Frantz Fanon, or to the author and critic Chinua Achebe, who finds Joseph Conrad's story 'The Heart of Darkness', for example, 'racist' and therefore unacceptable (where others might defend its value by historicising its combined complicity in, and critique of, colonialism).

A further move, suggested in these debates, is the adoption of the idea of a newly founded comparative world literature, or the use of terms such as 'multiculturalism' or 'cosmopolitanism' as an advance on the ambiguities and limitations of 'postcolonialism'. Any singular, essentialist or totalising term will now, however, be problematic. All of these suggested new terms, as well as the terms 'poststructuralism', 'postmodernism' and 'postcolonialism', bear witness to a contemporary crisis of signification and power relations, at least within literary and cultural criticism. These debates can seem hermetic and dilatory, to suspend rather than to promote change, but at the same time they show a readiness to interrogate and work through issues of language and meaning towards a new discourse of global literary and cultural relations.

SELECTED READING

N.B. For ease of reference this appears as two sections: 'Postmodernism' and 'Postcolonialism'. We have not distinguished between 'Introductions' and 'Further Reading' in these two cases.

Postmodernism

Basic texts

Baudrillard, Jean, *The Mirror of Production* (1973), trans. Mark Poster (Telos Press, St Louis, 1975).

Baudrillard, Jean, *For a Critique of the Political Economy of the Sign* (1976), trans. Charles Levin (Telos Press, St Louis, 1975).

Baudrillard, Jean, *Simulations* (1981), trans. P. Foss, P. Patton, and P. Beitchman (Semiotext(e), New York, 1983).

Baudrillard, Jean, *Fatal Strategies* (1983), trans. P. Beitchman and W. G. J. Nieluchowski, J. Fleming (ed.) (Pluto, London, 1990).

Baudrillard, Jean, *America* (1986), trans. Chris Turner (Verso, London, 1988).

Baudrillard, Jean, *Cool Memories* (1987), trans. Chris Turner (Verso, London, 1990).

Baudrillard, Jean, 'The Year 2000 Has Already Happened' in *Body Invaders: Panic Sex in America*, A. Kroker and M. Kroker (eds) (The New World Perspectives, Montreal, 1988).

Baudrillard, Jean, 'The Anorexic Ruins' in *Looking Back on the End of the World*, D. Kamper and C. Wulf (eds) (Semiotext(e), New York, 1989).

Benjamin, Andrew (ed.), *The Lyotard Reader* (Basil Blackwell, London and Cambridge, Mass., 1989).

Brooker, Peter (ed.), *Modernism/Postmodernism* (Longman, London, 1992).

Docherty, Thomas (ed.), *Postmodernism: A Reader* (Harvester Wheatsheaf, Hemel Hempstead, 1992).

Eagleton, Terry, 'Capitalism, Modernism and Postmodernism' (1985) in *Against the Grain: Selected Essays, 1975–85* (Verso, London, 1986).

Eco, Umberto, *The Role of the Reader* (Indiana University Press, Bloomington and London, 1979).

Eco, Umberto, *The Name of the Rose* (1980) (Picador, London, 1984).

Eco, Umberto, *Travels in Hyperreality*, trans. W. Weaver (Picador, London, 1987).

Hassan, Ihab, 'POSTmodernISM', in *Paracriticisms: Seven Speculations of Our Time* (Illinois University Press, Urbana, 1975).

Hassan, Ihab, *The Postmodern Turn: Essays in Postmodern Theory and Culture* (Ohio State University Press, Columbus, 1987).

Hutcheon, Linda, *A Poetics of Postmodernism: History, Theory, Fiction* (Routledge, London, 1988).

Hutcheon, Linda, *The Politics of Postmodernism* (Routledge, London, 1989).

Jameson, Fredric, 'Postmodernism, or the Cultural Logic of Late Capitalism' (1984) in *Postmodernism, or the Cultural Logic of Late Capitalism* (Verso, London, 1991).

Jameson, Fredric, 'Postmodernism and Consumer Society' in *Postmodern Culture*, Hal Fisher (ed.) (Pluto, London, 1985).

Lyotard, Jean-François, *Discours, figure* (Klincksieck, Paris, 1971)

Lyotard, Jean-François, *Economie libidinale* (Les Editions de Minuit, Paris, 1974).

Lyotard, Jean-François, *The Postmodern Condition: A Report on Knowledge* (1979), trans. G. Bennington and B. Massumi (Manchester University Press, Manchester, 1984).

Lyotard, Jean-François, *The Differend* (1983), trans. G. Van Den Abbeele (Manchester University Press, Manchester, 1988).

Lyotard, Jean-François, *Just Gaming*, trans. W. Godzich and B. Massumi (Minnesota University Press, Minneapolis, 1985).

Lyotard, Jean-François, *Inhuman*, trans. G. Bennington and R. Bowlby (Blackwell/Polity Press, Cambridge, 1991).

Poster, Mark (ed.), *Jean Baudrillard: Selected Writings* (Polity Press, Cambridge, 1988).

Waugh, Patricia (ed.), *Postmodernism: A Reader* (Arnold, London, 1992).

Further reading

Alexander, Marguerite, *Flights from Realism: Themes and Strategies in Postmodernist British and American Fiction* (Arnold, London, 1990).

Best, Steven and Kellner, Douglas, *Postmodern Theory: Critical Interrogations* (Macmillan, Basingstoke, 1991).

Callinicos, Alex, *Against Postmodernism* (Polity/Basil Blackwell, Cambridge, 1989).

Collins, Jim, *Uncommon Cultures: Popular Culture and Postmodernism* (Routledge, London, 1989).

Connor, Steven, *Postmodernist Culture: An Introduction to Theories of the Contemporary* (Basil Blackwell, Oxford, 1989).

Docherty, Thomas, *After Theory: Postmodernism/Postmarxism* (Routledge, London, 1990).

Docherty, Thomas, review of *The Lyotard Reader* (ed. Andrew Benjamin, Basil Blackwell, Oxford, 1989), *Paragraph*, vol. 15 (1992), 105–15.

Easthope, Anthony and Thompson, John O. (eds), *Contemporary Poetry Meets Modern Theory* (Harvester Wheatsheaf, Hemel Hempstead, 1991).

Fokemma, David and Bertens, H. (eds), *Approaching Postmodernism* (John Benjamins, Amsterdam and Philadelphia, 1986).

Kaplan, E. Ann (ed.), *Postmodernism and its Discontents: Theories, Practices* (Verso, London, 1988).

Kellner, Douglas, *Jean Baudrillard: From Marxism to Postmodernism and Beyond* (Polity/Basil Blackwell, Cambridge, 1988).

Kellner, Douglas, *Postmodernism/Jameson/Critique* (Maisonneuve Press, Washington, DC, 1990).

Lee, Alison, *Realism and Power: Postmodern British Fiction* (Routledge, London, 1990).

McHale, Brian, *Postmodernist Fiction* (Routledge, London, 1987).

Nicholls, Peter, 'Divergencies: Modernism, Postmodernism, Jameson and Lyotard', *Critical Quarterly*, vol. 33 (1991), 1–18.

Norris, Christopher, *What's Wrong with Postmodernism: Critical Theory and the Ends of Philosophy* (Harvester Wheatsheaf, Hemel Hempstead, 1991).

Norris, Christopher, *Uncritical Theory: Postmodernism, Intellectuals and the Gulf War* (Lawrence & Wishart, London, 1992).

Readings, Bill, *Introducing Lyotard: Art and Politics* (Routledge, London, 1990).

Sarup, Madan, *An Introductory Guide to Post-Structuralism and Postmodernism* (Harvester Wheatsheaf, Hemel Hempstead, 1988; 2nd edn, 1993).

Silverman, Hugh J. (ed.), *Postmodernism, Philosophy and the Arts* (Routledge, London, 1990).

Wakefield, Neville, *Postmodernism: The Twilight of the Real* (Pluto, London, 1990).

Waugh, Patricia, *Metafiction: The Theory and Practice of Self-Conscious Fiction* (Routledge, London, 1984).

Waugh, Patricia, *Feminine Fictions: Revisiting the Postmodern* (Routledge, London, 1989).

Waugh, Patricia, *Practising Postmodernism/Reading Modernism* (Arnold, London, 1992).

Postcolonialism

Basic texts

Bhaba, Homi, 'The Other Question: Difference, Discrimination and the Discourse of Colonialism' in Barker *et al.* (1986, below).

Bhaba, Homi (ed.), *Nation and Narration* (Routledge, London, 1990).

Derrida, Jacques, 'White Mythology' (1971) in *Margins of Philosophy*, trans. Alan Ball (Chicago University Press, Chicago, 1982).

Derrida, Jacques, 'Racism's Last Word' in Henry Louis Gates, Jr (ed.) *'Race', Writing and Difference* (Chicago University Press, Chicago and London, 1985).

Fanon, Frantz, *The Wretched of the Earth*, trans. C. Farrington (Penguin, Harmondsworth, 1961).

Fanon, Frantz, *Black Skin, White Masks*, trans. C. L. Markmann with a foreword by Homi Bhaba, 'Remembering Fanon: Self, Psyche and the Colonial Condition' (Pluto, London, 1986).

Gates, Henry Louis, Jr (ed.), *Black Literature and Literary Theory* (Routledge, London, 1984).

Gates, Henry Louis, Jr (ed.), *'Race', Writing and Difference* (Chicago University Press, Chicago and London, 1985). Contains essays by Bhaba, Spivak and Derrida.

Gates, Henry Louis, Jr, *Figures in Black: Words, Signs and the 'Racial' Self* (1987) (Oxford University Press, Oxford, 1990a).

Gates, Henry Louis, Jr, *The Signifying Monkey: A Theory of Afro-American Literary Criticism* (1988) (Oxford University Press, Oxford, 1990b).

Gilroy, Paul, *There Ain't No Black in the Union Jack: The Cultural Politics of Race and Nation* (Hutchinson, London, 1987).

Said, Edward, *Orientalism* (Routledge, London, 1978).

Said, Edward, *Covering Islam* (Routledge, London, 1981).

Said, Edward, *The World, the Text and the Critic* (Harvard University Press, Cambridge, Mass., 1983).

Said, Edward, 'Orientalism Reconsidered' in Barker *et al.* (1986, below).

Spivak, Gayatri Chakravorty, 'Three Women's Texts and a Critique of Imperialism' in *'Race', Writing and Difference*, Henry Louis Gates, Jr (ed.) (Chicago University Press, Chicago and London, 1985).

Spivak, Gayatri Chakravorty, *In Other Worlds: Essays in Cultural Politics* (Routledge, London, 1987).

Spivak, Gayatri Chakravorty in Sarah Harasym (ed.), *The Post-Colonial Critic: Interviews, Strategies, Dialogues* (Routledge, London, 1990).

Further reading

Ashcroft, Bill, Griffiths, Gareth and Tiffin, Helen (eds), *The Empire Writes Back: Theory and Practice in Post-Colonial Literature* (Routledge, London, 1989).

Barker, Francis, Hulme, Peter, Loxley, Diana and Iverson, Margaret, *Literature, Politics, Theory: Papers from the Essex Conference, 1976–84* (Routledge, London, 1986). Contains essays by Bhaba and Said.

Berman, Paul (ed.), *Debating PC: The Controversy over Political Correctness on College Campuses* (Dell, New York, 1992).

Clifford, James, *The Predicament of Culture: Twentieth-Century Ethnography, Literature and Art* (Harvard University Press, Cambridge, Mass., 1988).

Coyle, Martin, Garside, Peter, Kelsall, Malcolm and Peck, John (eds), *Encyclopaedia of Literature and Criticism* (Routledge, London, 1990). Section IX contains essays (with useful bibliographies) on new English, African, African-American, Australian, Canadian, Indian, New Zealand, Pacific, West Indian and Western/Chinese literatures.

Hirsch, E. D., Jr, *Cultural Literacy: What Every American Needs to Know* (Vintage, New York, 1988).

Hodge, Bob and Mishra, Vijay, *The Dark Side of the Dream: Australian Literature and the Postcolonial Mind* (Allen & Unwin, Sydney, 1991).

Hulme, Peter, *Colonial Encounters: Europe and the Native Caribbean, 1492–1797* (Routledge, London, 1992).

Hutcheon, Linda, 'Circling the Downspout of Empire: Post-colonialism and Postmodernism', *Ariel*, vol. 20 (1989), 151 *et seq.*

Jameson, Fredric, 'World Literature in an Age of Multinational Capitalism' (1986) in *The Current in Criticism*, Koelbe and Lokke (eds) (Purdue University Press, West Lafayette, 1987).

Kaye, Jacqueline and Zoubir, Abdelhamid, *The Ambiguous Compromise: Language, Literacy and National Identity* (Routledge, London, 1990).

Mills, Sara, *Discourses of Difference: An Analysis of Women's Travel Writing and Colonialism* (Routledge, London, 1991).

Porteus, Jim (ed.), *Heart of Darkness* (Arnold, London, 1991). Contains essays by Chinua Achebe and others.

Walden, Dennis (ed.), *Literature in the Modern World* (Oxford University Press with the Open University, Oxford, 1990). Sections V and VI contain a number of useful documents and essays about the 'End of Empire' and 'New Writings in English'.

Young, Robert, *White Mythologies: Writing, History and the West* (Routledge, London, 1990).

8 Feminist theories

Women writers and woman readers have always had to work 'against the grain'. Aristotle declared that 'the female is female by virtue of a certain lack of qualities', and St Thomas Aquinas believed that woman is an 'imperfect man'. When John Donne wrote 'Air and Angels' he alluded to (but did not refute) Aquinas's theory that form is masculine and matter feminine: the superior, godlike, male intellect impresses its form upon the malleable, inert, female matter. In pre-Mendelian days men regarded their sperm as the active seeds which give form to the waiting ovum which lacks identity till it receives the male's impress. In Aeschylus's trilogy, *The Oresteia*, victory is granted by Athena to the male argument, put by Apollo, that the mother is no parent to her child. The victory of the male principle of intellect brings to an end the reign of the sensual female Furies and asserts patriarchy over matriarchy. Throughout its long history, feminism (for while the *word* may only have come into English usage in the 1890s, women's conscious struggle to resist patriarchy goes much further back) has sought to disturb the complacent certainties of such a patriarchal culture, to assert a belief in sexual equality, and to eradicate sexist domination in transforming society. Mary Ellman, for example, in *Thinking about Women* (1968), apropos the sperm/ovum nexus above, 'deconstructs' male-dominated ways of seeing by suggesting that we might prefer to regard the ovum as daring, independent and individualistic (rather than 'apathetic') and the sperm as conforming and sheeplike (rather than 'enthusiastic'). Feminist *criticism*, in all its many and various manifestations, has also attempted to free itself from naturalised patriarchal notions of the literary and the literary-critical. As we implied in passing in the Introduction, this has meant a refusal to be incorporated by any particular 'approach' and to disturb and subvert all received theoretical praxes. In this respect, and again as we have suggested in the Introduction, feminism and feminist criticism may be better termed a cultural *politics* than a 'theory' or 'theories'.

Indeed, some feminists have not wished to embrace theory at all, precisely because, in academic institutions, 'theory' is often male, even macho – the hard, abstract, *avant-gardism* of intellectual work; and as part of their general project, feminists have been at pains to expose the fraudulent objectivity of male 'science'. Freud's theories, for example, have been castigated for their endemic sexism, particularly in their assumption that female sexuality is shaped by 'penis envy'. However, much recent feminist criticism – in the desire to escape the 'fixities and definites' of theory and to develop a female discourse which cannot be tied down as belonging to a recognised (and therefore probably male-produced) conceptual position – have found theoretical sustenance in the Lacanian and Derridean modes of poststructuralist thinking, not least because these seem to refuse the (masculine) notion of authority or truth. As we have noted above (chapter 6), psychoanalytic theories have been especially powerfully deployed by feminist critics in articulating the subversively 'formless' resistance of women writers and critics to male-formulated literary discourse.

But here, perhaps, we happen upon a central characteristic and also a problematic of contemporary feminist criticism: the competing merits – and the debate between them – on the one hand of a broad-church pluralism in which diverse 'theories' proliferate, and which may well result in the promotion of the experiential over the theoretical; and on the other of a theoretically sophisticated praxis which runs the risk of incorporation by male theory in the academy, and thereby of losing touch both with the majority of women and with its political dynamic. Mary Eagleton, in the introduction to her Critical Reader, *Feminist Literary Criticism* (1991), also draws attention to 'a suspicion of theory . . . throughout feminism' because of its tendency to reinforce the hierarchical binary opposition between an 'impersonal', 'disinterested', 'objective', 'public', 'male' *theory*, and a 'personal', 'subjective', 'private', 'female' *experience*. She notes that because of this there is a powerful element within contemporary feminist criticism which celebrates the 'personal' ('personal is political' has been a key feminist slogan, since it was coined in 1970 by Carol Hanisch), the 'experiential', the Mother, the Body, *jouissance* (see above, chapter 6, and below, under 'French Feminist Critical Theories'). However, she also notes that many feminists *are* engaged in debates with other critical theories – Marxism, psychoanalysis, poststructuralism, postmodernism, postcolonialism – because, simply, there is no 'free' position 'outside' theory, and to vacate the domain of theory on the assumption that there is such a position is at once to be embroiled in the subjectivism of an 'untheorized politics of personal experience', to disable oneself thereby, and 'unwittingly' to take up potentially reactionary positions. In this context, Eagleton cites Toril Moi's critique of Elaine Showalter's resistance to making her theoretical framework explicit (see below).

Mary Eagleton's own book is conscious of both the pros and the cons of pluralistic feminisms. On the one hand pluralism may represent feminism's 'creativity and flexibility'; on the other it may signal lack of direction, a 'liberal' abdication of political purpose, or a tendency to become complicit with the (controlling) pluralism of the 'masculinist establishment' (Gayatri Spivak's phrase). But what each of these alternative views amounts to is a *position* within feminist critical debate, and this returns us to the key characteristic (and problematic) of feminist criticism (which is also the structuring device for Eagleton's book). Over the past twenty-five years or so, feminist critical theory has meant, *par excellence*, contradiction, interchange, debate; indeed it is based on a series of creative oppositions, of critiques and counter-critiques, and is constantly and innovatively in flux – challenging, subverting and expanding not only other (male) theories but its own positions and agenda. Hence there is no one 'grand narrative' but many *'petits récits'*, grounded in specific cultural-political needs and arenas:

Marxist-feminist, black and African, Asian, women-of-colour, American, French, Irish, black-British, gynocritics, gynesis, psychoanalytic, myth, 'Third-World'/Third-Wave, deconstructive, lesbian-feminist – all are components of the scene, and most are in some degree of contention with each other. This is, in our view (as male critics), both the astonishingly 'open' dynamic of critical feminisms, and the very acute difficulty (*especially* as male critics) of writing a brief synoptic chapter on such a diverse, self-problematising field of intellectual activity.

What this chapter attempts, then, is an overview of contemporary feminist critical theories, briefly sketching in the pre-1960s so-called 'first-wave' feminist criticism; outlining the characteristic achievements of the 'second wave' from the 1960s onwards; identifying some of the central debates and 'differences' which traverse the period; and offering pointers to the newer feminisms which are emerging as part of the viviparous creative process noted above.

FIRST-WAVE FEMINIST CRITICISM: VIRGINIA WOOLF AND SIMONE DE BEAUVOIR

Feminism in general, of course, has a long *political* history, developing as a substantial force, in America and Britain at least, throughout the nineteenth and early twentieth centuries. The Women's Rights and Women's Suffrage movements were the crucial determinants in shaping this phase, with their emphasis on social, political and economic reform – in partial contradistinction to the 'new' feminism of the 1960s which, as Maggie Humm has suggested in her book *Feminisms*, emphasised the different 'materiality' of being a woman and has engendered (in two senses) both moral solidarities created by feminist positions and identities, and a new 'knowledge' about the embodiment of women drawing on psychoanalytic, linguistic and social theories about gender construction and difference. Feminist *criticism* of the earlier period is more a reflex of 'first-wave' preoccupations than a fully fledged theoretical discourse of its own. But two significant figures may be selected from amongst the many other feminists working and writing in this period (e.g. Olive Schreiner, Elizabeth Robins, Dorothy Richardson, Katherine

Mansfield, Rebecca West, Ray Strachey, Vera Brittain and Winifred Holtby): Virginia Woolf – in Mary Eagleton's phrase, 'the founding mother of the contemporary debate' – who 'announces' many of the issues later feminist critics were to focus on and who herself becomes the terrain over which some debates have struggled; and Simone de Beauvoir, with whose *The Second Sex* (1949), Maggie Humm suggests, the 'first wave' may be said to end.

Virginia Woolf's fame conventionally rests on her own creative writing as a woman, and later feminist critics have analysed her novels extensively from very different perspectives (see below). But she also produced two key texts which are major contributions to feminist theory, *A Room of One's Own* (1929) and *Three Guineas* (1938). Like other 'first-wave' feminists, Woolf is principally concerned with women's material disadvantages compared to men – her first text focusing on the history and social context of women's literary production, and the second on the relations between male power and the professions (law, education, medicine, etc.). Although she herself abjures the label 'feminist' in *Three Guineas*, Woolf nevertheless promotes a wide-ranging slate of feminist projects in both books, from a demand for mothers' allowances and divorce-law reform to proposals for a women's college and a women's newspaper. In *A Room of One's Own*, she also advances the notion that while women are indeed the victims of men, they collude in their own domestic and professional victimisation by acting as a 'looking glass' (her phrase) for the reflecting-back to men of their desired image. *Three Guineas* analyses militarism, fascism and legal injustice as all deriving from patriarchy, in particular from early sexual division within the family.

Woolf's general contribution to feminism, then, is her recognition that gender identity is socially constructed and can be challenged and transformed, but apropos of feminist criticism she also continually examined the problems facing women writers. She believed that women had always faced social and economic obstacles to their literary ambitions, and was herself conscious of the restricted education she had received (she was taught no Greek, for example, unlike her brothers). Rejecting a 'feminist' consciousness, and wanting her femininity to be unconscious so that she might 'escape from the confrontation with femaleness or maleness' (*A Room of One's Own*), she adopted the Bloomsbury sexual ethic of 'androgyny' and hoped to achieve a balance between a 'male' self-realisation and 'female' self-annihilation. Her repeated attacks of madness and eventual suicide may suggest that the struggle to transcend sexuality failed, although they may also be regarded psychoanalytically as symptoms of her resistance to a repressive patriarchy. In respect of her espousal of androgyny, Virginia Woolf has been presented (in particular by Elaine Showalter) as one who accepted a passive withdrawal from the conflict between male and female sexuality, but Toril Moi advances a quite different interpretation of Woolf's strategy. Adopting Kristeva's coupling of feminism with *avant-garde* writing (see below), Moi argues that Woolf is not interested in a 'balance' between masculine and feminine types but in a complete *displacement* of fixed gender identities, and that she dismantles essentialist notions of gender by dispersing fixed points of view in her modernist fictions. Woolf, Moi argues, rejected only that type of feminism which was simply an inverted male chauvinism, and also showed great awareness of the distinctness of women's writing. Woolf's account of the eccentric Duchess of Newcastle, for example, wittily draws attention to the very 'feminine' creativity of a seventeenth-century woman writer:

> though her philosophies are futile, and her plays intolerable, and her verses mainly dull, the vast bulk of the Duchess is leavened by a vein of authentic fire. One cannot help following the lure of her erratic and lovable personality as it meanders and twinkles through page after page. There is something noble and Quixotic and high-spirited, as well as crack-brained and bird-witted, about her.

Woolf seems to be saying that the Duchess's dull 'masculine' oeuvre ('vast bulk') is brightened by a playful 'female' waywardness ('erratic', 'meanders'). The last sentence is especially revealing: 'noble and Quixotic' sound like masculine attributes, while 'crack-brained and bird-witted' sound feminine. By combining the contrasting connotations, she reaches towards a sort of androgynous dispersal of fixed sexual identity which appeals strongly to later feminist critics (like Moi) influenced by

French (Lacanian and Kristevan) psychoanalytic theory and by the notion of *l'écriture féminine* (see below).

One of Woolf's most interesting essays about women writers is 'Professions for Women', in which she regards her own career as hindered in two ways. First, as with many nineteenth-century writers, she was imprisoned by the ideology of womanhood: the ideal of 'the Angel in the House' (in Coventry Patmore's condescending term) called on women to be sympathetic, unselfish and pure, and so, to create time and space for writing, a woman had to use feminine wiles and flattery. Second, the taboo about expressing female passion prevented her from 'telling the truth about [her] own experiences as a body'. This denial of female sexuality was never consciously subverted in Woolf's own work or life, in that she thought women wrote differently not because they were different psychologically from men but because their social positioning was different. Her attempts to write about the experiences of women, therefore, were aimed at discovering linguistic ways of describing the confined life of women, and she believed that when women finally achieved social and economic equality with men, there would be nothing to prevent them from freely developing their artistic talents. Contemporary feminist critics have deconstructed these male 'looking-glass' components of Woolf's work.

Simone de Beauvoir – French feminist, lifelong partner of Jean-Paul Sartre, pro-abortion and women's-rights activist, founder of the newspaper *Nouvelles féminisme* and of the journal of feminist theory, *Questions féministes* – marks the moment when 'first-wave' feminism begins to slip over into the 'second wave'. While her major and hugely influential book *The Second Sex* (1949) is clearly preoccupied with the 'materialism' of the first wave, it beckons to the second wave in its recognition of the vast difference between the interests of the two sexes and in its assault on men's biological and psychological, as well as economic, discrimination against women. The book established with great clarity the fundamental questions of modern feminism. When a woman tries to define herself, she starts by saying 'I am a woman': no man would do so. This fact reveals the basic asymmetry between the terms 'masculine' and 'feminine': man defines the human, not woman, in an imbalance which goes back to the Old Testament. Being dispersed among men, women have no separate history, no natural solidarity; nor have they combined as other oppressed groups have. Woman is riveted into a lop-sided relationship with man: he is the 'One', she the 'Other'. Man's dominance has secured an ideological climate of compliance: 'legislators, priests, philosophers, writers and scientists have striven to show that the subordinate position of woman is willed in heaven and advantageous on earth', and, *à la* Virginia Woolf's 'looking glass', the assumption of woman as 'Other' is further internalised by women themselves. De Beauvoir documents her argument with great erudition, giving her readers a wide sweep of women's history. Women have been *made* inferiors, and the oppression has been compounded by men's belief that women *are* inferiors by nature. The abstract notion of 'equality' receives male lip-service, but demands for real equality will usually be resisted. Women themselves, therefore, not sympathetic men, are in the best position to assess the true existential possibilities of womanhood.

De Beauvoir's work carefully distinguishes between sex and gender, and sees an interaction between social and natural functions but without any notion of *biological* determinism: 'One is not born, but rather becomes, a woman; . . . it is civilization as a whole that produces this creature . . . Only the intervention of someone else can establish an individual as an *Other*.' It is the systems of interpretation in relation to biology, psychology, reproduction, economics, etc. which constitute the (male) presence of that 'someone else'. Making the crucial distinction between 'being female' and being constructed as 'a woman', de Beauvoir can posit the destruction of patriarchy if women will only break out of their objectification. In common with other 'first-wave' feminists, she wants freedom from biological differ-ence and the social enfranchisement of women's rational abilities, and she shares with them a distrust of 'femininity' – thus marking herself off from some contemporary feminists' celebration of the body and recognition of the importance of the unconscious. Nevertheless, *The Second Sex* sold over 20,000 copies when it first came out, and was acclaimed by such early 'second-wave' feminists as Betty Friedan in *The Feminine Mystique* (1963) and Shulamith Firestone in *The Dialectic of Sex* (1970).

SECOND-WAVE FEMINIST CRITICISM

One, perhaps over-simplifying, way of identifying the beginnings of the 'second wave' is to record the publication of Betty Friedan's *The Feminine Mystique* in 1963, which, in its revelation of the frustrations of white, heterosexual, middle-class American women – careerless and trapped in domesticity – put feminism on the national agenda, substantively and for the first time. (Friedan also founded NOW, the National Organisation of Women, in 1966.) Suffice it to say that 'second-wave' feminism and feminist criticism are very much a product of – are shaped by and themselves help to shape – the liberationist movements of the mid-to-late 1960s. Although second-wave feminism continues to share the first wave's fight for women's rights in all areas, its focal emphasis shifts to the politics of reproduction, to women's 'experience', to sexual 'difference'. 'Sexuality', as at once a form of oppression and something to celebrate, becomes a key issue, which, in its coupling of the 'personal' and the 'political', has constituted a crucially influential challenge to traditional (male) political thinking.

Five main foci are involved in most discussions of sexual difference: biology; experience; discourse; the unconscious; and social and economic conditions. Arguments which treat biology as fundamental and which play down socialisation have been used mainly by men to keep women 'in their place'. The old Latin saying *'Tota mulier in utero'* ('Women is nothing but a womb') established this attitude early. If a woman's body is her destiny, then all attempts to question attributed sex-roles will fly in the face of the natural order. On the other hand, some radical feminists celebrate women's biological attributes as sources of superiority rather than inferiority, while others appeal to the special *experience* of woman as the source of positive female values in life and in art. Since only women, the argument goes, have undergone those specifically female life-experiences (ovulation, menstruation, parturition), only they can speak of a woman's life. Further, a woman's experience includes a different perceptual and emotional life; women do not see things in the same ways as men, and have different ideas and feelings about what is important or not important. An influential example of this approach is the work of Elaine Showalter (see below) which focuses on the literary representation of sexual differences in women's writing. The third focus, discourse, has received a great deal of attention by feminists. Dale Spender's *Man Made Language* (1980), as the title suggests, considers that women have been fundamentally oppressed by a male-dominated language. If we accept Foucault's argument that what is 'true' depends on who controls discourse, then it is apparent that men's domination of discourse has trapped women inside a male 'truth'. From this point of view it makes sense for women writers to contest men's control of language rather than create a separate, specifically 'feminine' discourse. The opposite view is taken by the female socio-linguist Robin Lakoff, who believes that women's language actually is inferior, since it contains patterns of 'weakness' and 'uncertainty', focuses on the 'trivial', the frivolous, the unserious, and stresses personal emotional responses. Male utterance, she argues, is 'stronger' and should be adopted by women if they wish to achieve social equality with men. Most feminists, however, consider that women have been brainwashed by this type of patriarchal ideology, which produces stereotypes of strong men and feeble women. The psychoanalytic theories of Lacan and Kristeva have provided a fourth focus – that of the unconscious. Some feminists have broken completely with biologism by associating the 'female' with those processes which tend to undermine the authority of 'male' discourse. Whatever encourages or initiates a free play of meanings and prevents 'closure' is regarded as 'female'. Female sexuality is revolutionary, subversive, heterogeneous and 'open' in that it refuses to define female sexuality: if there is a female principle, it is simply to remain outside the male definition of the female. As we have seen, Virginia Woolf was the first woman critic to include a sociological dimension in her analysis of women's writing. Since then, Marxist feminists in particular have related changing social and economic conditions to the changing balance of power between the sexes, thus underwriting feminism's rejection of the notion of a universal femininity.

Certain themes, then, dominate second-wave feminism: the omnipresence of patriarchy; the inadequacy for women of existing political organisation; and the celebration of women's difference as central to the cultural politics of liberation. And these can be found running through many major second-wave writings, from popular interventions like Germaine Greer's *The Female Eunuch* (1970), which explores the destructive neutralisation of women within patriarchy, through the critical reassessments of socialism (Sheila Rowbotham) and psychoanalysis (Juliet Mitchell), to the radical (lesbian) feminism of Kate Millett and Adrienne Rich. In feminist literary theory more particularly, it leads to the emergence of so-called 'Anglo-American' criticism, fronted by the 'gynocriticism' of Elaine Showalter, which concentrates on the specificity of women's writing, on recuperating a tradition of women authors, and on examining in detail women's own culture. In dispute with this, however, is the slightly later and more theoretically driven 'French' feminist criticism, which draws especially on the work of Julia Kristeva, Hélène Cixous and Luce Irigaray, and emphasises not the *gender* of the writer ('female') but the 'writing-effect' of the text ('feminine') – hence, *l'écriture féminine*. (Alice Jardine has named it – in contradistinction to 'gynocriticism' – 'gynesis': the textualising of 'woman', rather than an emphasis on specific *women*.) It is worth noting here that this distinction between 'Anglo-American' and 'French' feminist criticisms is a significant fault-line in second-wave developments, and distinguishes two dominant and influential movements in critical theory since the end of the 1960s. It is, however, problematical for three main reasons: one, it is not a useful *national* categorization (many British and American critics, for example, might be described as 'French'), and must be understood, therefore, to identify the informing intellectual tradition and not country of origin; two, set up as it is, it seems to exclude feminist critical input from anywhere else, and especially the 'Third World'; three, it reifies into too simple a binary opposition, suppressing at once the vast diversity of practices within both movements, the recognition by many critics of the problems and possibilities of both schools, and the fact – as we noted in the introduction to this chapter – that interaction and interchange are precisely the dynamic engine of feminist criticism. But before exploring these more recent developments, we must take note of a founding text from the late 1960s.

KATE MILLETT: SEXUAL POLITICS

Second-wave feminism in the United States took its impetus from the civil-rights, peace and other protest movements, and Kate Millett's radical feminism is of this order. First published in 1969, a year after Mary Ellman's *Thinking About Women* and just before Germaine Greer's *The Female Eunuch*, Eva Figes's *Patriarchal Attitudes* and Shulamith Firestone's *The Dialectic of Sex* (all in 1970), Millett's *Sexual Politics* at once marks the moment when second-wave feminism becomes a highly visible, self-aware and activist movement, and when it itself became the cause-célèbre text of that moment. It has been – certainly in the significant legacy of its title – perhaps the best-known and most influential book of its period, and it remains (despite its inadequacies: see below) a ferociously upbeat, comprehensive, witty and irreverent demolition-job on male culture; and in this, perhaps, it is a monument to its moment.

Millett's argument – ranging over history, literature, psycho-analysis, sociology and other areas – is that ideological in-doctrination as much as economic inequality is the cause of women's oppression, an argument which opened up second-wave thinking about reproduction, sexuality and representation (especially verbal and visual 'images of women', and particularly pornography). Millett's title, *Sexual Politics*, announces her view of 'patriarchy' (the book establishes this concept at the centre of the feminist agenda), which she sees as pervasive and which demands 'a systematic overview – as a political institution'. Patriarchy subordinates the female to the male or treats the female as an inferior male, and this power is exerted, directly or indirectly, in civil and domestic life to constrain women. Despite democratic advances, women have continued to be coerced by a system of sex-role stereotyping to which they are subjected from the earliest age. Millett borrows from social science the important distinction between 'sex' and 'gender', where sex is determined biologically but 'gender' is a psychological concept which refers to *culturally* acquired sexual identity. Margaret Mead, the anthropologist, had shown that in non-Western societies the attributes assigned to men and women can differ widely: men can be peace-loving, women warlike. Millett and other feminists have attacked social scientists who treat the culturally learned 'female' characteristics (passivity, etc.) as 'natural'. She recognises that women as much as men perpetu-ate these attitudes in women's magazines and family ideology; and the acting-out of these sex-roles in the unequal and repressive relations of domination and subordination is what Millett calls 'sexual politics'.

Sexual Politics was a pioneering analysis of masculinist historical, social and literary images of women, and in our context here is a formative text in feminist literary criticism. 'Representations of women', for example, as a topic for books and courses has been and remains a dominant approach, while Millett's privileging of *literature* as a source helped to establish writing, literary studies and criticism as domains especially appropriate for feminism. One crucial factor in the social construction of femininity is the way literary values and conventions have themselves been shaped by men, and women have often struggled to express their own concerns in what may well have been inappropriate forms. In narrative, for instance, the shaping conventions of adventure and romantic pursuit have a 'male' impetus and purposiveness. Further, the male writer addresses his readers as if they are always men, while advertising provides obvious parallel examples in mass culture. However, as we have noted in relation to Woolf and de Beauvoir, it is also possible for the female reader to collude (unconsciously) in this patriarchal positioning and read 'as a man'. In order to resist this indoctrination of the female reader, Millett exposes the oppressive representations of sexuality to be found in male fiction. By deliberately foregrounding the view of a *female* reader, she highlights the male domination which pervades sexual description in the novels of D. H. Lawrence, Henry Miller, Norman Mailer and Jean Genet, offering in the case of Lawrence, for example, often hilarious and devastatingly deflationary analyses of his phallocracy.

Millett's book provided a powerful critique of patriarchal culture, but other feminist critics believe that her sole selection of male authors was too unrepresentative and that she does not sufficiently understand the subversive power of the imagination in fiction. She misses, for instance, the deeply deviant and subversive nature of Genet's *The Thief's Journal*, and sees in the homosexual world depicted only an implied subjection and degradation of the female. It appears that, for Millett, male authors are compelled by their gender to reproduce the oppressive sexual politics of the real world in their fiction, an approach which would underestimate, say, James Joyce's treatment of female sexuality. Some feminists therefore have seen Millett as holding a one-dimensional view of male domination, treating sexist ideology as a blanket oppression which all male writers inevitably promote. Cora Kaplan, in a thoroughgoing critique of Millett, 'Radical Feminism and Literature: Rethinking Millett's *Sexual Politics*' (1979), has suggested that she sees 'ideology [as] the universal penile club which men of all classes use to beat women with', and goes on to question her (partial) reading of Freud, her simplistic understanding of sexual politics and the politics of literary criticism, and, in particular, her almost exclusive focusing on *male* fiction for her evidence. Kaplan points to the crudity and contradictoriness of much of Millett's analysis of fiction, which sees it at once as 'true' and 'representative' of patriarchy at large, and simultaneously as 'false' in its representation of women. It fails, in its reductive reflectionism, to take account of the mediating 'rhetoric of fiction'.

MARXIST FEMINISM

With Millett, Shulamith Firestone (*The Dialectic of Sex*, 1970) regards male domination as primary and quite independent of other social and economic forms of oppression. Firestone's theoretical aim is to substitute sex for class as the prime historical determinant, and to present the 'class struggle' as itself a product of the organisation of the biological family unit. Michèle Barrett has argued that the notion of 'patriarchy' as used by Millett and Firestone suggests a universal domination with no historical origins or variations. By ignoring the *articulation* of patriarchy and capitalism, she suggests, they over-simplify a complex process. Instead, several factors must be related, including: the economic organisation of households and its accompanying 'familial ideology'; the division of labour in the economic system; the systems of education and the state; the cultural processes in which men and women are differently represented; and the nature of gender identity and the relationship between sexuality and biological reproduction.

Socialist/Marxist feminism was a powerful strand of the second wave during the late 1960s and 1970s, in Britain in particular. It sought to extend Marxism's analysis of class into a women's history of their material and economic oppression, and especially how the family and women's domestic labour are constructed by and reproduce the sexual division of labour. Like other 'male' forms of history, Marxism had ignored much of women's experience and activity (one of Sheila Rowbotham's most influential books is entitled *Hidden from History*), and Marxist feminism's primary task was to open up the complex relations between gender and the economy. Juliet Mitchell's early essay, 'Women: The Longest Revolution' (1966), was a pioneering attempt, *contra* the ahistorical work of radical feminists like Millett and Firestone, to historicize the structural control patriarchy exerts in relation to women's reproductive functions; and Sheila Rowbotham, in *Women's Consciousness, Man's World* (1973) and later works, recognised both that working-class women experience the double oppression of the sexual division of labour at work and in the home, and that Marxist historiography had largely ignored the domain of personal experience, and particularly that of female culture.

In the literary context, Cora Kaplan's critique of the radical feminist Millett (above), especially in its concern with ideology, may be seen as an instance of socialist-feminist criticism, and Michèle Barrett, in *Women's Oppression Today: Problems in Marxist Feminist Analysis* (1980), presents a Marxist feminist analysis of gender representation. First, she applauds Virginia Woolf's materialist argument that the conditions under which men and women *produce* literature are materially different and influence the form and content of what they write: we cannot separate questions of gender-stereotyping from their material conditions in history. This means that liberation will not come merely from changes in culture. Second, the ideology of gender affects the way the writings of men and women are read and how canons of excellence are established. Third, feminist critics must take account of the *fictional* nature of literary texts and not indulge in 'rampant moralism' by condemning all male authors for the sexism of their books (*vide* Millett) and approving all women authors for raising the issue of gender. Texts have no fixed meanings: interpretations depend on the situation and ideology of the reader. Nevertheless, women can and should try to assert their influence upon the way in which gender is defined and represented culturally.

In the introduction to *Feminist Criticism and Social Change* (1985), Judith Newton and Deborah Rosenfelt argue for a materialist feminist criticism which escapes the 'tragic' essentialism of those feminist critics who project an image of women as universally powerless and universally good. They criticise what they consider the narrow literariness of Gilbert and Gubar's influential *The Madwoman in the Attic* (1979: see below, p. 219), and especially their neglect of the social and economic realities which play an important part in constructing gender roles. Penny Boumehla, Cora Kaplan and members of the Marxist-Feminist Literary Collective have instead brought to literary texts the kind of ideological analysis developed by Althusser and Macherey (see chapter 4), in order to understand the historical formation of gender categories. However, Marxist feminism currently does not have the highest of profiles, perhaps because of the overriding effect of the 'debate' between Anglo-American and French feminisms.

ELAINE SHOWALTER: WOMEN'S WRITING AND GYNOCRITICISM

Toril Moi's *Sexual/Textual Politics* (1985) is in two main sections: 'Anglo-American Feminist Criticism' and 'French Feminist Theory'. Not only does this bring into sharp focus one of the main debates in contemporary feminist critical theory, it also makes a statement. Moi's (conscious) slippage from 'criticism' to 'theory' indicates both a descriptive characterisation *and* a value-judgement: for Moi, Anglo-American criticism is either theoretically naive or refuses to theorise itself; the French, on the other hand, is theoretically self-conscious and sophisticated. In fact, of course, there is much common ground and interpenetration between these two 'approaches', and both continue to help define major modes of feminist critical address. The French we will consider a little more fully in a subsequent section.

The principal 'Anglo-Americans' are, in fact, Americans. As the 'images of women' criticism of the early 1970s (driven by Ellman and Millett's work, and best represented in the collection of essays edited by Susan Cornillon, *Images of Women in Fiction: Feminist Perspectives*, 1972) began to seem simplistic and uniform, several works appeared which promoted both the study of *women* writers and a *feminist* critical discourse in order to discuss them. Ellen Moers's *Literary Women* (1976) was a preliminary sketching in or 'mapping' of the 'alternative' tradition of women's writing which separately shadows the dominant male tradition; but the major work of this kind, after Elaine Showalter's, is Sandra Gilbert and Susan Gubar's monumental *The Madwoman in the Attic* (1979), where they argue that key women writers since Jane Austen achieved a distinctive female voice by 'simultaneously conforming to and subverting patriarchal literary standards'. The female stereotypes of 'angel' and 'monster' (madwoman) are simultaneously accepted and deconstructed. However, as Mary Jacobus has pointed out, Gilbert and Gubar tend to limit women writers' freedom by constructing them as 'exceptionally articulate victims of a patriarchally engendered plot'; and Toril Moi adds that this continual retelling of the 'story' of female repression by patriarchy locks feminist criticism into a constraining and problematical relation with the very authoritarian and patriarchal criticism it seeks to surmount. Moi, of course, is looking to the 'psychoanalytic' proponents of French theory for a way out of this impasse.

However, the most influential American critic of the second wave is Elaine Showalter, and especially her *A Literature of Their Own* (1977). Here Showalter at once outlines a literary history of women writers (many of whom had, indeed, been 'hidden from history'); produces a history which shows the configuration of their material, psychological and ideological determinants; and promotes both a feminist critique (concerned with women readers) and a 'gynocritics' (concerned with women writers). What the book does is to examine British women novelists since the Brontës from the point of view of women's experience. Showalter takes the view that, while there is no fixed or innate female sexuality or female imagination, there is nevertheless a profound *difference* between women's writing and men's, and that a whole tradition of writing has been neglected by male critics: 'the lost continent of the female tradition has risen like Atlantis from the sea of English Literature'. She divides this tradition into three phases. The first, 'feminine', phase (1840–80) includes Elizabeth Gaskell and George Eliot, and is one where women writers imitated and internalised the dominant male aesthetic standards which required that female authors remain gentlewomen. The main sphere of their work was their immediate domestic and social circle, and they suffered guilt about their 'selfish' commitment to authorship, accepting certain limitations in expression and avoiding coarseness and sensuality. The 'feminist' phase (1880–1920) includes such radical feminist writers as Elizabeth Robins and Olive Schreiner, who *protest* against male values and advocate separatist Amazonian utopias and suffragette sisterhoods. The third, 'female', phase (1920 onwards) inherited characteristics of the former periods and developed the idea of specifically female writing and female experience in a phase of *self-discovery*. For Showalter, Rebecca West, Katherine Mansfield and Dorothy Richardson were its most important early 'female' novelists. In the same period that Joyce and Proust were writing long novels of subjective consciousness, Richardson's equally long novel *Pilgrimage* took as its subject *female* consciousness. Her views on writing anticipate recent feminist theories, in that she favoured a 'multiple receptivity' which rejects definite views and opinions (she called them 'masculine things'). Showalter writes that 'she also rationalized the problem of her "shapeless outpourings" by working out a theory that saw shapelessness as the natural expression of female empathy, and pattern as the sign of male one-sidedness.' She consciously tried to produce elliptical and fragmented sentences in order to convey what she considered to be the shape and texture of the female mind. After Virginia Woolf, a new frankness about sexuality (adultery and lesbianism, for example) enters women's fiction, especially in Jean Rhys. Thereafter followed a new generation of university-educated women who no longer felt the need to express feminine discontents; this included A. S. Byatt, Margaret Drabble, Christine Brooke-Rose and Brigid Brophy. However, in the early seventies a shift once again towards a more angry tone occurs in the novels of Penelope Mortimer, Muriel Spark and Doris Lessing.

Showalter's title, of course, indicates her debt to Virginia Woolf, and as Mary Eagleton points out their projects are markedly similar: 'A passion for women's writing and feminist research . . . links both critics. Aware of the invisibility of women's lives, they are active in the essential work of retrieval, trying to find the forgotten precursors.' Showalter, however, criticises Woolf for her 'retreat' into androgyny (denying her femaleness) and for her 'elusive' style. This, as Eagleton points out, is exactly where Toril Moi disagrees with Showalter, and where the focus of the opposition between Anglo-American and French critical feminisms may be sharply perceived. For the 'French' Moi, Woolf's refusal and subversion of the unitary self and her 'playful' textuality are her strengths, whereas the 'Anglo-American' gynocritic wishes to centre on the female author and character, and on female *experience* as the marker of authenticity – on notions of 'reality' (in particular of a collective understanding of what it means to be a woman) which can be represented, and experientially related to, by way of the literary work. (In some respects, this whole debate is reminiscent of that between the realists and the modernists within Marxism earlier in the century: see especially the sections in chapter 4 on Lukács and Brecht.) For Moi, Showalter's Anglo-American feminist criticism is also characterised both by being untheorised and by the shakiness, therefore, of its theoretical underpinning – most particularly in the connections it makes between literature and reality and between literary evaluation and feminist politics. Although Showalter's later edited collections, *The New Feminist Criticism* (1985) and *Speaking of Gender* (1989), are more eclectic in range, they still cannot engage and contain French theoretical initiatives, for, almost by definition, they are deconstructed by them. Paradoxically, then, at a point when for the gynocritics women, and women's experience and culture, are becoming potently visible, poststructuralist feminism sees everything as textuality and the whole project of 'women writing and writing about women' as misconceived, if not impossible. It is to this more radically theoretical analysis of women's difference, opened up by modern psychoanalysis, that we now turn.

FRENCH FEMINIST CRITICAL THEORY:
KRISTEVA, CIXOUS AND IRIGARAY

Bearing in mind that the fallout from 'French' feminist critical theory is constrained by no national boundary, it is nevertheless the case that this other key strand of the 'second wave' originated in France. Deriving from Simone de Beauvoir's perception of woman as 'the Other' to man (see above, p. 210), sexuality (together with class and race) is identified as a binary opposition (man/woman, black/white) which registers 'difference' between groups of people – differences which are manipulated socially and culturally in ways which cause one group to dominate or oppress another. French feminist theoreticians in particular, in seeking to break down conventional, male-constructed stereotypes of sexual difference, have focused on language as at once the domain in which such stereotypes are structured, and evidence of the liberating sexual difference which may be described in a specifically 'women's language'. Literature is one highly significant discourse in which this can be perceived and mobilized. (Black and lesbian feminists in America and elsewhere have developed these ideas in relation to the ever more complex positionings of those whose 'difference' is overdetermined by race and/or sexual preference.)

French feminism has been deeply influenced by psychoanalysis, especially by Lacan's reworking of Freud (see chapter 6), and in this has overcome the hostility towards the latter hitherto shared by many feminists. Before Lacan, Freud's theories, especially in the United States (cf. Kate Millett above), had been reduced to a crude biological level: the female child, seeing the male organ, recognises herself as female because she lacks the penis. She defines herself negatively and suffers an inevitable 'penis envy'. According to Freud, penis envy is universal in women and is responsible for their 'castration complex', which results in their regarding themselves as 'hommes manqués' rather than a positive sex in their own right. Ernest Jones was the first to dub Freud's theory 'phallocentric', a term widely adopted by feminists when discussing male domination in general. Juliet Mitchell, however, in *Psychoanalysis and Feminism* (1975), defended Freud, arguing that 'psychoanalysis is not a recommendation *for* a patriarchal society but an analysis *of* one'.

Freud, she believes, is describing the *mental representation* of a
social reality, not reality itself. Her defence of Freud's concept of
penis envy and his notions of sexual difference helped provide
the basis for contemporary psychoanalytic feminism; but while
her rehabilitation of Freud owes something to Lacan, Mitchell,
as Jane Gallop shows in *Feminism and Psychoanalysis* (1982), fails
to engage with Lacan's strategic use of Saussurean linguistics.
Inevitably feminists have reacted bitterly to a view of woman as,
in Terry Eagleton's words, 'passive, narcissistic, masochistic and
penis-envying' – as nothing in herself, but only measurable in
relation to a male norm. However, some French feminists have
emphasised that Freud's 'penis' or 'phallus' is a 'symbolic'
concept and not a biological actuality, and Lacan's use of the
term draws upon the ancient connotations of the phallus in
fertility cults. The word is also used in theological and
anthropological literature with reference to the organ's symbolic
meaning as *power*.

One of Lacan's diagrams has been found useful by feminists
in making clear the linguistic, and then social, arbitrariness of
sexual difference:

TREE   LADIES   GENTLEMEN

   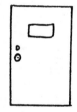

The first sign is 'iconic', describing the 'natural' correspondence
between word and thing, and it sums up the old pre-Saussurean
notion of language, according to which words and things
appear naturally unified in a universal meaning. The second
diagram destroys the old harmony: the signifiers 'ladies' and
'gentlemen' are attached to identical doors. The 'same' doors are
made to enter the differential system of language, so that we are
made to see them as 'different'. In the same way, the word
'woman' is a signifier, not the biological female: there is no

simple correspondence between a specific body and the signifier 'woman'. However, this does not mean that if we remove the distorting inscription of the signifier, a 'real', 'natural' woman will come to light as she would have been before the onset of symbolisation; we can never step outside the process of signification onto some neutral ground. Feminist resistance to phallocentrism (the dominance of the phallus as a signifier), then, must come from within the signifying process. As we saw in chapter 6, the signifier is more powerful than the 'subject', who 'fades' and suffers 'castration'. 'Woman' represents a subject position banished to outer darkness ('the dark continent') by the castrating power of phallocentrism, and indeed, because such oppression works through discourse, by 'phallogocentrism' (Derrida's term for the domination exercised by patriarchal discourse).

For Lacan, the question of phallocentrism is inseparable from the structure of the sign. The signifier, the phallus, holds out the promise of full presence and power, which, because it is unobtainable, threatens both sexes with the 'castration complex'. This complex is structured in the same way as language and the unconscious (see chapter 6) and both males and females, in different ways, lack the wholeness of sexuality symbolised in the phallus. Social and cultural factors, such as gender stereotypes, will accentuate or diminish the impact of this unconscious 'lack', but the phallus, being a signifier of full presence and not a physical organ, remains a universal source of 'castration complex'. Lacan sometimes calls this insistent signifier 'Name-of-the-Father', thus emphasising its non-'real', non-biological mode of existence. But the role of the father *is*, in fact, privileged in the process which leads to the formation of fully gendered individuals. The child arrives at a sense of identity by entering the 'symbolic' order of language, which is made up of relations of *similarity* and *difference*. Only by accepting the exclusions (if this, then not that) imposed by the Law of the Father can the child enter the gendered space assigned to it by the linguistic order. It is essential to recognise the *metaphoric* nature of the father's role: he is installed in the position of lawgiver not because he has a superior procreative function but merely as an effect of the linguistic system. The mother recognises the speech of the father because she has access to the *signifier* of the paternal function ('Name-of-the-Father'), which regulates desire in a 'civilised' (i.e. repressed) manner. Only by accepting the necessity of sexual difference (either/or) and regulated desire can a child become 'socialised'.

However, feminists have objected that, even if we take a strictly 'symbolic' view of the phallus, the privileged position in signification accorded to it in Lacan's theories is quite disproportionate. According to Jane Gallop, the application of Lacan's categories to sexual difference seems inevitably to involve a subordination of female sexuality. The man is 'castrated' by not being the total fullness promised by the phallus, while the woman is 'castrated' by not being male. Nevertheless, the advantage of Lacan's approach is that it supersedes biological determinism and puts Freudian psychoanalysis in touch with the social system (through language). Further, as Gallop has also noted, Lacan tends to promote a 'feminist' anti-logocentric discourse: though not consciously feminist, he is 'coquettish', playful and 'poetic', refusing to assert conclusions or to establish truths. When he recalls Freud's unanswered question: 'What does Woman want?' (*Was will das Weib?*), he concludes that the question must remain open since the female is 'fluid', and fluidity is 'unstable'. 'Woman never speaks *pareil* [similar, equal, like]. What she emits is flowing [*fluent*]. Cheating [*Flouant*].' There is here a danger, once again, of slipping back into a phallocentric system which relegates women to the margin, dismissing them as unstable, unpredictable and fickle; but what appears to prevent such a recuperation of female 'openness' to the patriarchal system is the positive *privileging* of this openness. Female sexuality is directly associated with poetic productivity – with the psychosomatic drives which disrupt the tyranny of unitary meaning and logocentric (and therefore phallogocentric) discourse. The major proponents of this theory are Julia Kristeva and Hélène Cixous.

Kristeva's work has frequently taken as its central concept a polarity between 'closed', rational systems and 'open', disruptive, 'irrational' systems. She has considered poetry to be the 'privileged site' of analysis, because it is poised between the two types of system, and because at certain times poetry has opened itself to the basic impulses of desire and fear which operate outside the 'rational' systems. We have already discussed (chapter 6) her important distinction between the 'semiotic' and the 'symbolic', which is the mother of many other polarities. In *avant-garde* literature, the primary processes (as described in Lacan's version of Freud's theory of dreams) invade the rational ordering of language and threaten to disrupt the unified subjectivity of the 'speaker' and the reader. The 'subject' is seen no longer as the source of meaning but as the site of meaning, and may therefore undergo a radical 'dispersal' of identity and loss of coherence. The 'drives' experienced by the child in the pre-Oedipal phase are like a language but not yet ordered into one. For this 'semiotic' material to become 'symbolic' it must be stabilised, and this involves repression of the flowing and rhythmic drives. The utterance which most approximates to a semiotic discourse is the pre-Oedipal 'babble' of the child. However, language itself retains some of this semiotic flux, and the poet is especially attuned to tapping its resonances. Because the psychosomatic drives are pre-Oedipal they are associated with the body of the mother; the free-floating sea of the womb and the enveloping sensuousness of the mother's breast are the first places of pre-Oedipal experience. The 'semiotic' is thus inevitably associated with the female body, while the 'symbolic' is linked with the Law of the Father which censors and represses in order that discourse may come into being. Woman is the silence of the 'unconscious' which precedes discourse: she is the 'Other', which stands outside and threatens to disrupt the conscious (rational) order of speech.

On the other hand, since the pre-Oedipal phase is undifferentiated sexually (although the semiotic is unequivocally 'feminine'), Kristeva does not identify the 'feminine' with the biological woman and 'masculine' with the biological man. Nevertheless, although she herself rejects the term 'feminist', we might say that Kristeva does, indeed, stake a claim on behalf of women to this unrepressed and unrepressive flow of liberating energy. The *avant-garde* poet, man or woman, enters the Body-of-the-Mother and resists the Name-of-the-Father. Mallarmé, for example, by subverting the laws of syntax subverts the Law of the Father, and identifies with the mother through his recovery of the 'maternal' semiotic flux. In literature, the meeting of the semiotic and the symbolic, where the former is released in the latter, results in linguistic 'play'. The resultant *'jouissance'* enacts a 'rapture' that is close to 'rupture'. Kristeva sees this poetic revolution as closely linked with political revolution in general and feminist liberation in particular: the feminist movement must invent a 'form of anarchism' which will correspond to the 'discourse of the avant-garde'. Anarchism is inevitably the philosophical and political position adopted by a feminism determined to destroy the dominance of phallogocentrism. Kristeva, unlike Cixous and Irigaray, does not treat the oppression of women as different in principle from that of other marginalised or exploited groups, since initial feminism was part of a larger and more general theory of subversion and dissent.

A number of French feminists have argued that female sexuality is a subterranean and unknown entity which can nevertheless represent itself in literary writing. Hélène Cixous is a creative writer and philosopher who argues for a positive representation of femininity in a discourse she calls *'écriture féminine'*, and her essay 'The Laugh of the Medusa' (1976) is a celebrated manifesto of 'women's writing' which calls for women to put their 'bodies' into their writing. While Virginia Woolf abandoned the struggle to speak of the female body, Cixous writes ecstatically of the teeming female unconscious: 'Write yourself. Your body must be heard. Only then will the immense resources of the unconscious spring forth.' There is no universal female mind; on the contrary, the female imagination is infinite and beautiful. The truly liberated woman writer, when she exists, will say:

> I . . . overflow; my desires have invented new desire, my body knows unheard-of songs. Time and again . . . I have felt so full of luminous torrents that I could burst – burst with forms much more beautiful than those which are put up in frames and sold for a stinking fortune.

Since writing is the place where subversive thought can germinate, it is especially shameful that the phallocentric tradition has, for the most part, succeeded in suppressing women's voice. Woman must uncensor herself, recover 'her goods, her organs, her immense bodily territories which have been kept under seal'; she must throw off her guilt (for being too hot or too frigid, too motherly or too unmaternal). But the heart of Cixous' theory is her rejection of theory: women's writing 'will always surpass the discourse that regulates the phallocentric system'. Always the 'Other' or negative of any hierarchies society may construct, *l'écriture féminine* will at once subvert 'masculine' symbolic language and create new identities for women, which, in their turn, will lead to new social institutions. However, her own work contains theoretical contradictions, whether strategic or not. Her concern for the free play of discourse rejects biologism, but her privileging of the female body seems to embrace it; she rejects the masculine/ feminine binary opposition and embraces Derrida's principle of *'différance'*, but she connects 'feminine writing' with Lacan's pre-Oedipal 'Imaginary' phase in which difference is abolished in a prelinguistic, utopian unity of the child and the mother's body.

This liberating return to the 'Good Mother' is the source of Cixous' poetic vision of women's writing, and it opens the possibility of a new type of sexuality. She opposes the sort of neutral bisexuality espoused by Virginia Woolf, and advocates instead what she calls 'the *other bisexuality*' which refuses to 'annul differences but stirs them up'. Barthes' study of *Sarrasine* (see chapter 6) is an excellent example of narrative bisexuality, and Cixous' account of female sexuality is often reminiscent of Barthes' description of the *avant-garde* text. 'A woman's body,' writes Cixous, 'with its thousand and one thresholds of ardor . . . will make the old single-grooved mother tongue reverberate with more than one language.' This is, of course, *'jouissance'* which, in Barthes and Kristeva, combines connotations of sexual orgasm and polysemic speech; the pleasure of the text, abolishing all repressions, reaches an intense crisis (the death of meaning). Such transgression of the laws of phallocentric discourse is the woman writer's special task, and having always operated 'within' male-dominated discourse, she needs 'to invent for herself a language to get inside of'.

Cixous' approach is essentially and strategically visionary, imagining a possible language rather than describing an existing one; but it runs the risk of driving women into a political and intellectual silence, interrupted only by 'uterine babble'. This danger is well understood by Kristeva, who sees women writers rather in the way that Virginia Woolf saw them, as caught between the father and the mother. On the one hand, as

writers, they inevitably collude with 'phallic dominance, associated with the privileged father–daughter relationship, which
gives rise to the tendency towards mastery, science, philosophy, professorships, etc.'. On the other, 'we flee everything
considered "phallic" to find refuge in the valorisation of a silent
underwater body, thus abdicating any entry into history'.

Luce Irigaray's *Spéculum de l'autre femme* (1974) develops, in
more rigorously philosophical terms, ideas which resemble
Cixous'. She considers that patriarchal oppression of women is
founded on the type of negative constructions associated with
Freud's theory of female sexuality. The concept of 'penis envy',
for example, is based upon a view of woman as man's 'Other',
lacking the penis which he possesses (precariously). She is not
viewed as existing at all except as a negative mirror-image of a
man. In this sense, women are invisible to the male gaze and
can only achieve a sort of phantasmal existence in hysteria and
in mysticism. Woman, like the mystic, is able to lose all sense of
personal subjective being, and is therefore able to slip through
the patriarchal net. While men are oriented to sight (they are
scopophilic), women find pleasure in touch; and therefore
woman's writing is connected with fluidity and touch, with the
result that 'Her "style" resists and explodes all firmly established
forms, figures, ideas, concepts.' Irigaray, in other words,
promotes the radical 'otherness' of women's eroticism and its
disruptive enactment in language. Only the celebration of
women's difference – their fluidity and multiplicity – can rupture
conventional Western representations of them.

'Gynesis', then – Alice Jardine's counter-term to 'gynocriticism' – is feminist criticism's development and mobilisation of
poststructuralist and postmodernist positions. Concerned with
the 'nonknowledge' or (feminine) 'space' which the *master*-
narratives always contain but cannot control, gynesis is the
putting into discourse of that 'Other' – 'Woman'. And it
recognises that 'woman' is not a person but a 'writing-effect',
that *'l'écriture féminine'*, in Mary Jacobus's phrase, 'asserts not
the sexuality of the text but the textuality of sex'. This, then, is a
kind of writing which is not specifically 'gendered' but disrupts
fixed meaning; which encourages textual free play beyond
authorial or critical control; which is anti-humanist, anti-realist

and anti-essentialist; and which is in effect a potent form of political, cultural and critical deconstruction. In terms specifically of literary studies, it revalues and reshapes (if not explodes) literary canons, refuses a unitary or universally accepted body of theory, and overtly politicizes the whole domain of discursive practice. It is fluid, multiplex, heteroglossic and subversive. And it is this condition which is the informing determinant for our final section in this Reader's Guide being little more than 'Notes' on the continuing feminist critical diaspora.

BLACK, WOMEN-OF-COLOUR, AND LESBIAN LITERARY THEORIES

It would be quite wrong to infer, however, that African-American, 'Third-World' or lesbian feminist critical theories are determinately 'influenced by' or 'dependent upon' the French or, more generally, white European and American theories described above. Monique Wittig, the French lesbian feminist, for example, rejects the use of the term 'woman' because, in its socially constructed form, it would not include a lesbian, who is not a 'woman' in that sense. She prefers the term 'lesbian' in that it suggests an unoppressed sexual identity and allows women to name and redefine themselves. Equally Gayatri Spivak (see above, chapter 7) has been deeply critical not only of Anglo-American ('First-World', white) feminist criticism in its ethnocentricity, but also of French theory (in particular Kristeva's *About Chinese Women*, 1977) in its willingness to export its analysis to 'Third-World' contexts without investigating its own relation to international feminism, and in its tendency to espouse a belief in the revolutionary potential of the metropolitan *avant-garde*. Indeed, as Cora Kaplan has pointed out ('Feminist Literary Criticism', 1990), Western feminist criticism, in particular, is becoming 'more aware than ever that critic and text both need to be understood in relation to their position within culture – any new reading practice . . . must first locate itself, and in doing so must reflect on its limitations and possibilities for its readers'.

Black feminists have long been concerned with problems of identity, in which race and sexuality are interlocking systems of oppression. *Contra* white feminists, race is not an 'added' problem but one which fundamentally changes notions of sexuality. 'Multiple identities', then, is a common link between many Asian, black-American, black-British and women-of-colour writers, and one basic strategy here has been to establish identifiable and separate discursive traditions in order to give voice to the particular experience of ordinary black, and other, women (Alice Walker's *In Search of Our Mothers' Gardens*, 1983, is an excellent case in point here). For women who have been 'invisible', 'hidden from history', simply putting on the record and valuing such experience is a major political initiative – especially in the context of a 'First-World' feminism which takes as its 'natural' coordinates its own ethnocentric norms. (Alice Walker, for example, in the book mentioned above, helps deconstruct our understanding of racial terminology by substituting the concept of 'womanism' for 'black feminism'.) Equally, drawing on cultural traditions (stories, songs, domestic practices) for a 'poetics' of black and Asian feminism at once 'degrades' Western notions of high art and establishes a very different, non-incorporated discourse for women, and one from which Western feminism can itself learn much. (Barbara Johnson, for example, a white American critic, has attempted in *A World of Difference*, 1987, to explore the feminist politics of deconstruction as non-coherent identity and ambivalent positionality through the work of African-American writers.)

In addition to Alice Walker, influential African-American feminist literary theorists and critics include Barbara Smith, the lesbian critic, who has produced a number of major collections of essays but whose *Toward a Black Feminist Criticism* (1977) is a pioneering work which sketches out the contours of black women's writing. It proposes a black feminist aesthetic which at once exposes the total silencing of the black lesbian writer, even in black male and white feminist criticism, and strategically brings her back into view; the lesbian poet and philosopher, Audre Lorde, who holds that sexual preference and race can be integrated to create a positive 'difference' which celebrates black women as the reverse of 'victims'; and Hazel Carby, whose

Reconstructing Womanhood: The Emergence of the Afro-American Woman Novelist (1987) focuses the need for historical and cultural specificity (e.g. the impact of black feminist discourse on literary conventions) when analysing the novels of early nineteenth-century black women writers.

Women of colour who should be mentioned in this context too, are Gloria Anzaldúa, the Chicana writer and teacher, whose book *This Bridge Called My Back* (1981) is a collection of essays by women of colour which broke the silence about Chicana lesbianism; and Rosario Morales, a Puerto-Rican feminist, who promotes a comprehensive and experiential concept of auto-biography in which cultural and historical differences give a distinctive perspective to political struggle.

Lesbian critics and theorists who have had an impact on feminist theory include Mary Daly, whose major work *Gyn/ Ecology* (1978) charts male dominance by way of sexual violence throughout history and all cultures, and offers women a new 'gynomorphic' vocabulary with which to renounce male discourses and myths; and Adrienne Rich, the poet and theorist, whose essay 'Compulsory Heterosexuality and Lesbian Existence' (1980) has been widely influential, arguing that, despite the rapacious power of a patriarchal, heterosexual culture which makes women's innate lesbianism invisible or 'abnormal', there is a possibility for all women to share, by way of a 'lesbian continuum', in the rich history and culture of the 'woman-identified-woman' tradition.

As Cora Kaplan has put it:

> the 'new colours and shadows' that inform feminist criticism today have put feminism itself, in its earlier paradigms and definitions, into question, shaking up, and in some cases breaking up, its philosophical, epistemological and political certainties, but confirming its importance as an analytic perspective.

In this context, we may end as we began: by noting the demise – particularly resonant in relation to feminist criticism – of the '*master*-narratives' of theory, and the dynamic emergence of particularised theoretical praxes in the international arena of cultural politics.

SELECTED READING

Basic texts

Abel, Elizabeth (ed.), *Writing and Sexual Difference* (University of Chicago Press, Chicago, 1982; Harvester Wheatsheaf, Hemel Hempstead, 1983).

Abel, Elizabeth *et al.* (eds), *The Voyage In: Fiction of Female Development* (University Press of New England, Dartmouth, 1983).

Barrett, Michèle, *Women's Oppression Today: Problems in Marxist Feminist Analysis* (Verso, London, 1980).

Bell, R. P., Perker, B. J. and Guy-Sheftall, B. (eds), *Sturdy Black Bridges: Visions of Black Women in Literature* (Anchor Press, Garden City, NY, 1979).

Belsey, Catherine and Moore, Jane (eds), *The Feminist Reader: Essays in Gender and the Politics of Literary Criticism* (Macmillan, Basingstoke, 1989).

Braxton, Joanne and McLaughlin, A. N. (eds), *Wild Women in the Whirlwind: Afro-American Culture and the Contemporary Literary Renaissance* (Serpent's Tail, London, 1990).

Cixous, Hélène, 'The Laugh of the Medusa' (1976), reprinted in Marks and de Courtivron (below).

Cixous, Hélène, *Writing Differences: Readings from the Seminar of Hélène Cixous*, Susan Sellers (ed.) (Open University Press, Milton Keynes, 1988).

Cixous, Hélène, *Readings: The Poetics of Blanchot, Joyce, Kafka, Kleist, Lispector and Tsvetayeva*, trans. and ed. Verena Andermatt Conley (Harvester Wheatsheaf, Hemel Hempstead, 1992).

Cornillon, S. K. (ed.), *Images of Women in Fiction: Feminist Perspectives* (Bowling Green University Popular Press, Bowling Green, Ohio, 1972).

de Beauvoir, Simone, *The Second Sex* (1949), trans. H. M. Parshley (Bantam, New York, 1961; Penguin, Harmondsworth, 1974).

Diamond, A. and Edwards, L. (eds), *The Authority of Experience: Essays in Feminist Criticism* (University of Massachusetts Press, Amherst, 1977).

Donovan, Josephine (ed.), *Feminist Literary Criticism: Explorations in Theory* (University Press of Kentucky, Lexington, 1975).

Eagleton, Mary (ed.), *Feminist Literary Theory: A Reader* (Basil Blackwell, Oxford, 1986).

Eagleton, Mary (ed.), *Feminist Literary Criticism* (Longman, London, 1991).

Ellman, Mary, *Thinking About Women* (Harcourt Brace Jovanovich, New York, 1968).

Fetterley, Judith, *The Resisting Reader: A Feminist Approach to American Fiction* (Indiana University Press, Bloomington, 1978).

Firestone, Shulamith, *The Dialectic of Sex* (1970) (The Women's Press, London, 1979).

Friedan, Betty, *The Feminine Mystique* (Dell, New York, 1963).

Gallop, Jane, *Feminism and Psychoanalysis: The Daughter's Seduction* (Macmillan, Basingstoke, 1982).

Gilbert, Sandra and Gubar, Susan, *The Madwoman in the Attic: The Woman Writer and the Nineteenth Century Literary Imagination* (Yale University Press, New Haven, 1979).

Gilbert, Sandra and Gubar, Susan, *No Man's Land: The Place of the Woman Writer in the Twentieth Century* (Yale University Press, New Haven, 1988).

Greene, Gail and Kahn, Coppelia (eds), *Making a Difference: Feminist Literary Criticism* (Methuen, London, 1985).

Hull, Gloria *et al.* (eds), *All the Women Are White, All the Blacks Are Men, But Some of Us Are Brave: Black Women's Studies* (The Feminist Press, New York, 1982).

Humm, Maggie, *The Dictionary of Feminist Theory* (Harvester Wheatsheaf, Hemel Hempstead, 1989).

Humm, Maggie (ed.), *Feminisms: A Reader* (Harvester Wheatsheaf, Hemel Hempstead, 1992).

Irigaray, Luce, *This Sex Which Is Not One* (Cornell University Press, Ithaca, 1985).

Jacobus, Mary (ed.), *Women Writing and Writing About Women* (Croom Helm, London, 1979).

Jacobus, Mary, *Reading Woman: Essays in Feminist Criticism* (Methuen, London, 1986).

Jardine, Alice, *Gynesis: Configurations of Women in Modernity* (Cornell University Press, Ithaca, 1985).

Johnson, Barbara, *A World of Difference* (Johns Hopkins University Press, Baltimore, 1987).

Kaplan, Cora, 'Pandora's Box' in *Sea Changes: Culture and Feminism* (Verso, London, 1986).

Kolodny, Annette, 'Dancing Through the Minefield: Some Observations on the Theory, Practice and Politics of a Feminist Literary Criticism', *Feminist Studies*, vol. 6, (1980), 1–25.

Kristeva, Julia, *Desire in Language: A Semiotic Approach to Literature and Art* (Columbia University Press, New York, 1980).

Kristeva, Julia, *The Kristeva Reader*, ed. Toril Moi (Basil Blackwell, Oxford, 1986).

Lorde, Audre, *Sister Outsider: Essays and Speeches* (Crossing Press, New York, 1984).

Marks, Elaine and de Courtivron, Isabelle (eds), *New French Feminisms: An Anthology* (Harvester Press, Brighton, 1981).

Millett, Kate, *Sexual Politics* (Doubleday, New York, 1970).

Mitchell, Juliet, *Psychoanalysis and Feminism* (Penguin, Harmondsworth, 1975).

Mitchell, Juliet, *Women: The Longest Revolution: Essays on Feminism, Literature and Psychoanalysis* (Virago, London, 1984). Includes her 1966 article as title essay.

Moers, Ellen, *Literary Women* (Anchor Press, Garden City, 1976).

Moi, Toril (ed.), *French Feminist Thought: A Reader* (Basil Blackwell, Oxford, 1987).

Newton, Judith and Rosenfelt, Deborah (eds), *Feminist Criticism and Social Change: Sex, Class, and Race in Literature* (Methuen, London, 1985).

Olson, Tillie, *Silences* (Delacorte Press, New York, 1978).

Pryse, M. and Spillers, Hortense (eds), *Conjuring: Black Women's Fiction and the Literary Tradition* (Indiana University Press, Bloomington, 1985).

Rich, Adrienne, 'When We Dead Awaken: Writing as Re-Vision' in *On Lies Secrets, Silence: Selected Prose 1956–1978* (W. W. Norton, New York, 1979).

Robinson, Lillian, *Sex, Class and Culture* (Indiana University Press, Bloomington, 1978).

Russ, Joanna, *How to Suppress Women's Writing* (University of Texas Press, Austin, 1983).

Showalter, Elaine, *A Literature of Their Own* (Princeton University Press, Princeton, 1977).

Showalter, Elaine (ed.), *The New Feminist Criticism: Essays on Women, Literature and Theory* (Pantheon, New York, 1985).

Showalter, Elaine (ed.), *Speaking of Gender* (Routledge, London, 1989).

Smith, Barbara, *Toward A Black Feminist Criticism* (Out and Out Press, New York, 1977).

Smith, Barbara (ed.), *Home Girls: A Black Feminist Anthology* (Kitchen Table Women of Color Press, New York, 1983).

Spivak, Gayatri Chakravorty – see 'Selected Reading' for chapter 7.

Todd, Janet (ed.), *Dictionary of British Women Writers* (Routledge, London, 1991).

Walker, Alice, *In Search of Our Mothers' Gardens: Womanist Prose* (Harcourt Brace Jovanovich, New York, 1983).

Walker, Alice, *Living By the Word: Selected Writings, 1973–1987* (Harcourt Brace Jovanovich, New York, 1988).

Wittig, Monique, *The Straight Mind and Other Essays* (Harvester Wheatsheaf, Hemel Hempstead, 1992).

Woolf, Virginia, *A Room of One's Own* (Hogarth Press, London, 1929).
Woolf, Virginia, *Three Guineas* (Hogarth Press, London, 1938).
Woolf, Virginia, *Women and Writing*, intro. Michèle Barrett (The Women's Press, London, 1979).

Introductions

Anzaldúa, Gloria (ed.), *Making Face, Making Soul: Haciendo Caras: Creative and Critical Perspectives of Women of Color* (Aunt Lute Foundation Books, San Francisco, 1990).
Benstock, Shari (ed.), *Feminist Issues in Literary Scholarship* (Indiana University Press, Bloomington, 1987).
Christian, Barbara, *Black Feminist Criticism: Perspectives on Black Women Writers* (Pergamon, New York, 1985).
Conley, Verena Andermatt, *Hélène Cixous* (Harvester Wheatsheaf, Hemel Hempstead, 1992).
Donovan, Josephine, 'Introduction to the Second Edition' in *Feminist Literary Criticism: Explorations in Theory*, Josephine Donovan (ed.) (University Press of Kentucky, Lexington, 2nd edn, 1989).
Evans, Mari (ed.), *Black Women Writers* (Pluto, London, 1985).
Gallop, Jane, *Around 1981: Academic Feminist Literary Theory* (Routledge, London, 1992).
Gates, Henry Louis, Jr (ed.), *Reading Black: Reading Feminist: A Critical Anthology* (Meridian, New York, 1990).
Grosz, Elizabeth, *Jacques Lacan: A Feminist Introduction* (Routledge, London, 1990).
Humm, Maggie, *Feminist Criticism: Women as Contemporary Critics* (Harvester Press, Brighton, 1986).
Jay, K. and Glasgow, J. (eds), *Lesbian Texts and Contexts: Radical Revisions* (New York University Press, New York, 1990).
Kaplan, Cora, 'Feminist Literary Criticism: "New Colours and Shadows"' in *Encyclopaedia of Literature and Criticism*, Martin Coyle, Peter Garside, Malcolm Kelsall and John Peck (eds) (Routledge, London, 1990).
Meese, Elizabeth, *Crossing the Double-Cross: The Practice of Feminist Criticism* (University of North Carolina Press, Chapel Hill, 1986).
Meese, Elizabeth, *(EX)Tensions: Re-Figuring Feminist Criticism* (University of Illinois Press, Urbana, 1990).
Mills, Sara, Pearce, Lynne, Spaull, Sue and Millard, Elaine, *Feminist Readings/Feminists Reading* (Harvester Wheatsheaf, Hemel Hempstead, 1989). Includes practical demonstrations.
Moi, Toril, *Sexual/Textual Politics: Feminist Literary Theory* (Methuen, London, 1985).

Sellers, Susan, *Language and Sexual Difference: Feminist Writing in France* (Macmillan, London, 1991).

Shiach, Morag, *Hélène Cixous: A Politics of Writing* (Routledge, London, 1991).

Stimpson, Catherine, *Where the Meanings Are: Feminism and Cultural Spaces* (Routledge, London, 1988).

Wall, C. A. (ed.), *Changing Our Own Words: Essays on Criticism, Theory and Writing by Black Women* (Rutgers University Press, New Brunswick, 1989).

Warhol, Robin and Price Herndl, Diane, *Feminisms: An Anthology of Literary Theory and Criticism* (Rutgers University Press, New Brunswick, 1991; Macmillan, Basingstoke, 1992).

Whitford, Margaret, *Luce Irigaray: Philosophy in the Feminine* (Routledge, London, 1991).

Further reading

Carby, Hazel V., *Reconstructing Womanhood: The Emergence of the Afro-American Woman Novelist* (Oxford University Press, Oxford, 1987).

Culler, Jonathan, 'Reading as a Woman' in *On Deconstruction: Theory and Criticism after Structuralism* (Routledge, London, 1983).

de Lauretis, Teresa (ed.), *Feminist Studies/Critical Studies* (Indiana University Press, Bloomington, 1986).

Gates, Henry Louis, Jr. – see 'Selected Reading' for chapter 7.

Humm, Maggie, *An Annotated Bibliography of Feminist Criticism* (Harvester Press, Brighton, 1987).

Jardine, Alice and Smith, Paul (eds), *Men in Feminism* (Routledge, London, 1987).

Jump, Harriet Devine (ed.), *Diverse Voices: Twentieth-Century Women's Writing from Around the World* (Harvester Wheatsheaf, Hemel Hempstead, 1991).

Kaplan, Cora, 'Radical Feminism and Literature: Rethinking Millett's *Sexual Politics*' (1979), reprinted in Eagleton, 1991 (see *Basic Texts* above).

Lakoff, Robin, *Language and Woman's Place* (Harper & Row, New York, 1975).

Lilly, Mark (ed.), *Lesbian and Gay Writing: An Anthology of Critical Essays* (Macmillan, Basingstoke, 1990).

McConnell-Ginet, S., Barker, Ruth and Furman, Nelly (eds), *Women and Language in Literature and Society* (Praeger, New York, 1980).

McDowell, Deborah E. and Rampersand, Arnold (eds), *Slavery and the Literary Imagination* (Johns Hopkins University Press, Baltimore, 1989).

Miller, Nancy (ed.), *The Poetics of Gender* (Columbia University Press, New York, 1986).

Miller, Nancy, *Subject to Change: Reading Feminist Writing* (Columbia University Press, New York, 1988).

Miller, Nancy, *Getting Personal: Feminist Occasions and Other Autobiographical Acts* (Routledge, London, 1991).

Milloy, Jean and O'Rourke, Rebecca, *The Woman Reader: Learning and Teaching Women's Writing* (Routledge, London, 1991).

Minogue, Sally (ed.), *Problems for Feminist Criticism* (Routledge, London, 1990).

Modleski, Tania, *Feminism Without Women: Culture and Criticism in a 'Postfeminist' Age* (Routledge, London, 1991).

Moi, Toril, *Feminist Literary Theory and Simone de Beauvoir* (Basil Blackwell, Oxford, 1990).

Munt, Sally (ed.), *New Lesbian Criticism: Literary and Cultural Readings* (Harvester Wheatsheaf, Hemel Hempstead, 1992).

Roe, Sue (ed.), *Women Reading Women's Writing* (Harvester Press, Brighton, 1987).

Rose, Jacqueline, *Sexuality in the Field of Vision* (Verso, London, 1986).

Sellers, Susan (ed.), *Feminist Criticism: Theory and Practice* (Harvester Wheatsheaf, Hemel Hempstead, 1991).

Todd, Janet, *Feminist Literary Theory: A Defence* (Polity, Oxford, 1988).

Waugh, Patricia, *Feminine Fictions: Revisiting the Modern* (Routledge, London, 1989).

Weedon, Chris, *Feminist Practice and Poststructuralist Theory* (Basil Blackwell, Oxford, 1987).

Wilcox, Helen, McWatters, Keith, Thompson, Ann and Williams, Linda (eds), *The Body and the Text: Hélène Cixous, Reading and Teaching* (Harvester Wheatsheaf, Hemel Hempstead, 1990).

Willis, Susan, *Specifying: Black Women Writing the American Experience* (Routledge, London, 1990).

Wisker, Gina (ed.), *Black Women's Writing* (Macmillan, Basingstoke, 1992).

Index